Date Due

Emotions, Aggression, and Morality in Children

Emotions, Aggression, and Morality in Children

Bridging Development and Psychopathology

Edited by William F. Arsenio and Elizabeth A. Lemerise

American Psychological Association
Washington, DC

Published by
American Psychological Association
750 First Street, NE
Washington, DC 20002
www.apa.org

To order
APA Order Department
P.O. Box 92984
Washington, DC 20090-2984
Tel: (800) 374-2721; Direct: (202) 336-5510
Fax: (202) 336-5502; TDD/TTY: (202) 336-6123
Online: www.apa.org/books/
E-mail: order@apa.org

In the U.K., Europe, Africa, and the Middle East, copies may be ordered from
American Psychological Association
3 Henrietta Street
Covent Garden, London
WC2E 8LU England

Typeset in Goudy by Circle Graphics, Inc., Columbia, MD

Printer: Edwards Brothers, Inc., Ann Arbor, MI
Cover Designer: Watermark Design Office, Alexandria, VA

The opinions and statements published are the responsibility of the authors, and such opinions and statements do not necessarily represent the policies of the American Psychological Association.

Library of Congress Cataloging-in-Publication Data

Emotions, aggression, and morality in children : bridging development and psychopathology / edited by William F. Arsenio and Elizabeth A. Lemerise. — 1st ed.
   p. cm.
 Includes bibliographical references and index.
 ISBN-13: 978-1-4338-0764-0 (print)
 ISBN-10: 1-4338-0764-5 (print)
 ISBN-13: 978-1-4338-0765-7 (electronic)
 ISBN-10: 1-4338-0765-3 (electronic)
1. Developmental psychology. 2. Psychology, Pathological. 3. Emotions in children.
4. Aggressiveness in children. 5. Ethics. I. Arsenio, William Frank II. Lemerise, Elizabeth A.

 BF713.E46 2010
 155.4'1825—dc22

                                   2009039843

British Library Cataloguing-in-Publication Data

A CIP record is available from the British Library.

Printed in the United States of America
First Edition

CONTENTS

CONTRIBUTORS

William F. Arsenio, PhD, Ferkauf Graduate School of Psychology, Yeshiva University, Bronx, NY

Tammy D. Barry, PhD, Department of Psychology, University of Southern Mississippi, Hattiesburg

R. J. R. Blair, PhD, Mood and Anxiety Disorders Program, National Institute of Mental Health, Bethesda, MD

Caroline L. Boxmeyer, PhD, Center for the Prevention of Youth Behavior Problems, University of Alabama, Tuscaloosa

Bram Orobio de Castro, PhD, Department of Developmental Psychopathology, Utrecht University, the Netherlands

Alison Edwards, Department of Psychology, Arizona State University, Tempe

Natalie D. Eggum, MA, Department of Psychology, Arizona State University, Tempe

Nancy Eisenberg, PhD, Department of Psychology, Arizona State University, Tempe

Paul J. Frick, PhD, Department of Psychology, University of New Orleans, New Orleans, LA

Jason Gold, PhD, Institute for the Study of Child Development, University of Medicine and Dentistry of New Jersey–Robert Wood Johnson Medical School, New Brunswick, NJ

Julie A. Hubbard, PhD, Department of Psychology, University of Delaware, Newark

Monika Keller, PhD, Max Planck Institute for Human Development, Berlin, Germany

Melanie Killen, PhD, Department of Human Development, University of Maryland, College Park

Elizabeth A. Lemerise, PhD, Department of Psychology, Western Kentucky University, Bowling Green

Michael Lewis, PhD, Institute for the Study of Child Development, University of Medicine and Dentistry of New Jersey–Robert Wood Johnson Medical School, New Brunswick, NJ

John E. Lochman, PhD, ABPP, Center for Prevention of Youth Behavior Problems, University of Alabama, Tuscaloosa

Tina Malti, PhD, Developmental and Clinical Child Psychology, Jacobs Center for Productive Youth Development, Zurich, Switzerland

Monica A. Marsee, PhD, Department of Psychology, University of New Orleans, New Orleans, LA

Jennifer Maulden, PhD, Department of Psychology, Ohio State University, Columbus

Meghan D. McAuliffe, PhD, Division of Behavioral Health, A.I. duPont Hospital for Children, Wilmington, DE

Michael T. Morrow, Department of Psychology, University of Delaware, Newark

Emily K. Newton, Department of Psychology, University of California, Davis

Nicole P. Powell, PhD, MPH, Center for the Prevention of Youth Behavior Problems, University of Alabama, Tuscaloosa

Lydia J. Romano, MA, Department of Psychology, University of Delaware, Newark

Ross A. Thompson, PhD, Department of Psychology, University of California, Davis

Elliot Turiel, PhD, Graduate School of Education, University of California, Berkeley

Laura Young, Department of Psychology, University of Alabama, Tuscaloosa

Emotions, Aggression, and Morality in Children

INTRODUCTION: AN INTEGRATIVE APPROACH TO EMOTIONS, AGGRESSION, AND MORALITY

WILLIAM F. ARSENIO AND ELIZABETH A. LEMERISE

Aggression and other moral transgressions, such as cheating, lying, and stealing, are by their basic nature emotionally charged. Whether the transgression involves a preschooler taking another child's toy, a middle school child lying about a peer to stay out of trouble, or an adolescent involved in an armed robbery, victimizers are likely to feel a range of intense emotions, whereas their victims will feel different, but no less intense, emotions. But how and why do these acts of victimization become charged with emotions? And what do these emotions tell us about both those who become routine victimizers and those who learn to inhibit victimizing behaviors? Finally, is victimization primarily a matter of affective influences, or do cognitive abilities also play an important role?

To answer these questions, it would help to start with a little background about this volume. The original impetus for this book came from our discussions and explorations of these questions in a series of theoretical/literature reviews (Arsenio & Lemerise, 2001, 2004; Lemerise & Arsenio, 2000). Early on in these exchanges, it became clear that for various historical reasons, several major divides had emerged in the psychological subdisciplines that could provide partial answers to these questions. One key divide is that two parallel, nearly independent fields have emerged that focus on children's victimizing behaviors and cognitions, that is, the literatures on aggression and moral development. Furthermore, this divergence seems especially surprising given the deep commonalties between what are arguably the current major theoretical and empirical approaches in each field—the social information processing (SIP) model (Dodge, Coie, & Lynam, 2006) for studying aggression and the domain approach (Turiel, 2006) for studying moral development. Both theories start with a focus on behaviors that involve intentional harm and victimization while also sharing a central focus on the vital (if complex) connections between children's morally relevant social cognitions and their related behaviors. In addition, both traditions present very similar sociomoral events as stimuli about which participants make judgments.

Given these similarities, why did the study of aggression and moral development follow such different paths, and, put simply, why should we care? Part of the answer is that these fields have very different pragmatic concerns and, consequently, quite different theoretical emphases, foundations, and subsequent empirical findings. For example, SIP research has focused almost exclusively on how individual differences in children's social reasoning relate to their aggressive victimizing behavior. By contrast, moral domain theory has been primarily concerned with normative age-related changes in how children understand victimization and its relation to other types of sociomoral limits (e.g., conventional and personal domains). Despite this difference, the present book reflects the view that by recognizing the deeper similarities in these two areas, it will be possible to develop a broader, more integrated understanding of how and why some children follow developmental trajectories toward increasing levels of aggression when most children do not.

The chapters included in this volume also share a second unifying theme: the need to understand how children and adolescents' emotions, moods, and other affective processes interact with their social cognitions to influence moral and aggressive tendencies. If, as Socrates and Aristotle claimed, simply "knowing the good" automatically compelled one to "do the good," there would be no real need to study why this process goes off track, because aggression and other forms of immoral behavior would be quite rare. So what is it that motivates some children to use their moral understanding to resist harming others while some children's understanding of "moral rules" seems to have no effect on their related behaviors?

One historical answer to this question has been to reduce concerns about aggression and morality to a conflict between cognitive and affective primacy. If there is a weak or uneven connection between morally relevant social cognitions and behavior, some would argue, it is simply because deep affective influences, ranging from fear of punishment and guilt induction to empathy and attachment, are so much more important than social cognition.

Why else, for example, would early empathic disruptions predict subsequent externalizing problems? In turn, others argue, putting arational, affective processes at the center of morality and aggression ignores the key role of volition and intention in how adults and children evaluate the moral nature of behavior. Why else would children's evaluations of others' intentions in provocative peer situations have such an important influence on behavior?

Debates about cognitive versus affective primacy date back more than a quarter of a century (e.g., Lazarus, 1984, vs. Zajonc, 1984) and probably much longer than that. The chapters in this book suggest that the debate is far from resolved. Some chapters focus on the more affective bases of behavior, including empathy and the potentially disruptive influence of emotion on cognition. By contrast, other chapters focus more strongly on social cognition, moral reasoning, and the central role of cognitive processes. A closer reading, however, reveals that even though the relative focus on cognitive and affective processes in each chapter varies greatly, all of the authors share an interest in how cognition and affect intertwine in the emergence of moral and aggressive tendencies. So, for example, in their chapter on empathy, Eisenberg, Eggum, and Edwards include a detailed section on how empathy and moral reasoning combine to affect morally relevant behaviors. Similarly, in their chapter, Turiel and Killen describe how their cognitive–developmental domain model of morality is built on affective processes such as empathy and a fundamental respect for persons.

Another central theme of this book is the attempt to bridge development and psychopathology as they relate to emotions, aggression, and morality. Ideally, it should be unnecessary to talk about "bridging" developmental and psychopathological approaches: The field of developmental psychopathology has both implicitly and explicitly incorporated this bridging for several decades now. But when it comes to emotions, aggression, and morality, some of the most basic assumptions in developmental psychopathology have not yet been met.

In a seminal, special issue of *Child Development* in 1984, guest editor Dante Cicchetti argued that it is "widely accepted that research into pathological conditions must go hand-in-hand with so called basic research into human functioning" (p. 4). Cicchetti further argued that several different fields, including developmental and clinical psychology, psychiatry, and other disciplines, were merging into a larger hierarchical integration that promised to be much more than the sum of its parts, both theoretically and empirically. From the perspective of developmental psychopathology, two things were clear: (a) if psychopathology is a process that unfolds over time, typically extending back into childhood, then a general understanding of development is necessary to inform when and why psychopathology first emerges, and (b) if normative development can go awry, then a focus on psychopathology is necessary to help explain the nature, range, and meaning of these significant individual differences.

Although the integrative approach of developmental psychopathology has had a major impact on numerous fields, to date it has a more restricted influence on our understanding of how emotions, aggression, and morality interact. One obstacle has already been briefly mentioned, and that is the distinct division between those who study moral development and those who study aggression. From the perspective of developmental psychopathology, moral development describes the developmental side of morality/immorality, whereas aggression describes the psychopathology of moral/immoral behavior. However, despite several initial attempts to combine these two fields (e.g., Arsenio & Lemerise, 2004; Guerra, Nucci, & Huesmann, 1994; Tisak, Tisak, & Goldstein, 2006), there is nothing approaching a hierarchical integration in this area. Consequently, another goal of this volume is to begin bridging the study of aggression and morality, development and psychopathology, in ways that may eventually lead to a more basic integration.

Although many of the chapters in this book include sections on theoretical foundations, research, and clinical implications, the relative balance of these dimensions differs greatly from chapter to chapter. Consequently, this book is organized into three broad categories focusing on (a) theoretical underpinnings, (b) different research perspectives, and (c) clinical and intervention implications. In Part I, Theoretical Foundations, the four chapters reflect several basic theoretical orientations regarding how emotions, aggression, and morality combine. In Chapter 1, Thompson and Newton describe how the earliest roots of young children's conscience first emerge. The authors argue that infants' and young children's sensitivity to others' feelings combines with parent–child emotional communication to lay a moral foundation that is based on interpersonal reciprocity. Similarly, Turiel and Killen (Chapter 2) also emphasize the central role that positive emotions and relationships (e.g., respect for persons) play in the cognitive developmental approach to moral understanding and behavior. Turiel and Killen also stress that attempts to reduce morality to arational, emotional forces ignore extensive research on children's ubiquitous attempts to make sense of their social worlds.

The other two chapters in the first, more theoretical, section of the book focus on when development goes awry. For example, de Castro (Chapter 3) describes how aggression results from dysregulated emotional processes (including both emotional tendencies and disrupted emotional knowledge) during interpersonal interactions. Although de Castro begins with the SIP model (see, e.g., Crick & Dodge, 1994, and Chapters 4, 7, 8, 10, and 12 in this volume), he argues that a more fundamental focus on emotion regulation and its "control precedence" in aggression is needed. Arsenio (Chapter 4) also argues that emotion dysregulation can play a key role in certain forms of aggression. However, Arsenio argues that neither emotion dyregulation nor the SIP model can explain all forms of aggression: Research on instrumental, proactive aggression and "happy victimization" (see also Chapter 8) suggests that some children's aggression is strongly related to disrupted moral reasoning as well.

Part II, From Neuroscience to Culture: Factors Influencing Aggression and Morality, includes five chapters summarizing research on some of the major empirical approaches to understanding how emotions, aggression, and morality are intertwined. So, for example, Blair (Chapter 5) begins with a review of work on the separable neurocognitive processes that underlie different aspects of empathy and morality. Blair's subsequent emphasis on how empathic dysfunctions are related to disrupted moral reasoning and increased risk of certain forms of antisocial behavior is also elaborated at length by Eisenberg, Eggum, and Edwards (Chapter 6). Specifically, Eisenberg et al. summarize the extensive developmental literature on empathy, sympathy, and personal distress and on their complex interconnections with children's prosocial behavior, aggression, and moral judgment. Chapter 7 by Marsee and Frick continues the focus on empathy-related processes, but with a specific focus on psychopathology. Marsee and Frick summarize the growing literature on callous-unemotional traits in children, adolescents, and adults (e.g., a lack of empathy and guilt) and the connection of this relatively stable personality trait with the related literature on proactive aggression and on the reactive/proactive aggression distinction (see, e.g., Chapters 3, 10, and 11).

The final two chapters of Part II follow somewhat different paths to understanding how emotions and emotional processes are connected with aggression and morality. Lemerise and Maulden (Chapter 8) provide the most extensive review to date of research related to Lemerise and Arsenio's (2000) model of how affective processes can be integrated into Crick and Dodge's (1994) mostly social cognitive SIP model. Lemerise and Maulden summarize research on how emotions in self and others, emotion regulation, and the nature of affective relationships with provocateurs systematically influence children's reasoning and aggressive tendencies at each of the different steps of the SIP model. In contrast, Malti and Keller (Chapter 9) start with an explicit focus on moral reasoning and children's related emotion attributions and then continue on to examine aggression and interpersonal relationships. Malti and Keller also provide extensive developmental and cross-national data on how children's moral emotion judgments differ as a function of age, culture, and aggression status.

Part III, Assessment, Interventions, and Clinical Perspectives, combines a focus on research with extended sections on some of the clinical and intervention-related implications of these approaches. In Chapter 10, Hubbard, Morrow, Romano, and McAuliffe begin with a discussion of research and measurement issues related to the reactive/proactive aggression distinction. Following this, they describe some of the different intervention strategies used to address children's overall aggressive tendencies, in addition to interventions specifically designed to target children's angry, reactive aggression as well as more instrumental, proactive forms of aggression. In contrast, Gold and Lewis (Chapter 11) present a model and related data on youth violence that stresses multiple contributors, beginning with poverty and racism and their relationship to parenting, and extending to how these factors relate to adolescents' attributions of blame and shame. In their view, interventions that target both adolescents' blame-related cognitions and emotions of shame, in addition to traditional delinquency-related cognitions, are likely to prove especially effective. Finally, Powell, Lochman, Boxmeyer, Barry, and Young (Chapter 12) begin by reviewing research on the role of emotional processes in children's angry, aggressive behaviors. Much of their chapter, however, describes the details of the Coping Power program and its demonstrated efficacy in reducing children's aggressive tendencies and improving their self-regulation and anger coping skills.

Overall, the chapters in this book provide a systematic, state-of-the-art overview of theory, research, and interventions from current and emerging views of how emotional processes underlie children's aggression and moral development. Across these chapters, it is clear that a consideration of how emotion and cognition interact is essential to further our understanding of both moral development and aggression. Emotional arousal in the form of empathy is a key motivator of prosocial moral behavior as well as an important inhibitor of aggressive and immoral acts. Too little emotion (as in callous-unemotional trait) may enable aggressive and immoral acts. However, too much emotion, especially intense, poorly regulated anger or shame, may be another pathway to aggressive and immoral acts (e.g., reactive aggression). Thus, although emotionality can contribute to adaptive functioning, it is clear that emotions must come to be well regulated. Here again, emotionality and cognitive processes are intertwined. For some children, their growing understanding of emotions in self and others, as well as their knowledge about how to manage strong emotions, contributes to the appropriate regulation of emotions and a subsequent avoidance of aggressive–immoral behaviors. In the following chapters, readers will find not only good summaries of what is known about how emotions and cognition interact in morality and aggression but also a road map of where we need to go to further our understanding of this important topic.

REFERENCES

Arsenio, W. F., & Lemerise, E. A. (2001). Varieties of childhood bullying: Values, emotion processes, and social competence. *Social Development, 10,* 59–73. doi:10.1111/1467-9507.00148

Arsenio, W. F., & Lemerise, E. A. (2004). Aggression and moral development: Integrating the social information processing and moral domain models. *Child Development, 75,* 987–1002. doi:10.1111/j.1467-8624.2004.00720.x

Cicchetti, D. (1984). The emergence of developmental psychopathology. *Child Development, 55,* 1–7. doi:10.2307/1129830

Crick, N., & Dodge, K. (1994). A review and reformulation of social-information-processing mechanisms in children's social adjustment. *Psychological Bulletin, 115,* 74–101. doi:10.1037/0033-2909.115.1.74

Dodge, K., Coie, J., & Lynam, D. (2006). Aggression and antisocial behavior in youth. In W. Damon & R. Lerner (Series Eds.) & N. Eisenberg (Vol. Ed.), *Handbook of child psychology: Vol. 3. Social, emotional, and personality development* (6th ed., pp. 719–788). New York, NY: Wiley.

Guerra, N., Nucci, L., & Huesmann, L. (1994). Moral cognition and childhood aggression. In L. Huesmann (Ed.), *Aggressive behavior: Current perspectives* (pp. 13–33). New York, NY: Plenum Press.

Lazarus, R. (1984). On the primacy of cognition. *American Psychologist, 39,* 124–129. doi:10.1037/0003-066X.39.2.124

Lemerise, E. A., & Arsenio, W. F. (2000). An integrated model of emotion processes and cognition in social information processing. *Child Development, 71,* 107–118. doi:10.1111/1467-8624.00124

Tisak, M., Tisak, J., & Goldstein, S. (2006). Aggression, delinquency, and morality: A social-cognitive perspective. In M. Killen & J. Smetana (Eds.), *Handbook of moral development* (pp. 611–629). Hillsdale, NJ: Erlbaum.

Turiel, E. (2006). The development of morality. In W. Damon & R. Lerner (Series Eds.) & N. Eisenberg (Vol. Ed.), *Handbook of child psychology: Vol. 3. Social, emotional, and personality development* (6th ed., pp. 789–780). New York, NY: Wiley.

Zajonc, R. (1984). On the primacy of affect. *The American Psychologist, 39,* 117–123. doi:10.1037/0003-066X.39.2.117

I

THEORETICAL FOUNDATIONS

1

EMOTION IN EARLY CONSCIENCE

ROSS A. THOMPSON AND EMILY K. NEWTON

Emotions are prominent in classic theories of moral development. From early in life, children are portrayed as being motivated to act morally owing to fear of punishment, anxiety over the loss of parental love, anticipated rewards, internalized guilt, the experience of shame, or other emotional incentives. Perhaps because early morality is usually viewed in terms of compliance to prohibitive expectations, it is important that these emotional incentives are primarily negative: Children comply because of the aversive consequences of failing to do so. This view of emotion in morality is especially apparent for young children, who are portrayed as premoral, externalized, consequentialist, obedience oriented, and egocentric in traditional portrayals of moral growth (e.g., Bandura, 1991; Freud, 1940/1949; Kohlberg, 1969; Piaget, 1932/1985; Skinner, 1971).

Recent years have witnessed, however, the emergence of a new view of the emotional foundations of moral growth from an unexpected source: studies of young children. Contrary to traditional portrayals of early egocentrism, this research literature highlights the early-emerging sensitivity of infants and toddlers to others' feelings, needs, and desires; the early growth of a "moral self" and of helping behavior; the positive relational incentives to cooperative behavior; and the influence of the emotional communication in parent–child conversation that connects moral conduct with the feelings of others. These studies of early socioemotional understanding and conscience development are leading to a new portrayal of early moral development that shares much in common with the more relational and humanistic morality of later years (Thompson, in press)—and also contributes to a more complex and constructive portrayal of the role of emotion in moral growth.

This chapter profiles this research and its implications for the future study of emotion and its role in moral development. We begin by considering the foundations of conscience development in the first 2 years, when infants and toddlers are constructing an understanding of others' feelings and how to respond to them. Studies of social referencing, toddlers' sensitivity to standards, and the emergence of self-conscious emotions and empathy together highlight the importance of emotion to morally relevant appraisals and evaluations. In the subsequent section, we turn to research on conscience development in preschoolers and consider the influence of parent–child relationships and, more specifically, how the emotional communication between parents and offspring is important to the growth of conscience. Taken together, the research discussed in this chapter, including work from our lab, suggests that emotions are significant for the positive—as well as aversive—incentives they offer to moral conduct, that relational experience is central to the early socialization of moral awareness, and that early conscience development shares many of the same constructive emotional incentives that older children and adults experience.

FOUNDATIONS OF CONSCIENCE IN THE FIRST 2 YEARS

What is conscience? *Conscience* can be defined as the cognitive, affective, and relational processes that enable children to construct and act according to internalized standards of conduct defined by experience, personal relationships, and societal expectations (Thompson, Meyer, & McGinley, 2006). Conscience is thus a much broader concept than moral judgment, which has been the longstanding focus of moral development research. Although it would be surprising to portray experiences in infancy and toddlerhood as important foundations to moral judgment, the study of conscience development has shown how the cognitive, affective, and relational foundations of conscience are established very early.

Sensitivity to Emotions and Goals in Infancy

Sensitivity to others' emotions is one of these early foundations. During the early months, infants can readily differentiate positive and negative emotional expressions in the face and voice and show a preference for facial and vocal expressions that are congruent rather than incongruent (Bornstein & Arterberry, 2003; Fernald, 1993; Walker-Andrews, 1997). Their early capacity to appropriately "read" others' emotional expressions provides a basis in subsequent months for implicit knowledge of how people's emotions occur in response to objects, people, or events in the environment and are associated with (fulfilled or frustrated) goals and desires. Infants and toddlers begin to understand, in other words, how emotions offer a window into the minds of other people.

Their early sensitivity to the meaning of emotional expressions causes infants to derive sophisticated inferences, for example, concerning others' intentions or desires. Experimental studies by Phillips, Wellman, and Spelke (2002) showed that 12-month-olds were unsurprised to find that an adult who had gazed and spoken warmly toward one of two stuffed kittens was subsequently observed to be holding the kitten, but they responded as if the sight of the adult subsequently holding the other kitten was unexpected—suggesting that the adult's emotional expressions led to expectations of the adult's intentions toward the two toys. In a similar manner, Liszkowski and colleagues showed that 12-month-olds pointed to the location of an object that a surprised and perplexed experimenter had misplaced, again using the adult's emotional signals to infer a desire that infants helped to fulfill (Liszkowski, Carpenter, Striano, & Tomasello, 2006). As these studies (and others) suggest, 1-year-olds not only interpret others' emotional expressions in a nonegocentric manner, but also use them as sources of information about the mental state of the emoter to which they respond appropriately.

Social Referencing

Another important example of early emotion understanding is social referencing, an easily observed behavior in which 1-year-olds look to the face of a trusted adult when they encounter an ambiguous event and then respond according to the adult's emotional expression (Moses, Baldwin, Rosicky, & Tidball, 2001; Sorce, Emde, Campos, & Klinnert, 1985). For example, if mother acts warmly toward an unfamiliar adult or novel object, infants are more likely to approach it; but if mother exhibits fear, the infant is more likely to avoid the person or object and stay close to mother. Social referencing is important because it indicates that infants are good interpreters and consumers of others' emotional cues, and that they use this information to vicariously learn about the emotional meaning of events.

Viewed in this light, it is apparent how the emotional cues of social referencing can become enlisted into young children's understanding of behavioral standards and evaluations. Parents commonly display cautionary facial and vocal expressions when infants approach potentially dangerous objects, and they exhibit anticipatory cues of disapproval when toddlers are about to engage in forbidden activity. In other circumstances, such as when young children witness another's distress (or have caused it), caregivers use their emotional signals to induce sympathy for another person. Sometimes social referencing is enlisted to communicate evaluations of other people (such as when the family witnesses a sibling's temper tantrum) or even of the child herself, such as when a parent looks disapprovingly at a toddler's intentional disobedience. In these and other ways, social referencing connects behavioral standards to the emotional signals of people to whom the child is emotionally attached to endow certain behaviors, objects, or people with emotional significance. Much more remains to be learned about how social referencing contributes to the young child's acquisition of morally relevant appraisals and evaluations in these ways.

Advances in Emotion Understanding and Helping in the Second Year

Toddlers are psychologically more sophisticated than infants, and one reflection of this is their enhanced understanding of the associations between emotions and goals, desires, and intentions. By 18 months they are much more competent at understanding another person's mental state, especially on the basis of emotional cues. Toddlers will imitate an adult's intended action, even if the action was not completed (Meltzoff, 1995), for example, and they respond appropriately to another's desire even if it is different from their own preferences (Repacholi & Gopnik, 1997). In the latter study, 18-month-olds gave a friendly experimenter the broccoli she clearly preferred as a snack (conveyed with evocative expressions of delight while tasting the broccoli) rather than the crackers the child preferred. In doing so, toddlers were capable of interpreting the adult's emotional expressions to indicate preferences, which the child satisfied even though those preferences were different from his or her own.

The view that toddlers are capable of helping other people achieve their goals in this manner is inconsistent with traditional conceptions of early egocentrism, but consistent with new understanding of their sensitivity to the mental and emotional states of other people. In a series of studies, Warneken and Tomasello (2006, 2007) showed that by 18 months, toddlers spontaneously offered assistance more than half the time to help experimenters achieve their goals in experimental trials when the adult's need for aid was clear and children knew how to help. By contrast, toddlers helped infrequently when the adult's need for assistance was not clearly apparent in control trials. For example, toddlers retrieved a marker 65% of the time when the adult accidentally dropped it on the floor and unsuccessfully reached for it, but did so less than 25% of the time when the adult intentionally dropped the marker on the floor without reaching (Warneken & Tomasello, 2006). Helping occurred in the absence of any reward for doing so and, indeed, seems to be undermined by extrinsic rewards in 20-month-olds (Warneken & Tomasello, 2008).

The experimenters in the Warneken and Tomasello studies were affectively neutral throughout the procedure to avoid rewarding toddlers for helping with positive emotional expressions or praise. But young children may not require another's manifest dismay or distress to infer sad affect when other cues of apparent need (e.g., reaching for a lost marker) are so apparent, especially in light of their understanding of the associations between emotion, desire, and intention. In an interesting follow-up study, Vaish, Carpenter, and Tomasello (in press) reported that when 18- and 25-month-olds observed an adult who acted harmfully toward another (by destroying or taking away his or her possessions) rather than benignly, they were more likely in a subsequent situation to help the victim, even though the latter showed no emotion in either circumstance. The researchers hypothesized that the young children in this study did so because of rudimentary affective perspective-taking skills. We are currently replicating the Warneken and Tomasello (2006, 2007) study in our lab, with the additional experimental factor that the adult looks either sad or indifferent in the experimental trials. Our findings will provide additional evidence of whether an adult's immediate emotional expressions are an important influence on young children's helping in this situation, or whether basic capacities for affective perspective taking contribute to toddlers' helping regardless of the adult's emotional expression.

Sensitivity to Standards

Although classic moral development theories emphasize the role of parents for instilling standards in their children, contemporary research has shown that young children contribute to their own sense of what is normative on the basis of their everyday experiences. Toddlers sometimes develop their own sense of what is or is not correct independently of parental efforts, manifested in their overregularizations in early word usage and their inflexibility about bedtime or morning rituals. In the moral domain, toddlers have also been observed to react to damaged objects with increased attention, interest, and negative emotional evaluations, reflecting their awareness that these objects deviate from implicit norms of wholeness and intactness (Kagan, 2005; Kochanska, Casey, & Fukumoto, 1995).

Kagan (2005) has reported that 19-month-olds have adverse reactions to broken, damaged, or marred objects, expressing dismay and curiosity about who is responsible for the damage. Kagan attributed these emotional responses to "morally" violated objects to parental socialization: Parents prohibit damaging objects and express dismay when children break things, often cautioning children against certain actions lest something gets broken. In his view, therefore, toddlers' sensitivity to damaged objects reflects an emergent moral sensitivity to violated standards deriving from parents' sanctions.

In a study conducted in our lab with 14- to 23-month-olds (reported in Thompson, in press), however, Thompson and McGinley found that toddlers responded comparably to objects that were morally violated (e.g., a broken cup, a Teddy bear with one eye missing), objects that were functionally impaired without being broken (e.g., a cup with a finished hole at the bottom, a Teddy bear without stuffing), and objects that simply appeared different from normal (e.g., a cup with a handle at an unusual angle, a Teddy bear with psychedelic colors and wings). Young children responded with comparable interest, emotion, and attention to all forms of atypicality and did not respond to morally violated objects in any consistently distinctive way. This suggests that at this age, emotional responses to atypicality reflect young children's emergent standards for how things should be on the basis of how they typically are, and they are fascinated by deviations from the norm. To the extent to which young children's responses to objects that are damaged or marred reflect an emergent moral sensitivity, therefore, these responses seem to derive from a more general response to atypicality that reflects toddlers' emerging standards for what is normative in their everyday experience.

Self-Conscious Emotions and Empathy

A significant emotional foundation to conscience development is the emergence of self-conscious emotions like guilt, pride, shame, and embarrassment and their association with morally relevant behaviors. Although preschoolers reliably exhibit behaviors reflecting self-conscious emotions, careful observational studies have revealed that toddlers exhibit constellations of guilt-like behaviors (e.g., spontaneous confession, efforts at reparation), shame-like behaviors (e.g., avoidance of the adult, anxious mannerisms), and embarrassment (e.g., gaze-aversion and self-touching) in appropriate situations (Barrett, 2005; Lagattuta & Thompson, 2007). Barrett (2005) showed, for example, that 17-month-olds exhibit predictable expressions of guilt, shame, and embarrassment in response to a rigged mishap in which the experimenter's beloved doll was apparently "broken" by the child. Using the same procedure, Kochanska, Gross, Lin, and Nichols (2002) found similar results in a longitudinal study of guilt in children from 22 to 56 months of age. Individual differences in young children's guilt-like behaviors at 22, 33, and 45 months were stable over time and each predicted independent measures of conscience at 56 months. These findings suggest that self-conscious emotions are early emerging and may provide an important emotional foundation to conscience development.

Early manifestations of pride, guilt, and shame are associated with parental responses to young children's successes and failures, compliance, and disobedience (Stipek, 1995; Stipek, Recchia, & McClintic, 1992). Indeed, children's emotional responses to their morally and achievement-related behaviors derive, in part, from their anticipation of parental reactions. As the experimental studies described above suggest, however, it is unlikely that the behavioral reactions reflecting pride, shame, or guilt are nothing more than anticipated parental reward or punishment, as traditional moral development theories argue. Rather, children's self-generated standards and, as we shall note in the next section, their emergent sense of themselves as moral are also important resources for conscience development and likely constitute another basis for their self-conscious emotional reactions in situations of moral compliance or noncompliance.

Empathy is another important emotional resource for moral conduct (Thompson, 1998; Zahn-Waxler, 2000). Research by Zahn-Waxler, Robinson, and Emde (1992), Spinrad and Stifter (2006), and others has shown that toddlers often look at a distressed person with concern and, more rarely, will offer assistance or comforting. These findings suggest, therefore, that early emotional sensitivity is manifested in empathy-like responses to distressed persons.

However, the low rates of helping by young children in these situations merits further attention. By contrast with the studies of early helping reviewed earlier, experimental empathy probes usually provide toddlers with few meaningful ways of assisting a distressed adult (e.g., if an experimenter hurts her finger in a distress simulation, there is little the child can do to fix the adult's finger, and it is uncharacteristic for a child to provide comfort to an adult). Thus, although empathy may be an early-emerging resource for moral conduct, its association with prosocial behavior is limited both because empathy is a motivationally complex emotional response (toddlers may seek personal comfort rather than comforting another) and because young children must know how to effectively help an adult in the situation. For similar reasons, empathy may not be the curb on aggressive conduct in very young children that it is for older children and adults because of the conceptual challenges of anticipating another's distress on the basis of one's actions. For this reason, it is common for caregivers to respond to a toddler who has been hurt by another's aggression, only to discover that the perpetrator of harm is also seeking comfort for her or his vicarious distress.

Interim Conclusion

The studies described in this section show that infants and toddlers are surprisingly sensitive to the emotional and mental states of other people, including others' needs, goals, and desires to which young children often respond appropriately. Toddlers exhibit a capacity to act helpfully toward adults when they know how to do so, and emotions are also important to the morally relevant appraisals and evaluations that develop in the early years. Viewed in this light, it appears that contrary to the primarily aversive influence of emotion on young children in classic moral developmental theories, emotional reactions of the child and others are complex, multifaceted catalysts to early moral sensitivity and the motivation to act cooperatively and prosocially toward others. Emotions motivate young children to act helpfully and prosocially as well as compliantly (i.e., resisting acting badly), and these emotions include awareness of others' feelings when they are in need, the emotional evaluations of other people, and young children's feelings of pride in good behavior as well as the aversive emotions when experiencing the consequences of misbehavior.

CONSCIENCE DEVELOPMENT IN
THE CONTEXT OF EARLY RELATIONSHIPS

With these emotional and conceptual foundations established during the first 2 years, conscience fully emerges during the preschool years. But conscience development does not resemble the premoral or preconventional morality of classic moral development theories. Instead, preschoolers develop a moral sense in response to a rich variety of emotions they perceive in other people, their emotional responses to others, and the affective consequences of their own moral conduct.

This is revealed in two recent studies. Wright and Bartsch (2008) analyzed the spontaneous verbal behavior of two young children using the archived CHILDES database, focusing especially on talk related to moral issues by Abe and Sarah recorded between the ages of 2 and 5 years. During this period of developing moral awareness, neither child talked much about moral rules and standards, but each frequently evaluated people's dispositions and actions with reference to feelings and human welfare. Thus at age 3.2 years, Sara commented "my cousin hit me, and she's a bad girl," and at age 2.11 years, Abe said "I think they are mean to that man because they put him in that glue." Positive emotions were also mentioned in the children's comments about approved and disapproved behavior: At age 3.4 years, Abe said, "I'm picking up mine because I want you to be happy." In their greater interest in the internal over the external motivators of good and bad behavior, emotions and emotional inferences were foremost. At age 3.9 years, Sara enlisted affective perspective, saying, "These hits hurts for you," and at 3.1 years, Abe cautioned (when his father threatened to harm a stuffed toy) "don't do that then

I will get sad." For both children, early moral sensibility was closely tied to positive and negative emotions in themselves and others.

In a second study, Kochanska (2002a) examined 5-year-olds' emerging views of themselves on moral dimensions, building on prior studies showing that children of this age characterize themselves in terms of internal characteristics and traits (e.g., Measelle, Ablow, Cowan, & Cowan, 1998). Emotional responses figure prominently in this early moral self: preschoolers with a strong moral component to their self-awareness were more likely to endorse statements describing themselves as someone who feels badly about doing the wrong thing ("when I do something wrong, sometimes I get a funny feeling in my tummy"), responds sympathetically and helpfully to others ("I try to make other people happy when they are sad"), and is concerned about violations of behavioral standards ("it upsets me when others do something wrong"). The validity of this assessment is supported by research showing that individual differences in the "moral self" were predicted by children's observed responses to wrongdoing in the lab and related morally relevant behaviors at earlier ages (Kochanska et al., 2002). Emotional reactions thus are important to children's appraisals of themselves as moral actors.

As noted in the preceding discussion, these emotion-laden evaluations of moral conduct arise from young children's rapidly developing understanding of the internal motivators of behavior together with the salience of emotional reactions in everyday interaction. Young children can thus be viewed as intuitive moral theorists who construct understanding of right and wrong conduct on the basis of their everyday experience (Thompson et al., 2006). But they are assisted in their understanding by adults, who are models, interpreters, and socializers of moral conduct in their interactions with young children and who offer incentives to cooperative behavior through the emotional quality of the parent–child relationship (Laible & Thompson, 2007).

Parent–Child Relationship and Early Conscience

Parent–child relationships offer potentially diverse emotional incentives for the growth of conscience in young children. In addition to the sanctions of the discipline encounter emphasized by some moral development theories, positive incentives arise through the warmth and mutual responsiveness of the parent–child relationship. Consistent with the views of attachment theory, researchers have found that preschoolers in secure parent–child relationships are more advanced in conscience development, reflected in their more cooperative conduct with the parent and their greater willingness to comply with the parent's requests when left alone (Kochanska, 1995; Laible & Thompson, 2000). The reason that attachment security is important is suggested by further findings of Kochanska (1991, 1995), who has shown that a secure attachment is especially influential for children who are temperamentally relatively fearless, for whom the emotional incentives of a positive mother–child relationship—rather than the anxiety provoked by maternal discipline practices—are motivational. Temperamentally bold children in secure relationships cooperate in order to maintain the warm reciprocity of the mother–child relationship. In addition, as discussed further below, secure attachments provide a forum for exploring emotion in oneself and others, including the emotions associated with good and bad behavior.

Taking a broader view, Kochanska (2002b) argued that a warm parent–child relationship is important to conscience development because it is a preschooler's first experience with the mutual obligations of close relationships. Although young children obviously cannot be equal contributors to such a relationship, the reciprocity of warmth and cooperation in relationships in which adults are positively responsive motivate young children to themselves respond cooperatively and positively to the parent's initiatives. Such a relationship also orients young children to the human dimensions of their conduct (e.g., consequences for the caregiver and others) and makes children generally more receptive to the parent's values and socialization initiatives (for similar views, see also Maccoby, 1984; Waters, Kondo-Ikemura, Posada, & Richters, 1991). Viewed in this manner, therefore, the parent–child relationship is important to conscience development not primarily as a source of the aversive emotional consequences of noncompliance (e.g., punishment, loss of parental love, shame), but primarily as a source of positive incentives for cooperative and, ultimately, self-motivated moral conduct.

In support of this view, several longitudinal studies have found that the mutual responsiveness and shared positive emotion of parent–child interaction early in childhood predict later measures of conscience development (e.g., Kochanska, Forman, & Coy, 1999; Kochanska & Murray, 2000; Laible & Thompson, 2000; see reviews by Kochanska, 2002b, Thompson et al., 2006). When mothers and young children are mutually responsive and positive toward each other, children subsequently are found to score higher on assessments of conscience development (e.g., cooperative compliance; internalized behavioral conduct in the parent's absence). One reason is that in such relationships, mothers use fewer power assertive discipline practices with young children and thus elicit less emotional reactivity from their offspring during discipline encounters (Kochanska, Aksan, Prisco, & Adams, 2008). In another study, Kochanska, Aksan, Knaack, and Rhines (2004) found that for securely attached children (assessed at 14 months), the parent's responsiveness and use of gentle discipline (from 14 to 45 months) predicted conscience development when children were 56 months old. By contrast, for insecurely attached children there was no such association.

It appears, therefore, that in parent–child relationships characterized by mutual responsiveness, the positive emotional incentives for preschoolers' cooperative conduct are complemented by fewer aversive parental practices to ensure compliance. Much more research remains to determine whether these are correlated or causal associations between parental socialization practices, but in light of the negative association between parental-power assertion and moral internalization found in studies with older children (Hoffman, 1970), these findings suggest that conscience development is fostered by early parent–child relationships characterized by mutual responsiveness and respect, shared positive emotion, and secure attachments.

Emotional Influences in Parental Discipline Practices and Parent–Child Conversation

Traditional moral development theories emphasize the influence of parental discipline practices on childhood moral development. Parents who use power-assertive discipline have children who are less morally mature and externalized in their reasons for compliance, whereas parents who primarily use reasoning have children with a more mature, internalized orientation (Hoffman, 1970). Studies with young children have also found this to be true: Parental discipline practices that enlist reasoning and provide young children with justifications for cooperation are more likely to foster the internalization of parental values—even though preschoolers are also likely to negotiate, bargain, and initially resist before complying (Crockenberg & Litman, 1990; Kuczynski & Kochanska, 1990).

Parental reasoning during discipline encounters may be especially important in early childhood for clarifying the conflicting feelings, motives, and intentions of the people in disagreement, as well as conveying attributions of responsibility, clarifying issues of causality, and instilling an understanding of social obligation. But parent–child conversation during discipline encounters may not be an optimal forum for fostering moral understanding in children (Thompson, 2006b). When confronted with misbehavior, children's negative arousal (whether distress, guilt, anger, or shame) may undermine their attention to and understanding and retention of the parent's values message, which is tied to a specific prohibitive violation rather than a broader message of moral obligation or positive values. In this respect, therefore, emotion enters into moral socialization in another manner: A child's emotional arousal when parental messages are being conveyed may have a significant influence on how these messages are understood and remembered by the child.

It is important to remember, however, that the discipline encounter is not the only conversational forum in which moral socialization occurs. Several researchers have found that early conscience is predicted by the quality of mother–child conversation about good and bad behavior independently of the discipline context. These situations, which are part of the reminiscing that frequently occurs in parent–child relationships, enable mothers and children to discuss past events apart from the adversarial context of confronting immediate misbehavior. Laible and Thompson (2000), for example, recorded conversations between 4-year-olds and their mothers about events in the recent past in which the child either misbehaved or behaved appropriately. Several features of the mother's conversational discourse were coded, including the frequency of her references to rules and the consequences of breaking them and references to people's feelings. Mothers who more often talked about people's feelings had children who, in independent assessments, were more advanced in conscience development. By contrast, the frequency of maternal references to rules and the consequences of breaking them was never a significant predictor of preschoolers' conscience development. Indeed, in another study, mothers who recounted the child's misbehavior in the recent past with a critical or negative attitude or with feelings of disappointment or anger, or who provided reproach or punishment, had preschoolers with lower scores on measures of moral cognition (Kochanska, Aksan, & Nichols, 2003). The content and emotional tone of mother–child reminiscing about good and bad behavior are each important to its broader influence on conscience.

Similar findings were obtained in a subsequent prospective longitudinal study in which maternal references to feelings (but not references to rules and the consequences of breaking them) during conflict with the child at 30 months predicted children's more advanced conscience development 6 months later (Laible, 2004a; Laible & Thompson, 2002). In another study, 2- to 3-year-old children whose mothers used reasoning and discussed the concerns of other people in resolving conflict with them, and who were more advanced in emotion understanding at 40 months, had a more mature moral orientation in kindergarten and first grade (Dunn, Brown, & Maguire, 1995). Taken together, these findings suggest that contrary to traditional moral theories that emphasize the rules-and-obedience orientation of young children, early conscience is stimulated by conversations with adults that sensitize young children to the human dimensions of misbehavior and good behavior and help children understand the effects of their actions on other people and their feelings. Conversations with caregivers are important to linking the young child's expanding emotion understanding with moral conduct.

There are other ways that parent–child conversations, even during conflict with the child, can enhance conscience development. Mothers who take the initiative to resolve conflict with young children, using explanations to justify and clarify their requests, are capable of negotiating and compromising, and mothers who manage to avoid aggravating tension (e.g., through threats or teasing) have children who are more advanced in subsequent assessments of conscience development (Dunn et al., 1995; Laible & Thompson, 2002). And in reminiscing about past episodes of child misbehavior, mothers who have an elaborative conversational style—which includes providing rich background information, asking the child open-ended questions about what happened, and otherwise enhancing the child's understanding of the event—also have preschoolers with more advanced conscience development (Laible, 2004b).

These conversational influences are consistent with a broader research literature documenting the importance of the quality of parental discourse for young children's understanding of their experiences, themselves, and relationships with others (see Harris & Koenig, 2006; Nelson & Fivush, 2004; Thompson, 2006a; Thompson, Laible, & Ontai, 2003). Together they suggest that young children rely on the secondary representations afforded by parent–child conversation to enrich and clarify their understanding of direct experiences, especially when they are seeking to comprehend the underlying causes of social events. With respect to the development of emotion and sociomoral understanding, conversation with a caregiver can be helpful to clarifying others' feelings, attributing responsibility, inducing sympathetic understanding, suggesting conflict-resolution strategies, and engaging in other forms of shared understanding that link emotion understanding with moral conduct. These conversational catalysts to conscience development may also help to explain the importance of secure attachments, because several studies have shown that mothers in secure relationships make more frequent references to others' feelings and speak more elaborately in conversation about past events with their children (Laible, 2004b; Ontai & Thompson, 2002; Raikes & Thompson, 2006). They also enlist greater compromise and conflict-resolution strategies during disputes with offspring (Laible, Panfile, & Makariev, 2008). These conversational stimulants may help to explain why securely attached preschoolers are more advanced on both emotion understanding and conscience development (see Thompson, 2008, for a review).

CONCLUSION

The portrayal of the development of early moral sensibility yielded by contemporary research is very different from traditional portrayals of the egocentric and externalized young child. Far from egocentric, infants and toddlers have an early and rapidly developing awareness of how others' subjective experiences are different from their own, and by the end of the first year emotion has become the gateway to their understanding of other mental states in people. And although young children are responsive to the incentives and sanctions of caregivers, which influence their early experiences of self-conscious (self-evaluative) emotions, they are also developing internal standards that derive from their own affectively based evaluations of nonnormative objects and conduct. Perhaps most important, young children's sensitivity to other people's feelings, desires, and needs motivate efforts to offer assistance when they are capable of doing so, providing a basis for positive moral conduct and prosocial behavior. These early emotional foundations for conscience development are expanded in the preschool years, with the conceptual catalysts of parent–child conversation in which discussions of the feelings of others, learning about the other person's intentions, tutoring in conflict-resolution strategies—all in the context of a warm, secure, mutually responsive relationship—provide further catalysts to conscience development.

The studies discussed in this chapter not only offer a new and different portrayal of early childhood morality, but also of the role of emotion in moral development, particularly in the early years. Although it is doubtlessly true that children are motivated to moral conduct by the anticipated sanctions of noncompliance, current research suggests that this is a fairly small part of the emotional picture of early moral socialization. Far more important are young children's natural sensitivity to and interest in the feelings of others, the pride they take in being helpful, their intuitive evaluations of conduct based on people's feelings and welfare, the affective dimensions of their emergent moral self, and the capacity for empathy with another's emotional experience. In these and other respects, the emotional dimensions of early childhood moral sensibility are very similar to those attributed to older children by traditional moral development theorists. Central to these emotional incentives to moral conduct are the feelings experienced and discussed in close relationships. The studies of our lab and elsewhere offer a fascinating picture of how the emotional quality of these relationships, the child's emotional experience in confronting moral issues with relational partners, and the emotion-related discussions with their partners combine to enlist emotional experience centrally into early sociomoral socialization.

The research described in this chapter also provides an agenda for future research. One of the most important questions for further study concerns how the various relational incentives to enhanced emotion and moral understanding fit together in early childhood. Experimental studies will be important to determining, for example, whether altering how mothers discuss misbehavior in the recent past can influence young children's conscience development without changing other incentives of the parent–child relationship (see Wareham & Salmon, 2006). Understanding better the conversational elements that contribute to early moral sensibility is also important. It is not surprising that young children do not particularly enjoy having their past misdeeds recalled for shared conversational analysis, and a recent study in our lab suggested that mothers' efforts to validate the child's emotional experience in a supportive manner can help to reduce child resistance. Likewise, a recent finding that diminished aggression in preschoolers was associated with the increased frequency of mothers' discussion of negative emotion in reminiscing with her child suggests that providing avenues for confronting negative feelings— which young children often experience as unsettling, confusing, and threatening—can have diverse positive consequences for young children, consistent with the predictions of attachment theory (Laible & Song, 2006). Other issues meriting future research inquiry include the influence of social referencing processes on young children's moral appraisals of events and people (including themselves) and how early helping behavior is affected by the emotional expressions (or their absence) in the recipient of aid.

It is almost always true that a renewed theoretical approach to a familiar topic generates renewed research interest. It is long past time for a new view of early childhood morality that takes into account contemporary understanding of early psychological growth and a new view of emotion in moral growth that takes into account its positive and constructive influences.

REFERENCES

Bandura, A. (1991). Social cognitive theory of moral thought and action. In W. M. Kurtines & J. H. Gewirtz (Eds.), *Handbook of moral behavior and development* (Vol. 1, pp. 45–103). Hillsdale, NJ: Erlbaum.

Barrett, K. C. (2005). The origins of social emotions and self-regulation in toddlerhood: New evidence. *Cognition and Emotion, 19,* 953–979. doi:10.1080/02699930500172515

Bornstein, M. H., & Arterberry, M. E. (2003). Recognition, discrimination, and categorization of smiling by 5-month-old infants. *Developmental Science, 6,* 585–599. doi:10.1111/1467-7687.00314

Crockenberg, S., & Litman, C. (1990). Autonomy as competence in 2-year-olds: Maternal correlates of child defiance, compliance, and self-assertion. *Developmental Psychology, 26,* 961–971. doi:10.1037/0012-1649.26.6.961

Dunn, J., Brown, J., & Maguire, M. (1995). The development of children's moral sensibility: Individual differences and emotion understanding. *Developmental Psychology, 31,* 649–659. doi:10.1037/0012-1649.31.4.649

Fernald, A. (1993). Approval and disapproval: Infant responsiveness to vocal affect in familiar and unfamiliar languages. *Child Development, 64,* 657–674. doi:10.2307/1131209

Freud, S. (1949). *A general introduction to psychoanalysis* (J. Strachey, Trans.). New York, NY: Modern Library. (Original work published 1940)

Harris, P. L., & Koenig, M. (2006). Trust in testimony: How children learn about science and religion. *Child Development, 77,* 505–524. Medline doi:10.1111/j.1467-8624.2006.00886.x

Hoffman, M. L. (1970). Moral development. In P. H. Mussen (Ed.), *Handbook of child psychology: Vol. 2* (3rd ed., pp. 261–354). New York, NY: Wiley.

Kagan, J. (2005). Human morality and temperament. In G. Carlo & C. Pope-Edwards (Eds.), *Nebraska Symposium on Motivation: Vol. 51. Moral motivation through the lifespan* (pp. 1–32). Lincoln, NE: University of Nebraska Press.

Kochanska, G. (1991). Socialization and temperament in the development of guilt and conscience. *Child Development, 62,* 1379–1392. Medline doi:10.2307/1130813

Kochanska, G. (1995). Children's temperament, mother's discipline, and security of attachment: Multiple pathways to emerging internalization. *Child Development, 66,* 597–615. doi:10.2307/1131937

Kochanska, G. (2002a). Committee compliance, moral self, and internalization: A mediated model. *Developmental Psychology, 38,* 339–351. Medline doi: 10.1037/0012-1649.38.3.339

Kochanska, G. (2002b). Mutually responsive orientation between mothers and their young children: A context for the early development of conscience. *Current Directions in Psychological Science, 11,* 191–195. doi:10.1111/1467-8721.00198

Kochanska, G., Aksan, N., Knaack, A., & Rhines, H. (2004). Maternal parenting and children's conscience: Early security as a moderator. *Child Development, 75,* 1229–1242. Medline doi:10.1111/j.1467-8624.2004.00735.x

Kochanska, G., Aksan, N., & Nichols, K. E. (2003). Maternal power assertion in discipline and moral discourse contexts: Commonalities, differences, and implications for children's moral conduct and cognition. *Developmental Psychology, 39,* 949–963. Medline doi:10.1037/0012-1649.39.6.949

Kochanska, G., Aksan, N., Prisco, T. R., & Adams, E. E. (2008). Mother–child and father–child mutually responsive orientation in the first 2 years and children's outcomes at preschool age: Mechanisms of influence. *Child Development, 79,* 30–44. Medline doi:10.1111/j.1467-8624.2007.01109.x

Kochanska, G., Casey, R., & Fukumoto, A. (1995). Toddlers' sensitivity to standard violations. *Child Development, 66,* 643–656. doi:10.2307/1131940

Kochanska, G., Forman, D., & Coy, K. (1999). Implications of the mother–child relationship in infancy for socialization in the second year of life. *Infant Behavior and Development, 22,* 249–265. doi:10.1016/S0163-6383(99)00009-0

Kochanska, G., Gross, J., Lin, M.-H., & Nichols, K. (2002). Guilt in young children: Development, determinants, and relations with a broader system of standards. *Child Development, 73,* 461–482. Medline doi:10.1111/1467-8624.00418

Kochanska, G., & Murray, K. (2000). Mother–child mutually responsive orientation and conscience development: From toddler to early school age. *Child Development, 71,* 417–431. Medline doi:10.1111/1467-8624.00154

Kohlberg, L. (1969). Stage and sequence: The cognitive-developmental approach to socialization. In D. A. Goslin (Ed.), *Handbook of socialization theory and research* (pp. 347–480). Chicago, IL: Rand McNally.

Kuczynski, L., & Kochanska, G. (1990). Development of children's noncompliance strategies from toddlerhood to age 5. *Developmental Psychology, 26,* 398–408. doi:10.1037/0012-1649.26.3.398

Lagattuta, K., & Thompson, R. A. (2007). The development of self-conscious emotions: Cognitive processes and social influences. In R. W. Robins & J. Tracy (Eds.), *Self-conscious emotions* (2nd ed., pp. 91–113). New York, NY: Guilford Press.

Laible, D. (2004a). Mother–child discourse about a child's past behavior at 30 months and early socioemotional development at age 3. *Merrill-Palmer Quarterly, 50,* 159–180. doi:10.1353/mpq.2004.0013

Laible, D. (2004b). Mother–child discourse in two contexts: Links with child temperament, attachment security, and socioemotional competence. *Developmental Psychology, 40,* 979–992. Medline doi:10.1037/0012-1649.40.6.979

Laible, D., Panfile, T., & Makariev, D. (2008). The quality and frequency of mother–toddler conflict: Links with attachment and temperament. *Child Development, 79,* 426–443. Medline doi:10.1111/j.1467-8624.2007.01134.x

Laible, D., & Song, J. (2006). Constructing emotional and relational understanding: The role of affect and mother–child discourse. *Merrill-Palmer Quarterly, 52,* 44–69. doi:10.1353/mpq.2006.0006

Laible, D. J., & Thompson, R. A. (2000). Mother–child discourse, attachment security, shared positive affect, and early conscience development. *Child Development, 71,* 1424–1440. Medline doi:10.1111/1467-8624.00237

Laible, D. J., & Thompson, R. A. (2002). Mother–child conflict in the toddler years: Lessons in emotion, morality, and relationships. *Child Development, 73,* 1187–1203. Medline doi:10.1111/1467-8624.00466

Laible, D. J., & Thompson, R. A. (2007). Early socialization: A relational perspective. In J. Grusec & P. Hastings (Eds.), *Handbook of socialization* (Rev. ed., pp. 181–207). New York, NY: Guilford Press.

Liszkowski, U., Carpenter, M., Striano, T., & Tomasello, M. (2006). Twelve- and 18-month-olds point to provide information for others. *Journal of Cognition and Development, 7,* 173–187. doi:10.1207/s15327647jcd0702_2

Maccoby, E. E. (1984). Socialization and developmental change. *Child Development, 55,* 317–328. doi:10.2307/1129945

Measelle, J. R., Ablow, J. C., Cowan, P. A., & Cowan, C. P. (1998). Assessing young children's views of their academic, social, and emotional lives: An evaluation of the self-perception scales of the Berkeley Puppet Interview. *Child Development, 69,* 1556–1576.

Meltzoff, A. N. (1995). Understanding the intentions of others: Re-enactment of intended acts by 18-month-old children. *Developmental Psychology, 31,* 838–850. doi:10.1037/0012-1649.31.5.838

Moses, L. J., Baldwin, D., Rosicky, J., & Tidball, G. (2001). Evidence for referential understanding in the emotions domain at twelve and eighteen months. *Child Development, 72,* 718–735. Medline doi:10.1111/1467-8624.00311

Nelson, K., & Fivush, R. (2004). The emergence of autobiographical memory: A social-cultural developmental theory. *Psychological Review, 111*, 486–511. Medline doi:10.1037/0033-295X.111.2.486

Ontai, L., & Thompson, R. A. (2002). Patterns of attachment and maternal discourse effects on children's emotion understanding from 3- to 5-years of age. *Social Development, 11*, 433–450. doi:10.1111/1467-9507.00209

Phillips, A. T., Wellman, H. M., & Spelke, E. S. (2002). Infants' ability to connect gaze and emotional expression to intentional action. *Cognition, 85*, 53–78. Medline doi:10.1016/S0010-0277(02)00073-2

Piaget, J. (1985). *The moral judgment of the child* (M. Gabain, Trans.). London, England: Routledge & Kegan Paul. (Original work published 1932)

Raikes, H. A., & Thompson, R. A. (2006). Family emotional climate, attachment security, and young children's emotion understanding in a high-risk sample. *The British Journal of Developmental Psychology, 24*, 89–104. doi:10.1348/026151005X70427

Repacholi, B., & Gopnik, A. (1997). Early reasoning about desires: Evidence from 14- and 18-month-olds. *Developmental Psychology, 33*, 12–21. Medline doi: 10.1037/0012-1649.33.1.12

Skinner, B. F. (1971). *Beyond freedom and dignity.* New York, NY: Knopf.

Sorce, J. F., Emde, R. N., Campos, J. J., & Klinnert, M. D. (1985). Maternal emotional signaling: Its effect on the visual cliff behavior of 1-year-olds. *Developmental Psychology, 21*, 195–200. doi:10.1037/0012-1649.21.1.195

Spinrad, T. L., & Stifter, C. A. (2006). Toddlers' empathy-related responding to distress: Predictions from negative emotionality and maternal behavior in infancy. *Infancy, 10*, 97–121. doi:10.1207/s15327078in1002_1

Stipek, D. (1995). The development of pride and shame in toddlers. In J. Tangney & K. Fischer (Eds.), *Self-conscious emotions* (pp. 237–252). New York, NY: Guilford Press.

Stipek, D., Recchia, S., & McClintic, S. (1992). Self-evaluation in young children. *Monographs of the Society for Research in Child Development, 57*, (1, Serial No. 226).

Thompson, R. A. (1998). Empathy and its origins in early development. In S. Braten (Ed.), *Intersubjective communication and emotion in early ontogeny* (pp. 144–157). Cambridge, England: Cambridge University Press.

Thompson, R. A. (2006a). Conversation and developing understanding: Introduction to the special issue. *Merrill-Palmer Quarterly, 52*, 1–16. doi:10.1353/mpq.2006.0008

Thompson, R. A. (2006b). The development of the person: Social understanding, relationships, self, conscience. In W. Damon & R. M. Lerner (Series Eds.) and N. Eisenberg (Vol. Ed.), *Handbook of child psychology: Vol. 3. Social, emotional, and personality development* (6th ed., pp. 24–98). New York, NY: Wiley.

Thompson, R. A. (2008). Early attachment and later development: Familiar questions, new answers. In J. Cassidy & P. R. Shaver (Eds.), *Handbook of attachment* (2nd ed., pp. 348–365). New York, NY: Guilford Press.

Thompson, R. A. (in press). Early foundations: Conscience and the development of moral character. In D. Narvaez & D. Lapsley (Eds.), *Moral self, identity and character: Prospects for a new field of study*. New York, NY: Cambridge University Press.

Thompson, R. A., Laible, D., & Ontai, L. (2003). Early understanding of emotion, morality, and the self: Developing a working model. In R. Kail (Ed.), *Advances in child development and behavior* (Vol. 31, pp. 137–171). San Diego, CA: Academic.

Thompson, R. A., Meyer, S., & McGinley, M. (2006). Understanding values in relationship: The development of conscience. In M. Killen & J. Smetana (Eds.), *Handbook of moral development* (pp. 267–297). Mahwah, NJ: Erlbaum.

Vaish, A., Carpenter, M., & Tomasello, M. (in press). Sympathy through affective perspective-taking and its relation to prosocial behavior in toddlers. *Developmental Psychology*.

Walker-Andrews, A. S. (1997). Infants' perception of expressive behaviors: Differentiation of multimodal information. *Psychological Bulletin, 121*, 437–456. Medline doi:10.1037/0033-2909.121.3.437

Wareham, P., & Salmon, K. (2006). Mother–child reminiscing about everyday experiences: Implications for psychological interventions in the preschool years. *Clinical Psychology Review, 26*, 535–554. Medline doi:10.1016/j.cpr.2006.05.001

Warneken, F., & Tomasello, M. (2006, March 23). Altruistic helping in human infants and young chimpanzees. *Science, 311*, 1301–1303. Medline doi:10.1126/science.1121448

Warneken, F., & Tomasello, M. (2007). Helping and cooperation at 14 months of age. *Infancy, 11*, 271–294.

Warneken, F., & Tomasello, M. (2008). Extrinsic rewards undermine altruistic tendencies in 20-month-olds. *Developmental Psychology, 44*, 1785–1788. Medline doi:10.1037/a0013860

Waters, E., Kondo-Ikemura, K., Posada, G., & Richters, J. (1991). Learning to love: Mechanisms and milestones. In M. Gunnar & L. Sroufe (Eds.), *Minnesota Symposia on Child Psychology: Vol. 23. Self processes and development* (pp. 217–255). Hillsdale, NJ: Erlbaum.

Wright, J. C., & Bartsch, K. (2008). Portraits of early moral sensibility in two children's everyday conversations. *Merrill-Palmer Quarterly, 54*, 56–85. doi:10.1353/mpq.2008.0010

Zahn-Waxler, C. (2000). The development of empathy, guilt, and internalization of distress: Implications for gender differences in internalizing and externalizing problems. In R. J. Davidson (Ed.), *Anxiety, depression, and emotion* (pp. 222–265). New York, NY: Oxford University Press.

Zahn-Waxler, C., Robinson, J. L., & Emde, R. N. (1992). The development of empathy in twins. *Developmental Psychology, 28*, 1038–1047. doi:10.1037/0012-1649.28.6.1038

2

TAKING EMOTIONS SERIOUSLY: THE ROLE OF EMOTIONS IN MORAL DEVELOPMENT

ELLIOT TURIEL AND MELANIE KILLEN

Some scholars are emotional about emotions. They tend to see human behavior through the prism of emotional reactions and heatedly criticize those who emphasize thought or reasoning or rationality as ignoring the essence of human functioning. Paradoxically, as scholars, theorists, and researchers of human psychology, they use reason (and evidence) to refute the relevance of reasoning (and the application of evidence) among laypersons. Insofar as the use of reasoning to refute reasoning is not paradoxical, it would be because of the implicit assumption that those who undertake to analyze human behavior use reasoning and evidence in ways not typically used by laypersons. In recent times, a number of constructs have been proposed to explain the ways that laypersons fail to use reasoning or to function rationally in their everyday decision making. These include intuitions, heuristics, frames, and, in recent neuroscience research, the idea that unconscious brain processes are the determinants of decisions and actions.

It is unclear from these formulations if laypersons are thought to be capable of using reasoning on a regular basis, as are the scholars. Presumably they would be, because we are all human beings with similar biological makeup and because it is education and specializations that allow scholars to reason in such intricate and flexible ways. If so, then it might be expected that people with education would be able to reason and act rationally in ways similar to those of scholars. Nevertheless, it could be argued that scholars have greater education and expertise in some areas and, therefore, reason more than educated laypersons. This opens up the possibility that there are group differences in the use of reasoning between the more and less educated.

All of this is to draw a contrast with the positions we take in this chapter—that those dichotomies between emotions and reasoning, and dichotomies between scholars and laypersons or the more and less educated with regard to thought or reasoning, are false dichotomies. Those who promote emotional determination and unconscious brain processes argue that an emphasis on thought and reasoning stems from the ideas of the Enlightenment and that current findings from the cognitive and neurosciences demonstrate that those ideas are false (Lakoff, 2008). Although many of the particulars of Enlightenment thought in general or propositions put forth by particular individuals may be questioned or revised, it is a radical and one-sided idea (and one might argue anti-intellectual and antiscientific) that the entire body of thinking about thinking, reasoning, rationality, and choice in decision making is to be supplanted. Of course, explanations of thought and choice in human functioning predated the Enlightenment, and in contemporary times, many in philosophy, social thought, and the psychological sciences (including evidence from much research) still provide analyses that give a coherent view of reasoning. One line of philosophical thought that has emphasized reasoning holds that "human beings are above all reasoning beings, and that the dignity of reason is the primary source of human equality" (Nussbaum, 1999, p. 71). As Nussbaum (1999) noted, this line of thought has important connections going back well before the Enlightenment to "the Greek and Roman Stoics, whose conception of the dignity of reason as a source of equal human worth profoundly influenced Kant, Smith, and others" (p. 71).

Our position on this issue is that emotions and morality include three main features. One is that emotions, in many instances, involve evaluative appraisals. A second is that emotions are connected with judgments. A third is that emotions, as evaluative appraisals in the moral domain, are often of a positive kind and not primarily aversive ones. Some of the focus in psychological research has been to attempt to explain morality as primarily avoidance behavior determined by strong emotions experienced as negative—such as fear, anxiety, guilt, and disgust. We propose, instead, that emotions like sympathy, empathy, attachments, promoting happiness, and desires to avoid experiencing pain and unhappiness are closely linked to morality and its development.

From childhood to adulthood, the acquisition of morality, we argue, is based, in part, on the emotions felt as a human being when contemplating what makes moral violations wrong. Although moral judgments can be generalized and impartial, the emotions that often lead an individual to infer a moral position may stem from personal experiences. Thus emotions as evaluative appraisals are associated with moral judgments, and moral judgments pertaining to harm or welfare, fairness or justice, and equality or rights include emotional appraisals. In this chapter, we elaborate on our view about these three points. We first examine the notion that emotions and reasoning are distinct entities. Second, we describe empirical research with children, which has demonstrated the developmental pattern of the intertwining of emotions and judgments. Third, we describe the emotions that form the basis of morality as it emerges throughout development, and which reflect positive dimensions of morality, such as empathy and respect for persons.

WHAT IS REASONING, AND ARE EMOTIONS AND JUDGMENTS DISTINCT?

There have been two interrelated misconceptions among psychologists, especially some psychologists attempting to explain morality about the proposition that human beings are reasoning beings. One is with regard to types and applications of reasoning and the other with regard to connections between reasoning and emotions. The first kind of misconception is that reasoning involves the application of formal and abstract principles without accounting for the particulars of social contexts or for competing claims in real situations people face. The interpretation of those who emphasize reasoning as referring to the application of formal principles is a misconception because, as much research shows, reasoning involves scrutiny, deliberation, and balancing of different types of considerations that arise in social situations and social relationships. Such reasoning can include reflection upon general or abstract concepts and how they can and cannot be applied in many situations. Reasoning can differ by domain, such that reasoning about logic or the physical world differs from reasoning about morality or the social world (Turiel & Davidson, 1986). Moreover, the process of deliberation involves reconciling conflicts, inconsistencies, and weighing different priorities.

Research on moral reasoning provides ample evidence of how seemingly formal, abstract concepts about welfare, justice, and rights are applied flexibly in social situations (see Helwig, 1995, on rights; Killen, Margie, & Sinno, 2006, on exclusion; and Turiel & Perkins, 2004, on honesty and trust). Moral reasoning does involve general concepts about welfare, justice, equality, and rights. As such, moral concepts are not monolithic, and moral ends can at times come in conflict with each other (e.g., welfare vs. rights). In fact, much of the philosophical and psychological developmental research has focused on how individuals evaluate situations with conflicting moral principles, demonstrating how complex situations are deliberated and debated. Furthermore, extensive developmental research has shown how concepts in the moral domain develop early in life and stand alongside other social, cultural, and personal concepts (Nucci, 2001; Smetana, 2006; Turiel, 1983, 2006). The existence of moral, social, and personal concepts means that people can perceive different and possibly competing considerations in social situations and that in order to understand how individuals come to their decisions, it is necessary to account for how different types of judgments are applied and balanced.

As a good deal of research on rights, honesty, and social inclusion and exclusion has shown, individuals draw on abstract concepts to evaluate, deliberate, and set priorities for making decisions in particular social contexts. As one example, children, adolescents, and adults understand concepts of rights in the abstract, which they apply in many situations; in other situations, they subordinate rights to avoid harm to persons or promote community interests (Helwig, 1995). As a second example, concepts of honesty and trust are often subordinated in situations that might require deception to prevent harm to persons (including to save lives) or promote fairness and justice (Perkins & Turiel, 2007; Turiel & Perkins, 2004).

As a third example, concepts of equality and fairness (e.g., with regard to race, gender, culture) are subordinated in some situations to considerations involving group cohesion, group identity, and the explicit goals of group norms (Killen et al., 2006). For example, in situations involving exclusion from groups, individuals weigh the reason for exclusion, such as preserving the group identity, with the reason for inclusion, such as treating people fairly and with respect. In these situations, the conflicts involve weighing multiple reasons for evaluating alternative courses of action, along with determining the salience of consequences (for both the group and the individual). The consequences for the group can include issues generally viewed as legitimate, such as group functioning as well as those that would be viewed as wrong from a moral viewpoint, such as prejudice or stereotyping. Thus, in this way, individuals weigh both the concepts associated with the acts along with the consequences to individuals, which include feelings and emotions (along with rights and fairness). As we argue here, deliberating various courses of action involves caring for others and using the emotional consequences of outcomes as significant considerations when deciding on the best or right course of action.

The second and related misconception of the view of humans as reasoning beings is most directly related to the main topic of this volume. It is that reasoning excludes and is distinct from emotions. On the assumption that reasoning is abstract, it is then seen as detached emotionally from situations. The philosophical and psychological traditions that take seriously the role of reasoning in human affairs also do not sharply separate emotions from reasoning.

Filling out her formulation of the philosophical traditions, Nussbaum (1999) stated that

> emotions such as fear, anger, compassion, and grief involve evaluative appraisals, in which people (or animals) survey objects in the world with an eye to how important goals and projects are doing. If one holds some such view of what emotions involve, the entire distinction between reason and emotion begins to be called into question, and one can no longer assume that a thinker who focuses on reason is by that move excluding emotion. (p. 72)

The idea that emotions involve evaluative appraisals is, indeed, contrary to the ways psychologists have often thought about emotions. By saying that they are evaluative, emotions are not conceived as forces that are simply there, or standing alone, in ways humans react to situations. It is not that our system, physiologically in-born or learned, reacts with a lack of control to experiences. Nor is it that emotions are the sole motivational force in driving cognitions or the attainment of goals. Instead, emotions are complex, and emotional reactions entail appraisals of the situation. (See Nussbaum, 2001, for an explication of how emotions like fear and grief can include judgments, perceptions of value, interpretations of objects and persons, and personal goals.)

FUNDAMENTAL EMOTIONS AND MORAL JUDGMENTS: SACREDNESS OF LIFE AND RESPECT FOR PERSONS

We propose that two general sentiments, the value of life and respect for persons, constitute broad and fundamental organizational features that significantly contribute to morality and its development. From a philosophical perspective, Dworkin (1993) has maintained that orientations to the intrinsic value of life include the strong emotional-conceptual sense of the sacredness or inviolability of life. In keeping with Dworkin's (1993) proposition that the sanctity of life is "a fundamental idea that almost all share in some form: that the individual human life is sacred" (p.13), we propose that most people maintain the sentiment of the sacredness and inviolability of life and hold the view that human life should flourish. In our view, in the study of morality from the psychological viewpoint, it is very important to take into account people's sense that lives have intrinsic value and that life is sacred, and to study how early in development this sense of respect for persons originates.

One important question is whether the sacredness of life and respect for persons are emotions. In significant respects they are emotions, in that people feel highly emotional about maintaining their own lives; the lives of close others (e.g., family, friends); and, in a general way, human life (including those one does not know). These orientations, however, are not solely emotional. Unlike current formulations of emotions as instinctual, unconscious processes, we agree with Nussbaum (2001) that emotions come with understandings about what one desires, the value of others in one's own life, the value of persons in each other's lives even when one is not part of those relationships, as well as the generalized value of persons.

Psychological research is also needed in order to explicate how the sense of the sacredness of life develops in individuals. A facile but very difficult to document explanation is the evolutionary one—that it has evolved for the preservation of the species. Evolutionary psychologists too often provide the circular story that if it exists, it must have evolved and that if it evolved, it exists to further preservation of the species. An alternative is to examine the process developmentally from the perspective of how emotions and thoughts are formed in people's social interactions and reflections on their experiences. A fundamental aspect of most people's experiences does relate to the feelings and ideas about one's desires to live and the awareness that others have the same desires. Study of the developmental processes related to the sense of sacredness of life is important but has not been done from the perspective that we have outlined in this chapter.

Unquestionably, the application of feelings and thoughts that lives have intrinsic value is complex. One of the complexities is that people do sometimes accept the taking of life. However, it is often the case that the sacredness of life is implicated in the taking of lives. Examples of such situations include suicide, capital punishment, self-defense, and war. With regard to these types of issues, research is needed to better understand how emotions and judgments pertaining to sacredness of life are applied and coordinated in situations of conflict involving decisions to terminate life that also have the goal of preserving lives.

The second phenomenon that forms broad and fundamental features in moral orientations—respect for persons—has been approached developmentally in the early work of Piaget (1932/1965) on children's moral judgments. The matter of respect has been considered in discussions of morality. For Kant (1785/1959), the central feature was the respect engendered for those who lay down obligatory rules, stemming from respect for moral rules. In Durkheim's (1925/1961) sociological perspective on morality, respect for the group or society was seen as a key sentiment that constitutes one of the main elements of morality. In Piaget's perspective, by contrast, it is respect for persons in relationships of mutuality and reciprocity that is essential for moral concepts of equality and justice. Emotions like fear, sympathy, and affection were all seen by Piaget to contribute to moral development. However, Piaget proposed that the early development of morality entailed a heteronomous orientation because of the unilateral respect young children feel for adult authority. The heteronomy of one-way respect for adults and obedience to their dictates and rules becomes transformed into an autonomous, reciprocal morality of mutual respect (to respect and be respected) that includes concerns with justice and fairness in serving the needs of persons and adjudicating competing interests. A good deal of research has cast doubt on the sequence proposed by Piaget that has children moving from heteronomy to autonomy. Research has demonstrated that young children form moral judgments that are not based on unilateral respect for authority or on adherence to their rules (Turiel, 1998). Young children form moral judgments about harm and fairness and display a respect for persons to be free of unnecessary hurt and unhappiness.

Research is needed to also ascertain how and at what ages children form sentiments of respect for persons in a generalized way that involves what Piaget termed mutual respect. Respect can take different forms. There is the respect for people with admired characteristics, such as their competence, achievements, or integrity. For the domain of morality, respect for persons as human beings is connected to concerns with their welfare, rights, and just treatment. It would appear that sentiments regarding the sacredness or inviolability of lives, respect for persons, and social justice are not disconnected from each other. Although we cannot yet adequately explain the intersection of sacredness of life and respect for persons, we propose that they are importantly intertwined with moral judgments that people's welfare should be promoted and that people should be free of unnecessary hurt and unhappiness, that people have rights and interests that should be protected, and that people should treat each other with justice. In fact, extensive research findings with children indicate that children evolve a respect for persons by early childhood; much less research has focused on children's recognition of the concept of the sacredness of life.

HARM, WELFARE, AND EMOTIONAL APPRAISALS

Consider the example of harm or welfare, which is an important aspect of moral judgments—including the moral judgments of young children. The evidence is clear that young children (by at least 5 or 6 years of age) and older people judge hitting (oneself being hit or someone else being hit) as morally wrong. To be sure, there are aversive emotions, or negative feelings, to experiences of physical hurt to self or in observing it occurring to others: It does not feel good, it is painful. However, these emotions are importantly combined with sympathy and empathy for the pain, as well as a sense of respect for the dignity of persons and desires of people to be free of pain.

Many studies in a wide range of cultures have shown that people judge hitting to be wrong because of the pain involved and the presumption that people do not want to be treated that way (Wainryb, 2006). In an early study conducted in the United States (Weston & Turiel, 1980), children from 5 to 9 years of age were presented with hypothetical situations in which the policy in a school is that hitting is permitted. The results of the study confirmed that moral judgments are not seen as contingent on authority dictates because most children stated that the policy is wrong and that children in the school still should not hit others. A 5-year-old boy's response helps illustrate how emotions are intertwined with moral judgments about harm, because he said that it is not all right for a school to allow hitting "because it is like making other people unhappy. You can hurt them that way. It hurts other people, hurting is not good" (Turiel, 1983, p. 62). This boy understood the emotions that people experience when pain is inflicted upon them, including that it makes them unhappy. His assessment reflects feelings of sympathy that are part and parcel of the moral judgment that hurting is not good and that it should not be done. It appears that he understood the following: "When you hit me it hurts me, and I get sad. When you get hit it hurts you, too, and you also feel sad."

These judgments about avoiding harm (along with judgments about promoting welfare) entail several complex features evident in many studies of moral judgments: that moral judgments about harm are not contingent on existing rules (judgments that acts are wrong even if no rule exists about them), or authority dictates (even if a teacher allows it), or institutional or common practice in a society or culture. Therefore, concerns with avoiding feelings of hurt and unhappiness, as well as promoting positive feelings, are intertwined not only with the judgment that it is wrong to hit but also with patterns of reasoning about rules, authority, generalizability, and common practices.

A set of studies by Arsenio and his colleagues have shown that the emotional outcomes children associate with moral acts differ from those they associate with other social domains, such as social conventional acts (Arsenio, 1988; Arsenio & Fleiss, 1996; Arsenio & Ford, 1985). In one study (Arsenio, 1988), for instance, children (5–12 years of age) were asked to attribute emotions to actors with different roles in different types of acts. The children differentiated among positive moral actions (helping, sharing), moral transgressions (stealing, hitting), and conventional transgressions. Children especially attributed positive emotions to actors, recipients, and observers with regard to positive moral acts. They attributed different emotions to recipients and instigators of moral transgressions, with recipients experiencing emotions of hurt feelings and instigators experiencing mixed emotions (some positive and some negative). Attributions to those who transgressed in the social conventional domain were of a different order in that emotions were neutral or feelings of sadness.

These studies have provided evidence for the proposition that emotions are evaluated and differentially connected to different types of events. Other research has illustrated some of the ways children as young as 3 or 4 years of age are aware of their own feelings and those of others in appraising social interactions they experience. In a study by Wainryb, Brehl, and Matwin (2005), children were asked to describe events involving harm they had experienced as either victims or perpetrators. The narratives analyzed by Wainryb et al. showed that children from preschool to high school ages take into account emotional experiences in their reactions to interactions with others. For example, a pre-school boy related the following experience as a victim:

> My friend Sydney . . . when I came inside her house, she said she really didn't want to play with me and she um she hit me and um and I felt bad and so I asked her mom . . . if I could go home and she said yes. (p. 54)

Another preschooler described his recollections as a perpetrator of harm:

> I was playing with my friend Adam and I said something that really hurt him and he said, "I don't like that." And I stopped. I also pushed him. And I said, "I'm sorry." Because he told me he didn't like it. (p. 54)

Both of these children recalled their actions based on feelings of hurt. The first child expressed the desire to remove himself from feelings of hurt stemming from acts of social rejection and hitting. Two other examples with older participants—a 1st-grade girl and a 10th-grade girl—illustrate that they think about feelings of self and others and connect them to their assessments of social relationships and concerns with mutual expectations. The 1st-grade girl, referring to a time she felt slighted by her best friend who referred to another child as her best friend, is both aware of the hurt feelings and ways to communicate to the other about it:

> And I kind of thought to myself that was kind of making me feel bad. So I wonder if I can go over there and tell her that I that that kind of hurt my feelings. . . . She's a best friend of mine and I just can't get it out of my mind because she, because, whenever I walked home from her home at night she would always give me a hug and I would always do that and we would and I would never want to leave her house. Then at the birthday. . . . I'm wondering if he's really her um best friend. (p. 56)

A more detailed concern with the feelings of another was expressed by the 10th-grade girl who talked about the time she evaded a planned evening with one of her best friends in order to spend time with other friends:

> And I remember uh I kind of lied to her but I mostly like avoided her one night . . . and then she figured it out and found out and she felt really bad and was hurt and so it wasn't good. Cause I bet she felt betrayed maybe even she thought I don't care about her but I do um I didn't want to hurt her feelings because she was one of my best friends. (p. 84)

This girl's portrayal included moral evaluations, and she attempted to account for the feelings of the other person and her own feelings about hurting the feelings of the other. With development and social experience, the types of emotions experienced become more psychological and complex, as do moral judgments. Although we do not have the space to discuss the multitude of ways in which this complexity changes over the lifespan, we illustrate our points about emotion and morality by focusing on judgments and experiences with inclusion and exclusion.

INCLUSION AND EXCLUSION: EMOTIONS AND SOCIAL JUSTICE

Inclusion and exclusion of people in groups and activities based on physical characteristics, abilities, gender, and ethnic or racial status are, of course, long-standing social and moral issues and constitute problems of social justice. People make moral judgments about equality and the need to include people in social interactions and group activities. People also exclude individuals from activities on the basis of their characteristics or perceived lack of certain characteristics (Abrams & Rutland, 2008; Killen, Sinno, & Margie, 2007). In dealing with inclusion and exclusion, children apply moral concepts about equality, fairness, and impartiality, as well as understandings of group cohesion and the needs for achieving the goals of group activities. Emotions are involved in such social interactions because people experience feelings of psychological hurt when they are excluded and because identification with groups includes attachments and care for others. Research findings on inclusion and exclusion provide good examples of how emotions and judgments are involved in social and moral decisions.

Attachments and affiliation to others result in relationships that create feelings of group loyalty that—although necessary for being a member of a culture, society, and community—can also potentially compete with concerns for impartiality in moral contexts. Impartiality is necessary to avoid serving selfish interests, but there are times when acting out of impartiality may also conflict with what underlies healthy social relationships, which includes positive emotional attachments. Contemporary philosophers, such as Appiah (2005), have written extensively about differentiations between the political and the personal sense of equality and impartiality, arguing that a personal sense of partiality may be consistent with a moral perspective. Taking this a step further, we propose that feelings of care for others are necessary for the acquisition of concepts of equality and fairness, which ultimately lead to inferences about the appropriateness of impartiality and justice.

Most generally, social development involves attachment to others, and from this beginning children form judgments about how to treat others (Dunn, 2006; Thompson, 2006). Through extensive interactions with peers at an early age, along with the larger infrastructure of communication with parents, children construct an understanding of reciprocity and fairness as well as caring about the welfare of others. As social attachments form in childhood (Cassidy, Kirsh, Scolton, & Parke, 1996), which reflect empathy, sympathy, and social friendships (Eisenberg, Spinard, & Sadovsky, 2006; Killen, 1991), social groups emerge as well, which contribute to children's social identity and group identity (Abrams & Rutland, 2008). Researchers working with adults have studied many of the outcomes of the emergence of group identity and have focused on the ways that social comparisons between the ingroup and the outgroup create negative emotions—those that lead to threat, fear, and ultimately, competition and prejudice (Brown & Gaertner, 2001).

Whereas most of this research was conducted with adults, recently there has been a focus on the emergence of group identity in childhood as it pertains to prejudice and stereotyping, the "negative" side of morality, that is, actions that lead to moral transgressions (Nesdale, 2008). Research on stereotyping and prejudice in childhood, for the most part, has focused on the negative emotions that accompany group identity. Yet, even from this perspective, there is a recognition that group identity plays an important role in the development of the person as a member of society and the positive emotions associated with group affiliation.

To a large extent, though, the findings from the research on intergroup relations reflect vastly different characterizations of the emotional underpinnings of children's social and moral orientations. On the one hand, research has demonstrated that for young children to acquire moral concepts of equality and fairness, it is necessary to form relationships with others that involve attachment, empathy, and reciprocity. On the other hand, research on group dynamics has shown that in forming their social identities, young children make comparisons with others that contribute to negative emotions associated with prejudice, discrimination, and bias.

There are a number of ways to view these different orientations. One could argue that when children give priority to group norms over norms of fairness, this implies that the emotional attachment to the group is more fundamental than the judgment of fairness. Alternatively, one could propose that for children who give priority to fairness, this implies that rationality is more basic than emotions. We argue that both of these interpretations reflect an oversimplification of the process, and that both emotions and judgments are implicated in different types of evaluations. As much as morality involves cognitive appraisals of situations, it also involves inferences about emotional assessments, such as those stemming from empathy and caring for others. Giving priority to group norms is emotional in terms of attachment to the group. It also involves cognitive understandings about group dynamics, in addition to the necessity of forming a group identity. In fact, children discuss their positive and negative emotions when making decisions that involve fairness in conflict with group norms.

Recent research on intergroup attitudes and group identity in childhood has provided some insights into this seemingly dichotomized characterization of moral development and moral emotions (Levy & Killen, 2008). As an example, one line of research (Killen, 2007; Killen, Richardson, & Kelly, in press; McGlothlin, Edmonds, & Killen, 2007) has investigated how children and adolescents evaluate exclusion from social groups and specifically exclusion based on group membership, such as gender, race, and ethnicity. Exclusion is an issue that involves a range of considerations including unfairness (when someone is excluded for arbitrary reasons that result in someone being denied access to resources), concerns about group functioning (making the group work well, creating an identity), and personal decisions (excluding someone from a social event because of psychological incompatibility). Moreover, exclusion involves prejudice and discrimination, as when someone is excluded solely on the basis of group membership such as gender, race, or ethnicity (Abrams, Rutland, & Cameron, 2003; Nesdale, 2004). Prejudice and discrimination have been theorized to be an outcome of group identity, a result of the threat and negative emotions that accompany outgroup derogation (Abrams, Hogg, & Marques, 2005). Exclusion, therefore, entails balancing moral judgments, social judgments, and both negative and positive emotions.

In some studies, children have been asked whether it is all right or not all right to exclude another child because of his or her gender or race/ethnicity. The findings indicate that the extent to which children and adolescents give priority to fairness or to group functioning is reflected, in part, by different types of emotional attributions about the experience of being excluded or the need to maintain group identity and group functioning. As in the following example from a large-scale study of children's evaluations of gender and racial exclusion in a range of peer groups (Killen, Lee-Kim, McGlothlin, & Stangor, 2002), children and adolescents often described the emotional consequences of what makes exclusion wrong. A 10th-grade ethnic minority girl explained her judgment about why it would be wrong for an adolescent ethnic majority boy to not invite another boy who is ethnic minority to sit with him at lunch with his friends:

> It's not okay. . . . Because he's going to see everybody. He's gonna see black people, he's gonna see white people, he's gonna see Asian people, he's going to see Cambodians, he's gonna see Ethiopians. I mean, yes, people do come from different places, and yes, they do speak different languages. But everybody has a heart, and they also have feelings, and they also know how it is to be put down. And it hurts. So I mean if you're the type of person who says "Okay, I don't like you because of a reason like that," it's just wrong and it's not fair. (Killen et al., 2002, p. 55)

In this case, the adolescent is incorporating her own attributions about how others will feel and using this information to make the moral judgment that it would be wrong to exclude someone from a different ethnic group. It is interesting that ethnic minority children were more likely to invoke emotional reactions of excluded recipients than were ethnic majority recipients and to use justifications based on empathy in addition to fairness (which was used by participants from all ethnic backgrounds). Most likely, judgments that involve empathy derive from prior personal experiences with exclusion, which, to some extent, enable individuals evaluating a decision to exclude someone as wrong.

Although the majority of children view exclusion as wrong because of unfairness, individuals who have experienced prior exclusion, such as girls (e.g., in sports) or ethnic minority youth, bring an empathic perspective to what makes exclusion wrong. In these cases, individuals who have experienced exclusion bring both emotional reactions of empathy and judgments about unfairness to bear on evaluations of exclusion. In these cases, negative emotions experienced while being excluded enabled positive emotions of empathy to lead to the judgment that exclusion is wrong in situations in which group membership is the sole basis for exclusion.

The distinction between the ingroup and the outgroup has the potential to interfere with morality, in that ingroup favoritism can result in inequalities, and outgroup negativity can result in prejudice and discrimination. The role of emotions in these processes is multifaceted, however. On the one hand, becoming attached to a group involves positive emotions of caring, loyalty, and empathy. On the other hand, social comparisons that result from distinguishing between the ingroup and the outgroup result in negative emotions such as threat and competition, which lead to prejudice and bias.

Research has also measured children's liking of others who are perceived to be from different groups and how the group dynamics surrounding exclusion involve both cognitive and emotional appraisals (Abrams & Rutland, 2008). It has been shown that, with age, children will more positively evaluate an outgroup member who supports the norms of the ingroup than an ingroup member who supports the norms of the outgroup. This indicates that knowledge about group norms is differentiated from the individuals who espouse the norms, and that this knowledge is reflected in judgments about liking and affect expressed for others. This often translates into evaluations of group loyalty, and the negative affect that gets expressed when group members are perceived to be disloyal to the group. Sometimes "disloyalty" may emerge in the expression of interest in outgroup members and what amounts to "cross-group" friendships. The fact that this type of social relationship may pose a threat to the ingroup (which it appears to do) provides information about why children begin to interact only with others who are perceived to be part of their own group. A negative aspect of "same group" preferences, however, is that research on prejudice has shown that intergroup contact (high-quality contact with the outgroup) reduces prejudice. Thus, if children begin to prefer to interact with same-group playmates, then this diminishes their outgroup contact, which means that group loyalty can have the negative outcome of contributing to prejudicial attitudes. This outcome would clearly constitute a negative dimension of group affiliation from a moral-fairness perspective.

In fact, additional evidence for the intertwining of judgments and emotions in intergroup relations is found in intergroup contact theory (Allport, 1954; Dovidio, Glick, & Rudman, 2005; Pettigrew & Tropp, 2005). Following Allport's theory (1954) that contact with members of outgroups reduces prejudice under certain conditions, current research has shown that the most significant predictor of prejudice reduction is cross-group friendship (other factors include cooperative goals, authority sanctions, and equal status; Pettigrew & Tropp, 2005). What is interesting about cross-group friendship is that the focus is on a positive emotional bond with another person from a different group. Thus, an underlying assumption is that the affective bonds with another individual from a different group background are directly connected to judgments about inclusion and exclusion.

Following this line of argument, Nesdale, Griffith, Durkin, and Maass (2005) found that children whose ingroup norm was exclusion reported that they disliked out-group members, whereas children whose ingroup norm was inclusion generally liked outgroup members (though to a lesser extent than ingroup members). Yet, children in these groups also reject exclusion in contexts in which the fairness dimensions are made explicit. All these findings provide evidence for the intertwined nature of emotions and reasoning for human social interactions.

Research with children and adolescents has demonstrated that moral judgments of fairness in groups have to be understood in the context of the basic processes of the formation of identification with a group. Thus it is necessary to consider children's social awareness about race, ethnicity, gender, and culture, as well as the extent to which identity with groups bears on social and moral judgments. As recent research has revealed, answers to these questions are complex. Giving priority to morality or to stereotypic expectations depends on the context and the target (gender, race, ethnicity) as well as the age, gender, and ethnicity of the individual making the decisions (Killen, 2007). As research findings with adults have indicated, individuals appear to hold both egalitarian views and intergroup biases (Fiske, 2002; Gaertner & Dovidio, 1986). How emotions play a role in moral judgments and group identity is equally complex.

CONCLUSIONS

We have presented a view of emotions in moral development that recognizes and attempts to account for the coherence of human functioning. Human beings do not function in disembodied ways; thought is not disjointed from emotions and emotions do not cause actions that are independent of thinking about social relationships. We have proposed that the sacredness or sanctity of life and respect for persons are fundamental sentiments for moral orientations and that these sentiments serve to organize moral judgments about welfare, justice, and rights. These sentiments do not stand alone but are closely connected to judgments that it is wrong to take a life, harm others, violate their rights, or treat them in unequal or unfair ways. Cognition about emotions and the importance of weighing emotional consequences when deciding how to treat others emerges very early in development (Dunn, 2006; Hastings, Zahn-Waxler, & McShane, 2006; Thompson, 2006). Young children use emotional information from others when determining whether to react to those in distress, to judge whether teasing is playful or harmful, and to engage in cooperative exchanges (Warneken & Tomasello, 2007). In conjunction with the fundamental sentiments of life and respect for persons, emotions like sympathy, empathy, compassion, affection, and attachment are important, as intertwined with moral reasoning, to the formation of morality from childhood to adulthood.

Experiences of these emotions are reciprocally related to moral judgments. For instance, feelings of sympathy or compassion for others lead individuals (including children) to the judgment that people should not be hurt or made unhappy, that they should be treated fairly, and that they should not be denied equal treatment. Correspondingly, moral judgments that people should not be hurt or made unhappy can result in emotions of sympathy or compassion for those who are hurt or made unhappy, treated unfairly, or denied equal treatment.

From this perspective, emotions like sympathy, empathy, compassion, and affection are more central to the origins and lifespan trajectory of moral development than emotions like fear, anxiety, guilt, and disgust. Others have placed the latter set of emotions at the forefront of moral acquisition and performance. This is because, as indicated at the outset, they believe that humans do not engage in purposeful, intentional, goal-directed thinking about the world around them and, especially about social relationships. Instead, humans are viewed either as organisms that are buffeted by their biological make-up (or at best guided by genetically encoded, deterministic brain processes of which they are unaware) or molded by their experiences of negative and aversive emotions. These are, of course, old stories in the field of psychology as seen in the instinctual and behaviorist positions of the first half of the 20th century (see Turiel, 2009). In recent times, we see a resurgence of explanations that draw sharp distinctions between emotions and thought and that place the onus of moral acquisition and behaviors on deterministic emotional reactions that render thought or rationality irrelevant (Killen & Smetana, 2008; Smetana & Killen, 2008). For some, it is primarily unconscious brain processes that determine emotional responses, which in turn control behavior (Greene, Sommerville, Nystrom, Darley, & Cohen, 2001). For others, it is built-in, automatic intuitions of a nonrational kind in conjunction with cultural acquisition that make for moral orientations (Haidt, 2001).

From these viewpoints, unlike the one asserted in this chapter, morality is mainly aversive; emotional reactions of disgust produce an aversion to certain acts that are then treated as moral injunctions. Two examples of acts that supposedly evoke nondeliberative intuitive emotional reactions are incest, and in some cultures, eating dog meat (Haidt, 2001; Haidt, Koller, & Dias, 1993). People regard these acts as morally wrong without thought or reflection. Insofar as people make judgments about the morality of these acts, it is merely to rationalize it to oneself and to try to convince others.

In our view, these types of issues are outliers to the central moral issues that have long been seriously grappled with (and using moral thought) regarding welfare, harm, benevolence, equality, social justice and injustices, ethnic, racial, gender and sexual prejudice, discrimination, war and peace, and much more. The use of examples like incest and eating dog meat represent reductionism and inappropriate generalizations to explain morality more broadly.

We propose that the aversive emotions play a much smaller role in morality than sympathy, empathy, compassion, and affection. Our view starts with the assumption that human beings do engage in thought and reflect upon their experiences, judgments, life goals, communications from others (Appiah, 2005; Habermas, 1990; Nussbaum, 2001), and the emotions they and others experience (for critiques of research and theory based on brain process and intuitions, see Killen & Smetana, 2008; Smetana, & Killen, 2008; Turiel, 2006, in press).

There is still much to uncover and explain about the integration of thought, emotions, and actions. To discount or deprecate the role of thought and deliberation in human functioning, and especially moral functioning, is to leave out some of the most important aspects that need to go into psychological explanation (and one of the reasons for the demise of behaviorism in the second part of the 20th century). Treating emotions as independent of thought ignores the embodied nature of human functioning. Emotions are central in moral development. But so is thought. To adequately understand moral development and moral decisions, it is necessary to examine the integration of emotions, thought, and action.

REFERENCES

Abrams, D., Hogg, M. A., & Marques, J. M. (2005). A social psychological framework for understanding social inclusion and exclusion. In D. Abrams, M. A. Hogg, & J. M. Marques (Eds.), *The social psychology of inclusion and exclusion* (pp. 1–24). New York, NY: Psychology Press.

Abrams, D., & Rutland, A. (2008). The development of subjective group dynamics. In S. R. Levy & M. Killen (Eds.), *Intergroup relations and attitudes in childhood through adulthood* (pp. 47–65). Oxford, England: Oxford University Press.

Abrams, D., Rutland, A., & Cameron, L. (2003). The development of subjective group dynamics: Children's judgments of normative and deviant in-group and out-group individuals. *Child Development, 74*, 1840–1856. Medline doi:10.1046/j.1467-8624.2003.00641.x

Allport, G. W. (1954). *The nature of prejudice.* Reading, MA: Addison Wesley.

Appiah, K. A. (2005). *The ethics of identity.* Princeton, NJ: Princeton University Press.

Arsenio, W. (1988). Children's conceptions of the situational affective consequences of sociomoral events. *Child Development, 59*, 1611–1622. Medline doi:10.2307/1130675

Arsenio, W., & Fleiss, K. (1996). Typical and behaviourally disruptive children's understanding of the emotional consequences of socio-moral events. *The British Journal of Developmental Psychology, 14*, 173–186.

Arsenio, W., & Ford, M. (1985). The role of affective information in social-cognitive development: Children's differentiation of moral and conventional events. *Merrill-Palmer Quarterly, 31*, 1–18.

Brown, R., & Gaertner, S. (Eds.). (2001). *Blackwell handbook in social psychology: Vol. 4. Intergroup processes.* Cambridge, MA: Blackwell.

Cassidy, J., Kirsh, S. J., Scolton, K., & Parke, R. D. (1996). Attachment and representations of peer relationships. *Developmental Psychology, 32*, 892–904. doi:10.1037/0012-1649.32.5.892

Dovidio, J. F., Glick, P., & Rudman, L. (Eds.). (2005). *Reflecting on the nature of prejudice: Fifty years after Allport.* Malden, MA: Blackwell.

Dunn, J. (2006). Moral development in early childhood and social interaction in the family. In M. Killen & J. G. Smetana (Eds.), *Handbook of moral development* (pp. 331–350). Mahwah, NJ: Erlbaum.

Durkheim, E. (1961). *Moral education* (E. K. Wilson & H. Schnurer, Trans.). Glencoe, IL: Free Press. (Original work published 1925)

Dworkin, R. (1993). *Life's dominion: An argument about abortion, euthanasia, and individual freedom.* New York, NY: Knopf.

Eisenberg, N., Spinard, T. L., & Sadovsky, A. (2006). Empathy-related responding in children. In M. Killen & J. G. Smetana (Eds.), *Handbook of moral development* (pp. 517–549). Mahwah, NJ: Erlbaum.

Fiske, S. T. (2002). What we know now about bias and intergroup conflict, the problem of century. *Current Directions in Psychological Science, 11,* 123–128. doi:10.1111/1467-8721.00183

Gaertner, S. L., & Dovidio, J. F. (1986). Prejudice, discrimination, and racism: Historical trends and contemporary approaches. In J. F. Dovidio & S. L. Gaertner (Eds.), *Prejudice, discrimination, and racism* (pp. 1–34). San Diego, CA: Academic Press.

Greene, J. D., Sommerville, R. B., Nystrom, L. E., Darley, J. M., & Cohen, J. D. (2001, September 14). An fMRI investigation of emotional engagement in moral judgment. *Science, 293,* 2105–2108. Medline doi:10.1126/science.1062872

Habermas, J. (1990). *Moral consciousness and communicative action.* Cambridge, MA: MIT Press.

Haidt, J. (2001). The emotional dog and its rational tail: A social intuitionist approach to moral judgment. *Psychological Review, 108,* 814–834. Medline doi:10.1037/0033-295X.108.4.814

Haidt, J., Koller, S. H., & Dias, M. G. (1993). Affect, culture, and morality, or is it wrong to eat your dog? *Journal of Personality and Social Psychology, 65,* 613–628. Medline doi:10.1037/0022-3514.65.4.613

Hastings, P. D., Zahn-Waxler, C., & McShane, K. (2006). We are, by nature moral creatures: Biological bases of concern for others. In M. Killen & J. G. Smetana (Eds.), *Handbook of moral development* (pp. 483–516). Mahwah, NJ: Erlbaum.

Helwig, C. C. (1995). Adolescents' and young adults' conceptions of civil liberties: Freedom of speech and religion. *Child Development, 66,* 152–166. Medline doi:10.2307/1131197

Kant, I. (1959). *Groundwork of the metaphysic of morals* (M. Gabain, Trans.). New York, NY: Harper & Row. (Original work published 1785)

Killen, M. (1991). Social and moral development in early childhood. In W. M. Kurtines & J. L. Gewirtz (Eds.), *Handbook of moral behavior and development* (Vol. 2, pp. 115–138). Mahwah, NJ: Erlbaum.

Killen, M. (2007). Children's social and moral reasoning about exclusion. *Current Directions in Psychological Science, 16,* 32–36. doi:10.1111/j.1467-8721.2007.00470.x

Killen, M., Lee-Kim, J., McGlothlin, H., & Stangor, C. (2002). How children and adolescents evaluate gender and racial exclusion. *Monographs of the Society for Research in Child Development, 67*(4, Serial No. 271). Oxford, England: Blackwell Publishers.

Killen, M., Margie, N. G., & Sinno, S. (2006). Morality in the context of intergroup relationships. In M. Killen & J. G. Smetana (Eds.), *Handbook of moral development* (pp. 155–183). Mahwah, NJ: Erlbaum.

Killen, M., Richardson, C., & Kelly, M. C. (in press). Developmental intergroup attitudes: Stereotyping, exclusion, fairness, and justice. In J. F. Dovidio, M. Hewstone, P. Glick, & V. M. Esses (Eds.), *Handbook of Prejudice and Discrimination.* Thousand Oaks, CA: Sage.

Killen, M., Sinno, S., & Margie, N. G. (2007). Children's experiences and judgments about group exclusion and inclusion. In R. Kail (Ed.), *Advances in Child Psychology* (Vol. 35, pp. 173–218). New York: Elsevier.

Killen, M., & Smetana, J. G. (2008). Moral judgment and moral neuroscience: Intersections, definitions, and issues. *Child Development Perspectives, 2,* 1–6. doi:10.1111/j.1750-8606.2008.00033.x

Lakoff, G. (2008). *The political mind: Why you can't understand 21st century American politics with an 18th century brain.* New York, NY: Penguin.

Levy, S. R., & Killen, M. (2008). *Intergroup attitudes and relations in childhood through adulthood.* Oxford, England: Oxford University Press.

McGlothlin, H., Edmonds, C., & Killen, M. (2007). Children's and adolescents' decision-making about intergroup peer relationships. In S. Quintana & C. McKown (Eds.), *The handbook of race, racism, and the developing child* (pp. 424–451). New York, NY: Wiley.

Nesdale, D. (2004). Social identity processes and children's ethnic prejudice. In M. Bennett & F. Sani (Eds.), *The development of the social self* (pp. 219–245). New York, NY: Psychology Press.

Nesdale, D. (2008). Peer group rejection and children's intergroup prejudice. In S. Levy & M. Killen (Eds.), *Intergroup attitudes and relations in childhood through adulthood* (pp. 32–46). Oxford, England: Oxford University Press.

Nesdale, D., Griffith, J., Durkin, K., & Maass, A. (2005). Empathy, group norms and children's ethnic attitudes. *Journal of Applied Developmental Psychology, 26,* 623–637. doi:10.1016/j.appdev.2005.08.003

Nucci, L. P. (2001). *Education in the moral domain.* Cambridge, England: Cambridge University Press.

Nussbaum, M. C. (1999). *Sex and social justice.* New York, NY: Oxford University Press.

Nussbaum, N. C. (2001). *Upheavals of thought: The intelligence of emotions.* Cambridge, England: Cambridge University Press.

Perkins, S. A., & Turiel, E. (2007). To lie or not to lie: To whom and under what circumstances. *Child Development, 78,* 609–621. Medline doi:10.1111/j.1467-8624.2007.01017.x

Pettigrew, T. F., & Tropp, L. R. (2005). Allport's intergroup contact hypothesis: Its history and influence. In J. F. Dovidio, P. Glick, & L. Rudman (Eds.), *Reflecting on the nature of prejudice: Fifty years after Allport* (pp. 262–277). Malden, MA: Blackwell.

Piaget, J. (1965). *The moral judgment of the child* (L. W. Beck, Trans.). London, England: Routledge and Kegan Paul. (Original work published 1932)

Smetana, J. G. (2006). Social domain theory: Consistencies and variations in children's moral and social judgments. In M. Killen & J. G. Smetana (Eds.), *Handbook of moral development* (pp. 119–153). Mahwah, NJ: Erlbaum.

Smetana, J. G., & Killen, M. (2008). Moral cognition, emotions, and neuroscience: An integrative developmental view [Special Issue]. *European Journal of Developmental Science*, *2*, 324–339.

Thompson, R. A. (2006). The development of the person: Social understanding, relationships, conscience, self. In N. Eisenberg (Ed.), *Handbook of child psychology: Vol. 3. Social, emotional, and personality development* (pp. 24–98). New York, NY: Wiley.

Turiel, E. (1983). *The development of social knowledge: Morality and convention*. Cambridge, England: Cambridge University Press.

Turiel, E. (1998). The development of morality. In W. Damon & N. Eisenberg (Eds.), *Handbook of child psychology: Vol. 3. Social, emotional, and personality development* (5th ed., pp. 863–932). New York, NY: Wiley.

Turiel, E. (2006). Thought, emotions, and social interactional processes in moral development. In M. Killen & J. G. Smetana (Eds.), *Handbook of moral development* (pp. 7–35). Mahwah, NJ: Erlbaum.

Turiel, E. (2009). The relevance of moral epistemology and psychology for neuroscience. In P. Zelazo, M. Chandler, & E. Crone (Eds.), *Developmental social cognitive neuroscience* (pp. 313–331). London, England: Taylor & Francis.

Turiel, E., & Davidson, P. (1986). Heterogeneity, inconsistency, and asynchrony in the development of cognitive structures. In I. Levin (Ed.), *Stage and structure: Reopening the debate* (pp. 106–143). Norwood, NJ: Ablex.

Turiel, E., & Perkins, S. A. (2004). Flexibilities of mind: Conflict and culture. *Human Development*, *47*, 158–178. doi:10.1159/000077988

Wainryb, C. (2006). Moral development in culture: Diversity, tolerance, and justice. In M. Killen & J. G. Smetana (Eds.), *Handbook of moral development* (pp. 211–240). Mahwah, NJ: Erlbaum.

Wainryb, C., Brehl, B. A., & Matwin, S. (2005). Being hurt and hurting others: Children's narrative accounts and moral judgments of their own interpersonal conflicts. *Monographs of the Society for Research in Child Development* 70(3, Serial No. 281).

Warneken, F., & Tomasello, M. (2007). Helping and cooperation at 14 months of age. *Infancy*, *11*, 271–294.

Weston, D. R., & Turiel, E. (1980). Act-rule relations: Children's concepts of social rules. *Developmental Psychology*, *16*, 417–424. doi:10.1037/0012-1649.16.5.417

3

RAGE, REVENGE, AND PRECIOUS PRIDE: EMOTIONS IN INFORMATION PROCESSING BY CHILDREN WITH AGGRESSIVE BEHAVIOR PROBLEMS

BRAM OROBIO DE CASTRO

Aggressive behaviors have large social consequences among all species. Aggression may serve to protect one's vital concerns, disrupt relations, and command dominance or subordination and may be a strong source of admiration or rejection (e.g., Aureli & de Waal, 2000). Because of its social importance, multiple biological and cultural mechanisms to regulate aggression have evolved over time, including emotion processes that are key agents in the regulation of aggression, both within and between persons. Humans and other animals are highly sensitive to signals of others' emotional states. Processing of such emotion signals directly affects the perceiver's own emotional state, predisposing both body and mind to respond appropriately. These processes appear partly "hardwired" in the lower brain regions, but they also have an important socially regulated side, in which humans are highly sensitive to the social norms and conventions concerning emotional behavior and the meaning of emotion signals in social interactions (Dodge, 2006; Frijda, 1988).

These emotion processes appear to be very relevant to our understanding of aggressive behavior problems in children. Could it be that aggressive behavior problems are triggered by dysregulation of emotional processes in social interaction? Can aggressive behavior problems result from lessened sensitivity to other people's emotional signals, misinterpretation of other people's emotions, over activation of physical systems involved in anger, and dysregulation of anger processes? Can excessive instrumental aggression be triggered by misinterpretations of one's own social dominance and the relevance of aggressive behavior to the attainment of one's goals, as well as by the relative underactivation of emotional processes that serve to inhibit aggression, such as empathy, guilt, and remorse? Can interventions influence these emotion processes and decrease aggressive behavior problems?

This chapter will present an overview of what is known about emotions in social information processing (SIP) by children with aggressive behavior problems. I first review theories concerning social cognition and emotion in aggressive behavior and present an overview of recent empirical findings. Finally, I present a tentative model of the development of emotion processes in SIP, with an emphasis on the development of aggressive behavior.

AGGRESSIVE BEHAVIOR PROBLEMS

Aggressive behavior, vandalism, extreme stubbornness, and other disruptive behavior problems are among the most frequent grounds for admission to child mental health services. Presently, disruptive behavior problems in children are rated among the largest concerns of the general public in Western countries (Netherlands Social Cultural Planning Agency, 1999). Researchers in psychology, psychiatry, criminology, sociology, and biology have increasingly cooperated to study the nature, causes, consequences, and malleability of disruptive behavior problems. To date, there is strong evidence that there is no single sufficient cause for disruptive behavior in children. Rather, complex interactions between multiple environmental and biological factors seem to cause various kinds of disruptive behavior (e.g., Dodge, Coie, & Lynam, 2006).

To further our understanding of aggressive behavior problems in children, it is crucial to know the exact processes causing individual aggressive acts. Research into these processes in aggressive children in the past decades has focused primarily on information processing in social interactions. By experimentally confronting children with provocative social stimuli and studying the consequent cognitive, emotional, and behavioral processes, we have learned a lot about the important roles that social-cognitive and emotional processes play in the development of aggressive behavior problems. It is important that this knowledge has been applied in promising cognitive–behavioral and emotion-focused interventions (e.g., Kazdin, 2003).

Notwithstanding these important advances in our understanding of the mechanisms involved in aggressive behaviors, there is still a lot to be learned. So far, relatively little attention has been paid to the role of emotion in behavior problems, as the dominant approaches to understanding information processing by aggressive children were originally oriented more toward cognitive than toward emotional aspects of behavior problems.

THEORETICAL APPROACHES TO SOCIAL COGNITION AND EMOTION IN AGGRESSIVE BEHAVIOR PROBLEMS

A key theory concerning cognition and aggressive behavior problems in children has been the SIP model (Crick & Dodge, 1994; Dodge, 1986). The theory proposes that, in order to react appropriately to social situations, a person processes social information in an orderly fashion. First, the information has to be encoded. Second, the encoded information has to be represented correctly. Third, this representation activates specific interaction goals. Fourth, this leads to the generation of response alternatives. Fifth, these response alternatives have to be evaluated against the interaction goals, and from these responses an optimal response has to be selected. Finally, the selected response has to be enacted. Each of these six steps draws information, such as schemata, from a database of past social experiences. The theory proposes that, through interactions between organismic and environmental influences, deviant SIP styles may develop that evoke specific aggressive behavior in specific situations. Specifically, problems in the first steps of information processing may lead to hypervigilance to threat and overattribution of hostile intentions to others, resulting in impulsive, angry, emotional aggressive behaviors named *reactive aggression*. Problems in the response decision and evaluation steps of SIP, in contrast, may lead to an underappreciation of the negative consequences and immorality of aggressive behaviors and an overappreciation of their efficacy, leading to aggressive behaviors aimed at instrumental gains or social dominance, named *proactive aggression* (Dodge, Lochman, Harnish, Bates, & Pettit, 1997; Dodge & Pettit, 2003).

SIP theory has several advantages over traditional approaches to information processing by aggressive children. It provides a very detailed description of the processes leading up to aggressive acts, is very specific about the putative causes of individual differences in these processes, and accommodates the possibility that children develop qualitatively different social cognitive styles, rather than "deficiencies" on a single developmental dimension.

Numerous studies have been conducted concerning SIP in children who are hindered or provoked by a peer. These studies demonstrate that aggressive behavior in children is related to atypical encoding, interaction goals, response generation, response evaluation, response enactment, and database schemata (e.g., Dodge et al., 1997; Lochman & Dodge, 1998). Results concerning representation are less consistent. Representation has primarily been studied in the sense of attribution of intent to other people's behavior (also known as "hostile attribution bias"). A meta-analysis indicated that attribution of intent and aggressive behavior are clearly related, but that results of empirical studies on this topic vary considerably (de Castro, Veerman, Koops, Bosch, & Monshouwer, 2002). The relations of specific SIP patterns with either reactive or proactive aggression has been supported by several studies, either completely (e.g., Crick & Dodge, 1996) or in part (Arsenio, Adams, & Gold, 2009; de Castro, Merk, Koops, Veerman, & Bosch, 2005; Dodge et al., 1997).

Less is known about the putative causes of atypical SIP by aggressive children. According to Dodge (2006; Dodge & Pettit, 2003), such patterns are caused by interactions between limited cognitive capacities and aversive environmental influences. Longitudinal studies have indeed shown that relations between early risk factors and later aggressive behavior are mediated by SIP patterns (e.g., Nelson & Coyne, 2009). However, the roles of limited cognitive capacities in the development of deviations in SIP is almost uncharted terrain, even though the few studies that do exist with children with mild intellectual disabilities, and on relations between executive functions and SIP, do find results in line with Dodge's theorizing (van Nieuwenhuijzen, de Castro, Van Aken, & Matthys, 2009; Waldman, 1996).

Last but not least, SIP by aggressive children is a target for cognitive–behavioral interventions to reduce behavior problems. Interventions including SIP modification (Hudley & Graham, 1993; Lochman & Wells, 2002) are relatively effective (Kazdin, 2003), and mediation analyses have indicated that the changes in aggressive behavior resulting from these interventions are indeed caused by changes in SIP (Lochman & Wells, 2002).

How adequately do SIP models describe the actual processes taking place in children when they behave aggressively? Several authors have noted the marked contrast between the subordinate role of emotions in the SIP approach to disruptive behavior and the experience of many clinicians that anger, tension, and disappointment play important roles in disruptive behavior (Crick & Dodge, 1994; Gottman, 1986; Lemerise & Arsenio, 2000). Emotions are increasingly seen as fundamental to human behavior, in that they constitute the basic action programs that drive behavior and enable social interaction. Emotions also seem to be fundamental to the regulation of social interactions. Indeed, Campos, Campos, and Barrett (1989) proposed that

> emotions are not mere feelings, but rather are processes of establishing, maintaining, or disrupting the relations between the person and the internal or external environment, when such relations are significant to the individual. (p. 395)

In this view, emotional involvement and "hot cognition," rather than "cold" rational decision making, determine our social behavior.

The original SIP model did not incorporate this eminent role of emotion explicitly. Emotions may be implicitly present in the model as "energy" driving the whole process (Dodge, 1991), but the model does not propose how this energy influences information processing. Accordingly, the model provides no clear, testable hypotheses concerning the roles emotions play in determining one's responses to situations. In contrast, in popular cognitive–behavioral interventions, the recognition and regulation of emotions play important roles (e.g., Promoting Alternative THinking Strategies [Cook, Greenberg & Kusche, 1994]; and Coping Power [Chapter 12, this volume]). It does seem quite possible to specify emotional processes in SIP, and several attempts to do so have been made. To discuss these models in detail, though, the term *emotion* first requires some clarification.

An emotion can be regarded as comprising an experiential/cognitive component, a motoric/behavioral component, and a neurophysiological component. The experiential/cognitive component represents the subjective experience of the emotion: the experience of being happy, angry, or sad. The motoric/behavioral component, also called *action tendency* represents a specific drive to perform a certain action, which is characteristic of emotions. A defining component of rage, for example, is the action tendency to rebel against the immediate environment, and a component of shame is the action tendency to creep away and hide. The neurophysiological component of emotion represents specific levels of the physical arousal characteristic of emotions. These three components are not mutually independent, but are considered different manifestations of the same process (e.g., Fischer, Shaver, & Carnochan, 1990; Frijda, 1988).

Exactly how emotions arise is the subject of wide debate. A central question concerns the causal relationship between emotion and cognition. One school of thought is that a relevant stimulus directly evokes an emotion, which then evokes a specific cognition. An alternative view is that a stimulus is first represented cognitively and that this representation then evokes a specific emotion. There is evidence in favor of both standpoints. A stimulus can elicit different emotions independent of the way it is consciously represented, and different emotions can call up different representations of stimuli (Fischer et al., 1990).

Models incorporating both these positions (e.g., Frijda, 1993) distinguish two types of representation called *primary* and *secondary appraisal*. As soon as a stimulus is perceived, a very rough appraisal is made of the valence of the stimulus for one's basic concerns (also called *interests* or *goals*). This appraisal is considered a mere automatic and preconscious "quick scan" of the most salient features of the stimulus. As such, it does not result in any abstract, symbolic, nuanced interpretation with complexities like "another person's intent," but rather in a signal of furthering or hindering one's concerns. If personal concerns are at stake, this primary representation leads directly to a specific action tendency that initiates behavior and also influences subsequent information processing. This process is believed to occur fast and automatically, and it appears to take place largely in the amygdala and related parts of the lower brain, outside of one's conscious awareness or control.

Before or during enactment of the action tendency, secondary appraisal can take place. The stimulus can be reappraised more in depth, involving preconscious or conscious judgments of more subtle qualities of the stimulus, including intentions of other actors involved. Consequently, action tendencies evoked by primary appraisal can be altered, and alternative responses can be considered and preferred. In secondary appraisal, one's own action tendency itself can also be appraised, resulting in an altered action tendency and other behavior. Secondary appraisal is believed to have evolved in primates as a regulatory system over the primary emotional system; is mainly rooted in the higher parts of the brain (particularly in the prefrontal areas); and is consequently slower, but also more flexible than the primary emotion system. In various areas of psychology, so-called "dual processing" models have been developed to account for the combination of fast automatic emotional processing with primary appraisal on the one hand and more controlled reflective processing involving secondary representation on the other (e.g., Anderson & Bushman's, 2002, general aggression model). Developmental psychologists have suggested that an important developmental task is to learn to use secondary appraisals in order to regulate emotions (e.g., Cole, Martin, & Dennis, 2004).

The above accounts of emotion processes are to some extent similar to SIP models. Both kinds of models postulate that perception and appraisal of stimulus information leads to certain behavior. Several authors (Graham, Hudley, & Williams, 1992; Lemerise & Arsenio, 2000; Lochman & Wells, 2002) have therefore suggested the following integrations of emotions in each step of the SIP model: Encoding and interpretation may concern one's own and other people's emotions. Such interpretations may trigger emotional action tendencies that trigger emotion-specific interaction goals, response generation, evaluation, and enactment. These emotion processes may be subject to regulatory processes subsumed under the general term emotion regulation—that is, attempts to control, modify, and manage the experience and expression of emotions (Cole et al., 2004).

Note that, over time, each adaptation of the SIP model has added more constructs to the model. The model evolved from five (Dodge, 1986) to six processing steps (Crick & Dodge, 1994), and emotion processes were then added to each of these steps (Lemerise & Arsenio, 2000). Notwithstanding sound theoretical grounds for each addition to the model, it is unclear whether all additions are parsimonious, because their added value has hardly been tested empirically yet. At face value, it does seem somewhat paradoxical that in the transformation from describing more reflective decision making to describing fast, automatic emotional information processing, the models have become larger rather than smaller. In the next sections, we discuss recent findings on emotional information processing and aggressive behavior problems in children. An important aim of this review is to identify opportunities to formulate a more parsimonious model of emotions in information processing than the present models.

EMPIRICAL STUDIES OF EMOTIONS IN INFORMATION PROCESSING BY CHILDREN WITH BEHAVIOR PROBLEMS

As described previously, in theory emotions are part and parcel of SIP. Aggressive behavior problems are thought to be related to inaccurate encoding and representation of other people's emotional states, greater intensity of a person's own anger, and lack of adequate regulation of a person's own emotions. However, research on these issues is scarce, particularly for children with severe behavior problems. Already in 1994, Crick and Dodge noted the following:

> Relatively little research has been conducted from an integrative perspective on social information processing and emotion. That is, few investigators have assessed the relation between social information processing and emotion and the impact of this relation on social adjustment. . . . Clearly, it will be important for future research to consider carefully the role that emotion plays in social information processing and adjustment. (pp. 81–82)

In 2000, Lemerise and Arsenio drew a similar conclusion on the basis of their comprehensive review of the literature.

To date, much progress has been made, but emotion processes and social information processing are still mostly studied separately, making it difficult to learn about their interrelatedness. Moreover, many studies of emotion in information processing by aggressive children have focused primarily on cognitive representations of (a person's own or others') emotions, not on emotion processes themselves. The following sections provide a short overview of research on emotions in SIP by aggressive children, with findings presented roughly in order of the SIP steps. See also Lemerise and Maulden (Chapter 8, this volume) for an extensive review.

Encoding and Representation of Others' Emotions

According to SIP theory, children with aggressive behavior problems primarily encode threatening information that makes hostile intent attribution likely and fail to encode information that would favor benign or accidental attributions. Encoding of emotion signals from others could play an important part in this phenomenon. In a provocation context, for example, sympathetic or apologetic facial and nonverbal expressions could signal that a provocation was not intended. If aggressive children would indeed fail to encode such emotion information, that might have serious consequences for the interpretation of events they consequently made.

Children with behavior problems do indeed appear to be inaccurate at identifying other children's emotions from pictures of emotion expressions in general (Cook et al., 1994; Izard, Schultz, & Ackerman, 1997; Schultz, Izard, & Bear, 2004). This inaccuracy includes a tendency to systematically misattribute sad facial expressions as angry and to miss out on reconciliatory emotion signals like regret or sympathy. Whether the inaccuracy also occurs when representing the social situations used in SIP research was recently investigated in a series of studies by Lemerise and colleagues (Lemerise, Fredstrom, Kelley, Bowersox, & Waford, 2006; Lemerise, Gregory, & Fredstrom, 2005). In this research, participants were presented with videotaped hypothetical provocation vignettes sometimes used in SIP research, but the facial emotion displays, vocal tone, and nonverbal behavior of protagonists were systematically manipulated. Variations in protagonists' emotion displays had systematic effects on all participants' goals and responses, but it is interesting that rejected aggressive children responded more aggressively to sad and angry displays than did their nonaggressive peers. Moreover, the deviations in information processing by the rejected-aggressive participants became smaller when these participants were explicitly asked about the emotions of the provocateurs, suggesting that reflective consideration of these emotion displays helps to form more adequate representations of the social situations presented.

Recently, eye-tracking methodology was used in an experiment designed to test whether children with aggressive behavior problems do indeed fail to attend to such emotional cues (Horsley, de Castro, & Van der Schoot, 2009). Participants were presented with provocation cartoons that randomly varied in the emotions expressed by the provocateur. Eye movements of participants were tracked in real-time while the cartoon scenario unfolded. Surprisingly, aggressive participants did not fail to look at facial emotion cues of sympathy or apology by the peers in the cartoons. Instead, they looked longer at this information than other participants, but nonetheless attributed hostile intent to the peer. This viewing pattern is consistent with findings on processing of schema-inconsistent information in general: Information that is at odds with preexisting expectations is generally looked at longer. It is interesting that the preexisting schemata concerning peers' hostility that cause the longer viewing times by aggressive children are apparently strong enough to make children disregard the emotion displays by their peers that we now know they actually do attend to. Or, as one participant put it to the (cartoon) peer, "and now you are lying on top of it, you sneaky ***hole."

Representation of other children's emotions does appear to be distinct from representation of others' intentions. In two studies, emotion representation and intent representation were studied in response to the same stimuli (de Castro, Bosch, Veerman, & Koops, 2003; de Castro et al., 2005). In both studies, the well-established relation between hostile intent attribution and aggression was found. In addition, aggressive behavior was found to be related to attributions of glee to others. That is, when distressed, children with aggressive behavior problems more often indicated that other children enjoyed their distress. The latter finding remained, even when stimuli were experimentally manipulated to attribute benign intentions to the children involved. Moreover, glee attributions explained variance in aggressive behavior over and above hostile intent attribution (cf. Arsenio et al, 2009).

In SIP models, others' emotion signals have effects on behavior via the representation step in the models. Therefore, most studies discussed so far in this section have focused on the meaning participants assign to emotion signals. However, one may wonder whether all effects of emotion signals are through cognitive representation. It is interesting that two recent studies showed that probing cognitive representation by asking SIP questions changes the aggressiveness of children's response tendencies (de Castro, Bosch, et al., 2003; Lemerise et al., 2005). It is likely that others' emotion signals have very direct "contagious" effects on one's own emotional state, through basal emotional systems in the brain that automatically "mirror" or simulate emotion signals (de Wied, Goudena, & Matthys, 2005). Signals of distress or regret from another person would thus automatically lead to empathic feelings, which would induce prosocial tendencies and reduce aggressive response tendencies. It has been suggested that aggressive behavior problems may result from lessened sensitivity of empathic emotion systems. Studies on emotional empathy in children with aggressive behavior problems do indeed suggest that these children may be less empathic to others' distress (de Wied et al., 2005; Schultz et al., 2004). However, much is still unclear about the exact relations between emotion representation and empathy, because it would seem that any empathic response would require a degree of emotion representation (cf. Frijda, 1993).

Encoding and Representation of One's Own Emotions

Intense anger in disruptive children is seen as an important source of reactive aggression. Greater intensity of anger in children with behavior problems may lead these children to react more aggressively than other children (Graham et al., 1992; Lochman & Lenhart, 1993). Intensity of own emotions has been related to aggressive behavior in two distinct ways. On the one hand, stable individual dispositions to respond with a certain emotional intensity have been studied by temperament and personality psychologists. On the other hand, the emotional intensity of responses to specific situations has been investigated by developmental social psychologists. Even though these two traditions have rarely been integrated in a single empirical study (but see Schultz et al., 2004), findings from both traditions do tend to converge.

From a personality perspective, researchers have used terms like negative emotionality, irritability, difficult temperament, negative affectivity, low effortful control, and undercontrol to denote a stable disposition to react with strong negative emotions to frustration and goal blocking. Notwithstanding important differences in definitions and measurement of these constructs, evidence converges on consistent relations between a tendency to react with relatively strong negative emotions to frustration (e.g., Sallquist et al., 2009). It has been suggested that this relation holds specifically for reactive aggression, and preliminary evidence is in line with this idea (Vitaro, Brendgen, & Barker, 2006).

From an information processing perspective, research has focused on individual differences in the intensity of emotional reactions to social stimuli and on the extent to which children are aware of their own emotions in such situations. Studies concerning physiological indices of intensity of emotional reactions have generally looked at heart-rate reactivity in response to negative stimuli. Even though this approach is fairly novel and still suffers from unresolved inconsistencies in findings between studies, there appear to be relations between aggressive behavior and heart-rate reactivity in response to negative stimuli in children (Lorber, 2004). Concerning self-perceived anger after provocation, results of studies in nonreferred samples are inconsistent. Although Graham et al. (1992) and Vlerick (1994) did find that aggressive-rejected children became angrier than did their nonaggressive peers, other studies (Quiggle, Garber, Panak, & Dodge, 1992; Waas, 1988) did not. These inconsistent findings may be due to different kinds of aggression studied. Theoretically, intense anger in response to provocation should be related to reactive but not proactive aggression. This specific relation of own anger representation with reactive aggression has indeed been found (de Castro et al., 2005).

Interaction Goals

The importance of atypical goals for aggressive behavior is supported by studies concerning children's (Erdley & Asher, 1996; Lemerise et al., 2006) and adolescent boys' (Lochman, Wayland, & White, 1993) explanations for their responses to hypothetical social events. In these studies, behavior problems were found to be associated with goals of dominance and revenge (i.e., instrumental goals) that were best attained by aggressive responses, whereas nonaggressive behavior was associated with affiliative goals (i.e., relational goals) best attained by nonaggressive responses. In addition, proactively aggressive children are found to select more instrumental than relational goals when given the choice (Salmivalli, Ojanen, Haanpää, & Peets, 2005).

These studies provide important information on relations between goal preference and aggressive behavior, but they do not provide evidence that aggressive behavior does actually result from pursuing goals. From a rational stance, the inclusion of "interaction goals" in the SIP model makes sense: One can only select an optimal response if one uses a goal as a standard to evaluate possible responses against. However, from an emotional point of view, it is possible that reactive aggression does not result from a deliberate response in order to attain a goal. Rather, responses may simply result from a strong emotional action tendency that is executed without any goal or outcome in mind. This is exactly what a recent study indicated for boys with reactively aggressive behavior problems (de Castro, Verhulp, & Runions, 2009). These boys generally responded aggressively but did not select responses they expected to have the best outcome. They frequently indicated that their responses resulted from intense anger that "made them" act aggressively (e.g., "I'll go mad with anger"), even though they did understand that these responses would get them in to trouble and away from their actual goals. In contrast, nondisruptive boys generally responded nonaggressively and selected responses that would best help them attain their predominantly prosocial goals. Thus, whereas goal setting does appear to be an important step in social information processing by children with few behavior problems, in reactively aggressive boys emotional action tendencies do seem to take precedence over goal setting. The implications of these findings are discussed below.

In contrast, proactive aggression may be expected to be driven by atypical interaction goals, because this kind of aggression by definition concerns goals of dominance and instrumental gain. Studies that distinguished between reactive and proactive aggression have indeed found this specific relation of proactive aggression with a preference for instrumental and dominance goals over prosocial goals (de Castro et al., 2005; Salmivalli et al., 2005), as well as endorsement of the efficacy and legitimacy of aggressive behaviors.

Response Generation and Selection

Relations between aggressive behavior problems and response generation are a robust finding in SIP research. Numerous studies have established strong relations between aggressive behavior and various problems in response generation, such as limitations in the number of responses generated, higher aggressiveness of dominant responses, higher aggressiveness of all generated responses, and limited cognitive availability of alternative responses (see Dodge, 1986, for an in-depth investigation).

Findings concerning response evaluation and response selection have generally found aggressive behavior to be related to less negative evaluations of aggressive responses to provocation and to lower self-efficacy for prosocial responses. Whenever a distinction was made between reactive and proactive aggression, these findings have been specific to proactive aggression (Crick & Dodge, 1996; Dodge et al., 1997). It should, however, be noted that in a number of studies aggressive children do not actually prefer aggressive responses over other responses, but are merely less negative about aggressive responses than are their nonaggressive peers: Their preferred response would be non-aggressive (de Castro et al., in press). Similarly, in children with aggressive behavior problems and mild intellectual disabilities, aggressive behavior seems not to be predicted by response selection, but by enactment of the dominant generated response (van Nieuwenhuijzen et al., 2009).

Concerning emotions in response selection processes, relatively little attention has been paid to responses aimed to regulate one's own emotion. This is surprising, given the fact that a considerable part of cognitive–behavioral interventions aimed to reduce aggressive behavior consists of training such emotion-regulation responses. I therefore devote a separate section to this important issue.

EMOTION REGULATION

Even intense anger does not necessarily lead to aggression. Most children learn to regulate anger and other negative emotions in circumstances in which expression of these emotions would have aversive consequences (Cole et al., 2004). In fact, young children are remarkably apt at emotion regulation, for instance, by distracting themselves or by intentionally devaluing the goal they were pursuing (Cole et al., 2004). Numerous studies have indeed shown that emotion-regulation problems are related to the development of aggressive behavior problems (see Hubbard, Morrow, Romano, & McAuliffe, Chapter 10, this volume).

The discriminant validity of emotion-regulation responses from aggressive response generation and response evaluation was assessed in a study using hypothetical vignettes. In this study (de Castro et al., 2005) we considered solutions, distractions, or cognitive strategies as adaptive emotion-regulation strategies. As expected, reactive aggression was related with less adaptive emotion-regulation strategies. Nonaggressive children often mentioned solutions and distraction, whereas children in the disruptive group more often did not know a strategy to regulate their emotion and more often said emotion could only be regulated by others. Proactive aggression was related with mentioning aggression as a way to regulate negative emotions, for example, by stating "If I smudge his painting too, then he'll cry and it's my turn to laugh," or by simply stating that fighting with the peer would be fun. It is interesting that aggressive behavior problems were best explained by difficulties in generating emotion regulation responses, not by response selection or response evaluation.

THE INFLUENCE OF EMOTIONAL STATE
ON INFORMATION PROCESSING

Research on information processing, in general, has shown that information processing is strongly affected by a person's emotional state. Effects of emotional states on information processing have been indirectly involved in research on the SIP model. It seems that deviations in SIP only occur when children are personally involved in the situation presented, and that these deviations increase when participants feel threatened. The influence of participant involvement in presented situations was investigated in two studies with aggressive, rejected boys (Dodge & Frame, 1982; Dodge & Somberg, 1987) and one study with boys referred for disruptive behavior problems (de Castro, Slot, Bosch, Koops, & Veerman, 2003). In the first study, subjects were asked to imagine themselves as being either an onlooker or the injured party in vignettes presented to them. Hostile representation of intent was only found when subjects imagined themselves as the injured party. In the second study, during a pause in SIP tasks, subjects were confronted with the so-called real problem (staged by the experimenter) that a child in the corridor was threatening to pick a quarrel with the subject. The aggressive-rejected group did not differ from the popular-nonaggressive group in their representation of hostile intent before the threat, but represented more hostile intent after the threat. In the third study, a manipulated computer game was used to induce negative emotions in boys with severe behavior problems, aggressive boys in regular education, and non-aggressive boys. Both before and after the affect manipulation, participants completed SIP tasks comparable to those used in the previous experiments. The affect manipulation led to an increase in hostile attributions of intent for the disruptive boys, but not for the other groups. Together, these three studies suggested that boys with disruptive behavior problems are particularly susceptible to the effect of negative emotions on subsequent information processing.

DIFFERENCES BETWEEN EMOTIONAL AND REFLECTIVE
INFORMATION PROCESSING

Appreciating the importance of emotions in SIP necessitates a reappraisal of results obtained in previous SIP studies. An important aspect of emotions—also mentioned by our disruptive participants—is that they take "control precedence" (Frijda, 1988). That is, emotions invoke a tendency to interpret and act on a situation in a specific emotional way. Anger, for example, is believed to invoke both a tendency to encode and represent potentially threatening information, and a tendency to act aggressively. Such emotional processing is clearly different from the extensive, rational information processing the SIP model prescribes. Yet, by asking children a series of questions about hypothetical events, studies of SIP have generally tempted children to calmly process information in the way the SIP model prescribes. The results of such studies are then believed to apply to automatic, emotional processing as well, even though there is no evidence to support this claim. This issue is particularly important, because cognitive–behavioral intervention programs aim to train children in reflective processing, under the assumption that this will reduce aggressive behavior.

To test this assumption, a number of studies have contrasted conditions of reflective processing with conditions of more automatic processing. In the first of these studies (de Castro, 2000), children's direct automatic responses to hypothetical vignettes were compared with their responses following extensive prompts to reflect by following the SIP model before responding. Reflection did not lead to an overall increase or decrease in aggressiveness of responses. However, response aggressiveness did increase for some children, whereas it decreased for others. Increased response aggressiveness was found to be associated with hostile attribution of intent in the reflective condition. This suggests that whether reflection decreases or increases, aggressiveness depends on what children think during reflection. This finding seems to go against the popular advice that aggressive children should "take another's perspective" before they act: If they take the other's perspective and represent the other's perspective as hostile, perspective taking will only increase aggressiveness.

In a second study (de Castro, Bosch, et al., 2003), we pursued this issue by studying the differential effects of different kinds of reflection in disruptive and comparison boys. Participants were asked to either monitor their own feelings and emotion regulation, to consider the other's intentions and feelings, to wait 10 seconds, or to answer a distracting question. The effects of reflection were found to depend on the type of reflection required. In line with the previous findings, considering another's emotions and intentions tended to increase aggressiveness in disruptive boys and decreased it in comparison boys. Consistent with the idea that unregulated anger plays an important role in aggressive responding, monitoring their own emotions and emotion regulation significantly reduced aggressiveness in the disruptive group. Further support for the hypothesis that reflective processing may decrease response aggressiveness was found by Lemerise et al. (2005), who found lower response aggressiveness in children randomly assigned to a condition stimulating reflection on a protagonist's emotional state through a series of questions than in a spontaneous response condition.

In sum, emotion processes appear to be important in SIP. The combined effects of both fast, automatic, emotionally driven SIP and more reflective and controlled SIP may perhaps best be described with a dual processing model (de Castro, 2004; cf. Anderson & Bushman, 2002; Berkowitz, 2008; Dodge, 2006, 2008). The model specifies an emotional and a reflective route from social stimulus to response. On the emotional route, basic cues are encoded, and if the cues are associated with promoting or hindering one's personal concerns, an emotional action tendency is triggered. Note that no complex representation of others' intent or generation and selection of multiple responses occurs on this route. A mere association between a stimulus characteristic and a concern may suffice. The reflective route is superimposed on the emotional route. Association of a stimulus characteristic with personal concerns may trigger reflective processing, including allocation of attention to the stimulus and reappraisal of the encoded information, including representation of intent and emotional state of others involved in the social event. This reappraisal triggers a response that is evaluated and enacted when evaluated positively. If the response is evaluated negatively, an alternative is generated, and so on. The emotional and reflective routes are proposed to operate in parallel, with a number of factors determining which process overrides the other (see de Castro, 2004, for details). This model is clearly highly speculative. However, there are indications of its tenability in the literature reviewed previously. The distinction between the two routes may be particularly useful to explain differential development of reactive and proactive aggressive behavior, as I will explain in the following section.

A DEVELOPMENTAL MODEL OF EMOTIONS IN INFORMATION PROCESSING

The present SIP models do not explicitly specify how SIP develops over time (cf. Gottman, 1986). It does seem, however, that clear hypotheses concerning SIP development may be formulated and tested. Considering SIP as a dance between fast, basic emotional processing and slower, more controlled reflective processing seems a good starting point to hypothesize about the development of SIP and the relations between differential development of SIP and aggressive behavior. The basic ideas of the developmental hypotheses formulated in this section are that (a) humans are born with strong dispositions to react with specific emotional action tendencies to stimuli that threaten or further their concerns (cf. Frijda, 1993) and (b) over development, these basic emotional action tendencies remain but are increasingly regulated by more elaborate information processing skills, acquired through transactions between maturation and social learning. This line of reasoning parallels Dodge (2006), who recently put forth clear hypotheses concerning the development of intent attribution, which are also based on the idea that, with development, basic emotional response tendencies become regulated by more elaborate representation.

From soon after birth, nearly all children behave aggressively. In most children, this aggressive behavior diminishes, whereas in a small proportion it remains present and diversifies (Tremblay, 2000). So, what needs to be understood is not how changes in SIP cause the "onset" of aggressive behavior, but the opposite: We need to study how most children's SIP changes to make them less aggressive. This reversal from studying onset of aggression to studying "offset" of aggression has fundamental implications for our understanding of SIP and aggressive behavior. It suggests that SIP involved in aggressive behavior must be a very basic, simple process, whereas SIP in nonaggressive behavior may be more complex and acquired over time (Dodge, 2006). In early childhood, following the emotional route may be normative. With maturation and experience, the reflective route may become more elaborate and dominant in most children, under most circumstances. But for children with strong negative emotionality, limited cognitive capacities, and/or little scaffolding social experiences to promote reflective processing, this may not be so.

From the dual-processing model previously suggested, we may tentatively derive specific hypotheses, which we would like to test in the near future, concerning the development of SIP and its relations with reactive and proactive aggression in line with current theories on emotional and social cognitive development. One may propose that three trajectories in the development of SIP and reactive and proactive aggressive behavior can be identified: (a) a general trajectory, followed by most children, from reactive aggression and emotional processing to little aggression and reflective processing; (b) a persistent reactive trajectory with stable high levels of reactive aggression, undercontrol, and emotional processing; and (c) a proactive trajectory, with increasing levels of proactive aggression and an atypical reflective information processing style.

On the general trajectory, SIP in infants and young children may be described by the emotional route: Any cue associated with goal blocking will evoke an anger action tendency that directly leads to aggressive behavior. As their cognitive capabilities mature and they are engaged in more complex social interactions, children acquire reflective SIP skills that enable them to inhibit emotional SIP and follow the reflective route both by taking into account others' intentions and feelings and by considering the likely consequences of multiple response alternatives. They come to appreciate the social norm that the extent to which aggressive responses are appropriate depends on others' intentions and feelings. Thus, what develops is not a tendency to attribute hostile intent, but the skill to detect benign intent and to modify one's response accordingly. Similarly, alternative responses to aggression are tried out and reinforced. These reflective SIP skills do not replace the emotional route, but adjust it under those circumstances in which society deems it inappropriate.

On the persistent reactive trajectory, emotions in information processing may remain dominant in undercontrolling children, as either the reflective skills are never learned or emotional action tendencies are so strong that they are hard to regulate. Persistent reactive aggression is present from an early age and is associated with difficult temperament, attention problems, negative mood, social problems, and low intelligence. Reactive aggression may persist in children who do not develop skills to use the reflective route. This proposition is in line with findings that reactively aggressive children encode more negative cues, and their aggressive responses are hardly related to reflective SIP steps of response selection and response evaluation. Failure to develop reflective information processing may result from transactions between temperament, undercontrol, and an unsuitable environment in which to learn reflective skills.

On the proactive trajectory, reflective processing may develop atypically when aggressive responses are reinforced. Proactive aggression emerges almost exclusively in children who already display reactively aggressive behavior. It is not associated with social problems, but rather with effective use of aggression in the child's own interests. Possibly, proactive aggression emerges when reflective SIP skills do develop. Such could be the case if the reinforcement of aggressive behavior, together with the examples provided by aggressive models, lead to different contents of reflection than those found in most children, particularly to less attribution of benign intent, instrumental interaction goals, and positive outcome expectancies for aggressive behavior. Clearly, the developmental trajectories proposed above are speculative.

DISCUSSION

Emotion processes are important aspects of information processing by children with aggressive behavior problems. A dual-processing model of information processing may tentatively integrate these emotion processes with the social-cognitive processes included in earlier models. Transactions between emotional dispositions, cognitive capacities, and social experience may cause individual differences in information processing and aggressive behavior. Many aspects of the proposed model and its development are only supported indirectly by empirical findings, and much remains to be learned. Yet, at the very least, the formulation of information processing models can stimulate discussion and research into the exact nature and development of information processing.

An important limitation of the information-processing research reviewed is that most studies concern responses to hypothetical rather than actual situations. This is particularly troublesome, because part of the studies concerns emotions, and children would presumably be more emotional in real situations that concern them than when listening to stories. The relation between findings with hypothetical vignettes and information processing in actual emotionally salient situations is far from clear and requires direct empirical study.

In nearly all studies reviewed here, the accent was on responses to provocation and, consequently, on anger and its regulation as determinants of disruptive behavior. In situations that evoke other kinds of disruptive behavior than reactive aggression, other emotions may be more relevant. For example, (lack of) guilt and feelings of pride and grandiosity may be associated with proactive aggression (Thomaes, Bushman, Stegge, & Olthof, 2008).

Another limitation of the studies reviewed is the heterogeneity of the samples. Aggressive behavior is a very broad term, and participants in these studies differed considerably with regard to type of behavior problems, developmental history, and severity of associated problems. The heterogeneity of behavior problems makes it especially important to note that most findings on deviant SIP in aggressive children presented here did not apply to all children in the disruptive groups, but concern differences between mean scores of groups of children. One of the challenges for future research will be to link specific SIP patterns to children with specific kinds of behavior problems and specific life histories. Interactions between limited information processing capacities, aversive social experiences, and training in deviant SIP by peers or parents may result in the display of different kinds of emotions in information-processing patterns. The relative contributions of these factors also may differ between children. For one child, impulsive behavior and attention problems may prohibit learning of social skills and give rise to peer rejection, causing the child to expect hostile behavior from these children. Another child may learn hostile attributions and aggressive responses as survival strategies in an abusive–coercive family climate.

Another striking feature of the participants in the studies reviewed in this chapter is that nearly all samples with severe behavior problems were exclusively male. This selection bias may be explained by the overrepresentation of boys in prevalence and treatment of behavior problems, but it does strongly limit the generalizability of findings.

Finally, I hope a better understanding of emotion processes in children with aggressive behavior problems will help enhance the "emotions in information processing" by adults working with children with behavior problems. Understanding other people's intentions and feelings is difficult not only for aggressive children; parents and professionals facing problematic behavior have a hard time understanding the feelings and motives of the children involved. A better understanding of the processes involved in children's aggressive behavior may help improve the quality of our social interactions and interventions with them.

REFERENCES

Anderson, C. A., & Bushman, B. J. (2002). Human aggression. *Annual Review of Psychology, 53*, 27–51. Medline doi:10.1146/annurev.psych.53.100901.135231

Arsenio, W. F., Adams, E., & Gold, J. (2009). Social information processing, moral reasoning, and emotion attributions: Relations with adolescents' reactive and proactive aggression. *Child Development, 80*, 1739–1755.

Aureli, F., & de Waal, F. B. M. (2000). *Natural conflict resolution*. Berkeley, CA: University of California Press.

Berkowitz, L. (2008). What I meant to say: Some thoughts in response to Pahlavan and Dodge. *Aggressive Behavior, 34,* 136–138. doi:10.1002/ab.20246

Campos, J. J., Campos, R. G., & Barrett, K. C. (1989). Emergent themes in the study of emotional development and emotion regulation. *Developmental Psychology, 25,* 394–402. doi:10.1037/0012-1649.25.3.394

Cole, P. M., Martin, S. E., & Dennis, T. A. (2004). Emotion regulation as a scientific construct: Methodological challenges and directions for child development research. *Child Development, 75,* 317–333. Medline doi:10.1111/j.1467-8624.2004.00673.x

Cook, E. T., Greenberg, M. T., & Kusche, C. A. (1994). The relations between emotional understanding, intellectual functioning, and disruptive behavior problems in elementary-school-aged children. *Journal of Abnormal Psychology, 22,* 205–219.

Crick, N. R., & Dodge, K. A. (1994). A review and reformulation of social information processing mechanisms in children's social adjustment. *Psychological Bulletin, 115,* 74–101. doi:10.1037/0033-2909.115.1.74

Crick, N. R., & Dodge, K. A. (1996). Social information-processing mechanisms in reactive and proactive aggression. *Child Development, 67,* 993–1002. Medline doi:10.2307/1131875

de Castro, B. O. (2000) *Social information processing in antisocial boys*. Unpublished doctoral dissertation, Vrije Universiteit, Amsterdam.

de Castro, B. O. (2004). The development of social information processing and aggressive behavior: Current issues. *European Journal of Developmental Psychology, 1,* 87–102. doi:10.1080/17405620444000058

de Castro, B. O., Bosch, J. D., Veerman, J. W., & Koops, W. (2003). The effects of emotion regulation, attribution, and delay prompts on aggressive boys' social problem solving. *Cognitive Therapy and Research, 27,* 153–166. doi:10.1023/A:1023557125265

de Castro, B. O., Merk, W., Koops, W., Veerman, J. W., & Bosch, J. D. (2005). Emotions in social information processing and their relations with reactive and proactive aggression in referred aggressive boys. *Journal of Clinical Child and Adolescent Psychology, 34,* 105–116. Medline doi:10.1207/s15374424jccp3401_10

de Castro, B. O., Slot, N. W., Bosch, J. D., Koops, W., & Veerman, J. W. (2003). Negative feelings exacerbate hostile attributions of intent in highly aggressive boys. *Journal of Clinical Child and Adolescent Psychology, 32,* 56–65. Medline doi:10.1207/S15374424JCCP3201_06

de Castro, B. O., Veerman, J. W., Koops, W., Bosch, J. D., & Monshouwer, H. J. (2002). Hostile attribution of intent and aggressive behavior: A meta-analysis. *Child Development, 73,* 916–934. Medline doi:10.1111/1467-8624.00447

de Castro, B. O., Verhulp, E., & Runions, K. (2009). *Rage and Revenge: Highly aggressive boys' explanations for their aggressive behavior*. Manuscript submitted for publication.

de Wied, M., Goudena, P. P., & Matthys, W. (2005). Empathy in boys with disruptive behavior disorders. *Journal of Child Psychology and Psychiatry, and Allied Disciplines, 46*, 867–880. Medline doi:10.1111/j.1469-7610.2004.00389.x

Dodge, K. A. (1986). A social information processing model of social competence in children. In M. Perlmutter (Ed.), *The Minnesota Symposium on Child Psychology: Vol. 18* (pp. 77–125). Hillsdale, NJ: Erlbaum.

Dodge, K. A. (1991). Emotion and social information processing. In J. Garber & K. A. Dodge (Eds.), *The development of emotion regulation and dysregulation* (pp. 159–181). Cambridge, England: Cambridge University Press.

Dodge, K. A. (2006). Translational science in action: Hostile attributional style and the development of aggressive behavior problems. *Development and Psychopathology, 18*, 791–814. Medline doi:10.1017/S0954579406060391

Dodge, K. A. (2008). On the meaning of meaning when being mean: Commentary on Berkowitz's "On the consideration of automatic as well as controlled psychological processes in aggression." *Aggressive Behavior, 34*, 133–135. Medline doi:10.1002/ab.20242

Dodge, K. A., Coie, J. D., & Lynam, D. (2006). Aggression and antisocial behavior in youth. In W. Damon, R. M. Lerner, & N. Eisenberg (Eds.), *Handbook of child psychology: Vol. 3. Social, emotional, and personality development* (6th ed., pp. 719–788). New York, NY: Wiley.

Dodge, K. A., & Frame, C. L. (1982). Social cognitive biases and deficits in aggressive boys. *Child Development, 53*, 620–635. Medline doi:10.2307/1129373

Dodge, K. A., Lochman, J. E., Harnish, J. D., Bates, J. E., & Pettit, G. S. (1997). Reactive and proactive aggression in school children and psychiatrically impaired chronically assaultive youth. *Journal of Abnormal Psychology, 106*, 37–51. Medline doi:10.1037/0021-843X.106.1.37

Dodge, K. A., & Pettit, G. S. (2003). A biopsychosocial model of the development of chronic conduct problems in adolescence. *Developmental Psychology, 39*, 349–371. Medline doi:10.1037/0012-1649.39.2.349

Dodge, K. A., & Somberg, D. R. (1987). Hostile attributional biases among aggressive boys are exacerbated under conditions of threats to the self. *Child Development, 58*, 213–224. Medline doi:10.2307/1130303

Erdley, C. A., & Asher, S. R. (1996). Children's social goals and self-efficacy perceptions as influences on their responses to ambiguous provocation. *Child Development, 67*, 1329–1344. Medline doi:10.2307/1131703

Fischer, K. W., Shaver, P. R., & Carnochan, P. (1990). How emotions develop and how they organize development. *Cognition and Emotion, 4*, 81–127. doi:10.1080/02699939008407142

Frijda, N. H. (1988). The laws of emotion. *The American Psychologist, 43*, 349–358. Medline doi:10.1037/0003-066X.43.5.349

Frijda, N. H. (1993). The place of appraisal in emotion. *Cognition and Emotion, 7*, 357–387. doi:10.1080/02699939308409193

Gottman, K. (1986). Commentary in Dodge, K. A., Pettit, G. S., McClaskey, C. L. & Brown, M. M. Social Competence in Children. *Monographs of the Society for Research in Child Development, 51*, 86–90.

Graham, S., Hudley, C., & Williams, E. (1992). Attributional and emotional determinants of aggression among African-American and Latino young adolescents. *Developmental Psychology, 28*, 731–740. doi:10.1037/0012-1649.28.4.731

Horsley, T., de Castro, B. O, & Van der Schoot, M. (2009). *In the eye of the beholder: Eye-tracking assessment of social information processing in aggressive behavior. Journal of Abnormal Child Psychology.* Advance online publication. www.springerlink.com/content/b711720604655312/

Hudley, C., & Graham, S. (1993). An attributional intervention to reduce peer-directed aggression among African-American boys. *Child Development, 64*, 124–138. Medline doi:10.2307/1131441

Izard, C. E., Schultz, D., & Ackerman, B. P. (1997). *Emotion knowledge, social competence, and behavior problems in disadvantaged children.* Paper presented at the biennial meeting of the Society for Research in Child Development, Washington, DC.

Kazdin, A. E. (2003). Psychotherapy for children and adolescents. *Annual Review of Psychology, 54*, 253–276. Medline doi:10.1146/annurev.psych.54.101601.145105

Lemerise, E. A., & Arsenio, W. F. (2000). An integrated model of emotion processes and cognition in social information processing. *Child Development, 71*, 107–118. Medline doi:10.1111/1467-8624.00124

Lemerise, E. A., Fredstrom, B. K., Kelley, B. M., Bowersox, A. L., & Waford, R. N. (2006). Do provocateurs' emotion displays influence children's social goals and problem solving? *Journal of Abnormal Child Psychology, 34*, 559–571. Medline doi:10.1007/s10802-006-9035-x

Lemerise, E. A., Gregory, D. S., & Fredstrom, B. K. (2005). The influence of provocateurs' emotion displays on the social information processing of children varying in social adjustment and age. *Journal of Experimental Child Psychology, 90*, 344–366. Medline doi:10.1016/j.jecp.2004.12.003

Lochman, J. E., & Dodge, K. A. (1998). Distorted perceptions in dyadic interactions of aggressive and nonaggressive boys: Effects of prior expectations, context, and boys' age. *Development and Psychopathology, 10*, 495–512. Medline doi:10.1017/S0954579498001710

Lochman, J. E., & Lenhart, L. A. (1993). Anger coping intervention for aggressive children: Conceptual models and outcome effects. *Clinical Psychology Review, 13*, 785–805. doi:10.1016/S0272-7358(05)80006-6

Lochman, J. E., Wayland, K., & White, K. (1993). Social goals: Relationship to adolescent adjustment and to social problem solving. *Journal of Abnormal Child Psychology, 21*, 135–151. Medline doi:10.1007/BF00911312

Lochman, J. E., & Wells, K. C. (2002). Contextual social-cognitive mediators and child outcome: A test of the theoretical model in the Coping Power program. *Development and Psychopathology, 14*, 945–967. Medline doi:10.1017/S0954579402004157

Lorber, M. F. (2004). Psychophysiology of aggression, psychopathy, and conduct problems: A meta-analysis. *Psychological Bulletin, 130,* 531–552.

Nelson, D. A., & Coyne, S. M. (2009). Children's intent attributions and feelings of distress: Associations with maternal and paternal parenting practices. *Journal of Abnormal Child Psychology, 37,* 223–237. Medline doi:10.1007/s10802-008-9271-3

Netherlands Social Cultural Planning Agency. (1999). *Social and cultural explorations.* The Hague, the Netherlands: Author. Quiggle, N. L., Garber, J., Panak, W. F., & Dodge, K. A. (1992). Social information processing in aggressive and depressed children. *Child Development, 63,* 1305–1320. Medline doi:10.2307/1131557

Sallquist, J. V., Eisenberg, N., Spinrad, T. L., Reiser, M., Hofer, C., Zhou, Q., . . . & Eggum, N. (2009). Positive and negative emotionality: Trajectories across six years and relations with social competence. *Emotion, 9,* 15–28. Medline doi:10.1037/a0013970

Salmivalli, C., Ojanen, T., Haanpää, J., & Peets, K. (2005). "I'm OK but you're not" and other peer-relational schemas: Explaining individual differences in children's social goals. *Developmental Psychology, 41,* 363–375. Medline doi:10.1037/0012-1649.41.2.363

Schultz, D., Izard, C. E., & Bear, G. (2004). Children's emotion processing: Relations to emotionality and aggression. *Development and Psychopathology, 16,* 371–387. Medline doi:10.1017/S0954579404044566

Thomaes, S., Bushman, B. J., Stegge, H., & Olthof, T. (2008). Trumping shame by blasts of noise: Narcissism, self-esteem, shame, and aggression in young adolescents. *Child Development, 79,* 1792–1801. Medline doi:10.1111/j.1467-8624.2008.01226.x

Tremblay, R. E. (2000). The development of aggressive behavior during childhood: What have we learned in the past century? *International Journal of Behavioral Development, 24,* 129–141. doi:10.1080/016502500383232

van Nieuwenhuijzen, M., de Castro, B. O., Van Aken, M. A. G., & Matthys, W. (2009). Impulse control and aggressive response generation as predictors of aggressive behaviour in children with mild intellectual disabilities and borderline intelligence. *Journal of Intellectual Disability Research, 53,* 233–242. Medline doi:10.1111/j.1365-2788.2008.01112.x

Vitaro, F., Brendgen, M., & Barker, E. D. (2006). Subtypes of aggressive behaviors: A developmental perspective. *International Journal of Behavioral Development, 30,* 12–19. doi:10.1177/0165025406059968

Vlerick, P. (1994). The development of socially incompetent behavior in provocative situations. *Psychologica Belgica, 34,* 33–55.

Waas, G. A. (1988). Social attributional biases of peer-rejected and aggressive children. *Child Development, 59,* 969–975. Medline doi:10.2307/1130263

Waldman, I. D. (1996). Aggressive boys' hostile perceptual and response biases: The role of attention and impulsivity. *Child Development, 67,* 1015–1033. Medline doi:10.2307/1131877

4

INTEGRATING EMOTION ATTRIBUTIONS, MORALITY, AND AGGRESSION: RESEARCH AND THEORETICAL FOUNDATIONS

WILLIAM F. ARSENIO

There are a variety of ways of understanding how emotions and affective processes, in general, can influence children's aggression and moral development. The other chapters in this book, for example, focus on empathic tendencies, callous-unemotional traits, and conscience development and how they are intertwined with culture, biology, and cognition. The goal of the present chapter is to take a single, important thread from this complex weave and follow it across several studies and theoretical frameworks. The starting point is that emotions do not just happen to us and are forgotten, but rather that we tend to remember the situations in which strong emotions arise, and these memories then affect our future behavioral decisions. As Damasio (1994) put it, an important evolutionary step for humans involves "*the feeling of the emotion* in connection to the object that excited it" (p. 132). By becoming consciously aware of the links between our feelings and certain types of situations, we become more capable of unpacking certain relatively automatic event-emotion connections in ways that can provide us with more cognitive and behavioral flexibility. And a critical aspect of this transition is our developing understanding and memory of environmentally important affect–event links.

The present chapter addresses these topics in several major sections. The first section provides a more detailed description of the nature of affect–event links (or moral emotion attributions) and of a study that illustrates how this focus relates to emotions and aggressive conduct disorders. This is followed by a section on "happy victimization"—both in its conceptual and behavioral manifestations. The last two major sections (a) begin with a description of some of the complex theoretical issues involved in trying to understand how emotions, social information processing, and moral concerns are implicated in the distinction between reactive and proactive aggression and (b) subsequently describe a study designed to assess this integrated focus.

EMOTION ATTRIBUTIONS: AN INTRODUCTION

> Feelings are not superfluous. All that gossip from deep within turns out to be quite useful. It is not a simple issue of trusting feelings as the necessary arbiter of good and evil. It is a matter of discovering the circumstances in which feeling can indeed be an arbiter and using the reasoned coupling of *circumstances and feelings* as a guide to human behavior. (Damasio, 2003, p. 179)

> Affects, by being represented, last beyond the presence of the object that excites them. This ability to conserve feelings makes interpersonal and moral feelings possible, and allows the latter to be organized into normative scales of values. (Piaget 1954/1981, p. 44)

One way of understanding how emotions are involved in morally relevant behaviors is to examine children's conceptions of the emotional consequences of different sociomoral events. In essence, what do children know about the likely emotional antecedents and consequences of common moral events (e.g., hurting vs. helping), and how does that knowledge affect behavior? This approach begins with several basic claims. The first is that many salient person–environment interactions are inherently affectively charged, and secondly, as the two quotes above highlight, these affective states are often retained as part of our basic mental representations of these events. So, for example, the child who gets pushed off a swing by a peer who does not want to wait his or her turn is likely to remember the event as eliciting strong emotions—including perhaps surprise, anger, and sadness. In brief, children and adults often remember the emotions associated with events, and they can then use those affect–event links, or emotion attributions, for interpreting the likely outcomes of different types of future events.

Arsenio and Fleiss (1996) were interested in whether this focus on affect–event links (or emotion attributions) could prove useful for understanding group differences in children's aggressive and disruptive behaviors. Earlier studies (e.g., Barden, Zelko, Duncan, & Masters, 1980) revealed that children across a wide age range (5- to 12-year-olds) had broadly similar views of the emotional outcomes of various "common social events" except for the one specifically moral event examined, acts involving theft. But what did this moral variability mean? If some children expect different emotional outcomes for theft than do their peers, would this have any effect on their behavior? And do these differences just apply to theft or to other morally relevant behaviors including aggression?

In an initial attempt to address these questions, Arsenio and Fleiss examined the emotion attributions and related emotion justifications of two groups of 24 6- to 12-year-olds. One group of behaviorally disruptive children had been diagnosed with either oppositional defiant or conduct disorder (*Diagnostic and Statistical Manual of Mental Disorders*, 3rd. ed., rev.; *DSM–III–R*; American Psychiatric Association, 1987), and the other group included nondiagnosed elementary school children (the two groups did differ in cognitive ability, maternal education, race/ethnicity, or gender composition [84% male]). During individual interviews, children were presented with several different types of stories, including simple prosocial stories (e.g., helping a peer pick up some dropped papers) as well as acts of aggressive victimization (threatening a peer so he or she would clean up the aggressor's mess). Participants predicted how the two story characters (actors and their targets) would feel and provided rationales to explain these emotion choices.

Although many of the emotion attributions for the two groups were similar, several key group differences emerged. For example, more than half of both groups expected that prosocial actors would feel happy, and yet significantly fewer behaviorally disruptive (BD) children had this expectation than did typical children (55% vs. 81%). In addition, compared with their peers, BD children less often expected that both participants in aggressive acts of victimization would feel afraid (5% vs. 30%). Children's explanations for these emotion attributions also differed: BD children explained aggressive victimizers' emotions by referring to the potential gains resulting from these victimizing acts much more than did their typical peers (61% vs. 33%). Overall, then, children's conceptions of sociomoral events differed systematically, both as a function of the nature of the event and a person's particular role in that event. In addition, however, behaviorally disruptive children differed from their peers in several key emotion attributions and related rationales in ways that seem likely to promote ongoing behavior problems.

HAPPY VICTIMIZATION

Despite the evidence of important behavior group differences in several categories of moral emotion attributions (see Dunn & Hughes, 2001), one specific moral attribution has received the most attention to date—the "happy victimizer" (see also Chapter 9, this volume). A brief description of this literature (see Arsenio, Gold, & Adams, 2006; Arsenio & Lover, 1995, for extensive reviews) will illustrate why this work has generated so much interest and also provide a background for several subsequent chapter sections.

Results from early studies (e.g., Arsenio, 1988) revealed that young children under the age of 5 years expect that successful acts of victimization (e.g., getting the other person's candy or seizing a turn on a swing) will make the victimizer (including oneself) feel happy as a result of the gains resulting from the act (although see Chapter 9, this volume, on self/other victimizer distinctions and cross-cultural differences in this distinction). Other studies revealed that young children's happy victimizer expectancy emerged even when young children were explicitly directed to the resulting harm for the victim (Nunner-Winkler & Sodian, 1988) or when it was supposedly their best friend doing the victimizing to them (Arsenio & Kramer, 1992). By contrast, slightly older children (6 years and up, depending on the study) attributed far fewer positive emotions to victimizers, in part because older children expected that the pain and loss experienced by the victim would affect the victimizer emotionally.

The early research on young children's happy victimizer expectancy seemed both unexpected and potentially problematic. For one thing, this conception fit poorly with several major theories that emphasized that children's awareness of the harm for victims, empathic distress, and concerns about punishment should lead children to expect that victimizers would feel distinctly mixed emotions, including sadness, guilt, and fear (Arsenio & Kramer, 1992). And if young children actually hold this expectation, it could support ongoing acts of peer victimization ("If I steal her lunch cookies, I can eat them and feel good!"). Although some recent studies (e.g., Lagattuta, 2005) have included more benign explanations for young children's happy victimizer expectancy (involving, e.g., theory of mind-related constraints), results from observational studies have revealed that happy victimization is far from uncommon. Perhaps more important, these observational studies revealed that individual differences in children's happy victimization are related to aggression, peer acceptance, and overall social competence.

In our own lab, we have conducted three observational studies on preschoolers' victimization-related emotions. In the most extensive of these (Arsenio, Cooperman, & Lover, 2000), we assessed 4-year-olds' aggressive interactions and the emotions they displayed both during their aggressive conflicts (including physical harm and taking others' objects) and at other times. We found that, overall, most children were angry when they were the targets of aggressive victimization, whereas aggressive victimizers were happy about 40% of the time and angry about 40% of the time. However, it was only those children who were especially likely to be happy victimizers (as a proportion of their overall aggression-related emotion expressions) who were more aggressive and less liked by their peers. In addition, the targets of aggressive victimization were much more likely to be distressed (sadness or anger) when victimizers were happy.

A short-term longitudinal study by Miller and Olson (2000) underscored the developmental significance of children's actual happy victimization. The participants were a group of 60 4- to 5-year-olds from a Head Start center that served low-income European American families. Children were videotaped once early in the school year and again 9 months later as they engaged in 15 min of mostly free play in groups of 5 preschoolers. Teachers and peers assessed the preschoolers at both time points using a variety of measures, and, in addition, the videotapes were scored for children's conflicts and emotion displays. A single emotion category called gleeful taunting, "high intensity inappropriate positive affect" (Miller & Olson, 2000, p. 344) during the videotaped conflicts at the beginning of the school year was the strongest predictor of negative outcomes 9 months later. Specifically, children with initially higher levels of gleeful taunting were subsequently less liked by peers and rated by teachers as having more disruptive, problematic behaviors. Not surprisingly, the authors argued that gleeful taunting was likely to have negative consequences for these children well beyond the preschool years.

Collectively, the research on children's morally relevant emotion attributions and their views of happy victimization, in particular, has supported several major conclusions. First, research involving school-age children has shown that individual differences in a group of sociomoral emotion attributions and rationales (including victimization, helping, and social conventions) are related to children's aggressive and disruptive behaviors (Arsenio & Fleiss, 1996; Dunn & Hughes, 2001). Second, although many studies find surprisingly little variability in preschoolers' happy victimizer conceptions (see Arsenio et al., 2006, for a review), observational studies have shown that preschoolers who actually display more happy victimization are both aggressive and considered less socially competent by their teachers and peers. In the remaining sections, evidence is presented that individual differences in older children's and adolescents' happy victimizer conceptions become predictive of a range of problematic behaviors as well as one particular type of aggression—proactive aggression.

INTEGRATING EMOTIONS, AGGRESSION, AND MORAL DEVELOPMENT: THEORETICAL CONSIDERATIONS

Theoretical work on emotion attributions has typically viewed these attributions as part of a broader model of how emotional processes inform children's social reasoning and behavior. For example, one theoretical model (Lemerise & Arsenio, 2000) describes how children's affective processes—

including affective relationships (e.g., being friends vs. enemies) and emotion recognition and regulation abilities—are likely to influence each of the six processing steps in Crick and Dodge's (1994) social information processing (SIP) model (see Chapter 8, this volume, for details of the model and a review of related research). These affective interests also provided a framework for Arsenio and Lemerise's (2001) subsequent attempt to explore a theoretically important debate about the nature of bullying and aggression between Crick and Dodge (1999) and Sutton, Smith, and Swettenham (1999a, 1999b).

Although both of these groups acknowledged the deeply problematic nature of childhood bullying, they differed strongly in how they viewed the role of social cognitive mediators of aggression and whether bullies could ever be considered socially competent. On one side, Sutton et al. (1999a) disagreed with the "popular stereotype of a bully supported by theories based on the social skills model . . . of a powerful but oafish person with little understanding of others" (p. 117). Instead, these authors argued that at least some bullies (a) had advanced social cognitive abilities (especially involving theory of mind), which they used to manipulate and control others, and (b) were socially competent because they were able to achieve their goals effectively.

In response, Crick and Dodge (1999) challenged the notion that bullying could ever be considered socially competent given the negative long-term developmental outcomes associated with all forms of aggression (e.g., peer rejection and declining academic performance; Dodge, Coie, & Lynam, 2006). Moreover, Crick and Dodge (1999) argued that Sutton et al. (1999a) had misunderstood a key feature of the SIP model: Aggression can result from either social cognitive deficits (e.g., difficulties with encoding and/or hostile attributions) or from chronic processing biases, including "nonnormative" beliefs about one's self-efficacy for being aggressive and the utility of using aggression to achieve instrumental goals.

This debate raised a number of important and unanswered questions about the connections among children's affective processes, aggressive tendencies, and related social cognitions (Arsenio & Lemerise, 2001). First of all, Sutton et al. (1999a, 1999b) sometimes seemed to focus on early SIP studies, work that revealed that when aggressive boys encountered negative outcomes in ambiguous contexts (e.g., getting hit in the head by a ball), they attributed more hostile intentions to "provocateurs" than did nonaggressive children. Sutton et al.'s (1999a) emphasis was understandable: The hostile attribution bias is arguably the most studied of all SIP biases or deficits, and it has been observed in a wide range of populations, from aggressive school-age children to violent incarcerated offenders (see de Castro, Veerman, Koops, Bosch, & Monshouwer, 2002, for a review). SIP researchers, however, have also begun to identify other forms of aggression that have had little to do with responding to misperceived aggression.

One important distinction involves the differences between reactive and proactive aggression, with reactive aggression appearing to be a "frustration response . . . associated with a lack of control, whereas the latter type [proactive aggression] appears to be less emotional and more likely driven by the expectation of reward" (Dodge, Lochman, Harnish, Bates, & Pettit, 1997, p. 30). Although these two forms of aggression are often highly related (see Chapter 10, this volume), there is growing evidence that they are associated with distinctly different patterns of SIP-related biases and deficits. Reactive aggression is typically related to early SIP steps, especially problems (i.e., deficits) related to judging others' intentions in potentially provocative situations (the "hostile attribution bias"). By contrast, proactive aggression is associated with a mix of later SIP stage "biases," starting with differences in children's social goals. For example, in contexts involving potential aggression, proactively aggressive children typically are more concerned with getting what they want (instrumental goals) rather than maintaining relationships with others. Proactively aggressive children also are more likely to generate aggressive responses (SIP, Step 4) and to evaluate those responses more favorably, both in term of aggressive self-efficacy and the expected material and emotional outcomes. In short, for some children aggression "is easy, it works, and it makes me feel good" (Arsenio & Lemerise, 2001, p. 64).

This description of proactive aggression and aggressors raises obvious concerns at several levels. Although Sutton et al. (1999a) may have linked the SIP model too exclusively with reactive aggression, they recognized that for some children the problem "may lie in the values of the bully rather than the accuracy of the cognitions, they view the costs and benefits of aggression differently" (p. 122). Moreover, these aggressive values seemed to reflect both a lack of empathic responsiveness for the costs inflicted on proactive aggressors' victims, as well as any sense that harming others in pursuit of instrumental gains is not just socially incompetent (as described in the SIP model), but also morally wrong from the standpoint of both adults and those children who are likely to be directly affected (see, e.g., Turiel, 2006).

In recent work (e.g., Arsenio, 2006; Arsenio & Lemerise, 2004), we examined the different moral implications of these claims. One implication, we argued, is that reactive aggressors appear to have similar core concerns with fairness and moral legitimacy as do nonaggressive children. Both groups share the view that if a peer deliberately harms them, then it is legitimate to respond aggressively (see, e.g., Astor, 1994); that is, "it's not ok (right/fair) for someone to do something to me bad on purpose" (Arsenio & Lemerise, 2001, p. 62). The difference between the two groups, however, is in their ability to interpret others' intentions accurately (the hostile attribution bias of reactive aggressors) and in the intensity of their expected reactions. Consequently, reactively aggressive children can be described as suffering from a

SIP-related deficit that undermines their largely intact moral orientation. Interventions that target this deficit and/or help these children regulate emotions when they become aroused during provocative situations are likely to be quite helpful (see Chapters 10 and 12, this volume).

What about proactive aggression and aggressors? The problem for proactive aggressors may have less to do with the accuracy of their social reasoning than with some aspect of their moral values. Proactive aggressors, for example, do not seem to have any particular problems understanding others' intentions, even during potentially emotionally dysregulating situations. And even though proactive aggressors seem to care about the intentions and associated moral legitimacy of others' actions, proactively aggressive children are still willing to use illegitimate aggression to advance their own goals, even when it means directly harming others. This intention asymmetry ("my harm is ok, yours is not") may initially seem puzzling, especially given most adults' and some philosophers' longstanding assumption that "to know the good is to do the good." But for some children and adults, just knowing what is "right" and "good" is not necessarily enough to motivate them when it conflicts with their own needs, desires, and potentially self-serving interests. As Sutton et al. (1999a) put it, "Could it be the case that bullies can do all this [SIP] very accurately and in fact use this skill to their advantage, lacking the empathy . . . to integrate such information into their interactions?" (p. 118).

INTEGRATING SOCIAL INFORMATION PROCESSING, MORAL REASONING, AND EMOTION ATTRIBUTIONS

Do children's and adolescents' aggressive tendencies result from being "hot-headed" and misinterpreting others' social cues or from being cold-blooded and victimizing others for personal gain without regard for victims? (Arsenio, Adams, & Gold, 2009, p. 1739)

The Sutton et al. (1999a, 1999b) and Crick and Dodge (1999) debate has suggested that both answers are true, depending on the nature of the aggression being studied. Furthermore, the Arsenio and Lemerise (2001) review suggested that any attempts to answer this question would require a theoretical framework that can address children's social information processing errors and biases as well as the moral aspects of victimization-related decisions and behavior. Unfortunately, research on children's aggressive tendencies and moral development, to date, has followed mostly separate empirical and theoretical tracks. This division is surprising given how many acts of aggression involve clear moral transgressions against others, and how often moral transgression take the form of either verbal or physical aggression. For example, aggression has been described as "behavior that is aimed at harming or injuring another person"

(Dodge et al., 2006, p. 721), with morality defined in terms of an act's harmful consequences (Turiel, 2006). Moreover, both approaches focus on intentional harm and victimization; accidents and other mishaps may be unfortunate, but they are neither inherently aggressive nor moral.

Recently, Arsenio and Lemerise (2004; see also Tisak, Tisak, & Goldstein, 2006) argued that two highly influential approaches within these fields, the social information processing (SIP) model for aggression (Crick & Dodge, 1994) and the domain approach for morality (Turiel, 2006), share a number of important similarities that point to a larger integrative theory. Both models emphasize the essential connections that exist between children's and adults' social cognitions and their behavior: An individual's understanding (or misunderstanding) of the others' social behaviors and intentions often has a strong influence on their subsequent short- and long-term aggressive and moral patterns. Second, until recently, neither model has had much to say about emotions or emotion processes (although see Lemerise & Arsenio, 2000; Wainryb, Brehl, & Matwin, 2005, among others), a surprising gap given that victimization, deliberate harm, and aggression are all likely to elicit especially strong emotions in both participants and witnesses.

Guided by the general outline of the integrative model proposed by Arsenio and Lemerise (2001, 2004), my colleagues and I recently completed a study designed to assess the unique social cognitive correlates of reactive and proactive aggression. As described above, our general interest was in whether reactive aggression is more closely related to being "hot-headed" and misinterpreting others' social cues, whereas proactive aggression is more related to being "cold-blooded" and victimizing others for personal gain. Specifically, we expected that adolescents' proactive aggressive tendencies would be associated with lower levels of moral concerns (e.g., less emphasis on fairness and harm) when adolescents were asked to justify hypothetical acts in which they victimized others for material and psychological gains. By contrast, we expected that adolescents' reactive aggressive tendencies would be linked with their SIP-related judgments (especially those involving hostile attribution biases in ambiguous situations), but not with their moral reasoning. Another research goal was to examine whether adolescents' emotion attributions for various events involving harm and/or victimization would have differential links with reactive and proactive aggression. Guided by recent happy victimization studies, it was expected that proactive aggression would be related to adolescents' expectations that they would feel happier after successfully victimizing others. Reactive aggressive tendencies, however, would be linked with greater expected anger following acts of ambiguous provocation.

The participants included 100 adolescents (69 boys and 31 girls) who attended public high schools in a lower socioeconomic status (SES), urban community. More than 60% of the adolescents lived in poor, female-headed households (Hollingshead, 1975; $M = 29.46$, $SD = 9.49$), and about two thirds of the sample was African American and most of the remainder was Latino. In addition, classroom teachers who knew each of the adolescents well participated. Half of the adolescents had previously been diagnosed as meeting *Diagnostic and Statistical Manual of Mental Disorders* (4th ed.; *DSM–IV*; American Psychiatric Association, 1994) criteria for conduct or oppositional defiant disorder, and the other half of the group came from the same school district, but with no reported *DSM* diagnoses. The groups, however, did not differ in terms of gender or racial/ethnic composition, SES, or age. Moreover, despite the existence of some mean group differences (see Arsenio et al., 2004), subsequent moderation analyses revealed that very few of the results described in this section were moderated by participants' group status. Consequently, the findings are described for the total sample.

Adolescents were individually presented with a multipart, orally administered interview that included an assessment of verbal ability (Peabody Picture Vocabulary Test; Dunn & Dunn, 2001) and separate measures focusing on three categories of aggressive stimulus events involving (a) ambiguously caused negative outcomes, (b) deliberate provocation, and (c) unprovoked acts of aggression that resulted in clear gains for the victimizer. The first two assessments—(a) and (b)—were taken from standard instruments used to assess reactive and proactive aggressive tendencies (Crick & Dodge, 1996; Dodge et al., 1997), and the last was taken from a previous study used to assess the moral reasoning of adolescents (Arsenio, Shea, & Sacks, 1995).

For the stories involving deliberate provocations (e.g., a peer cuts in front of you in line and says "I want this spot"), adolescents were asked to imagine that they had responded aggressively and to answer a series of questions about the effectiveness (will the other person stop?) and ease of responding aggressively and how they would feel subsequently (from *very bad* to *very good*). For stories involving ambiguous provocations (e.g., you get hit in the head by a football during gym class), adolescents judged whether the act had been done intentionally and how they would feel as a result (almost all expected to be angry). For the last instrument, adolescents were asked to imagine that they victimized someone else for a specific gain (e.g., "you knocked the kid down so you would get the last concert ticket"), and they judged how they and their victim would feel and why. In addition teachers (a) rated adolescents' reactive and proactive aggressive tendencies using an instrument development by Dodge and Coie (1987) and (b) completed Child Behavior Checklist (Achenbach, 1991) measures of adolescents' externalizing tendencies (delinquent and aggressive subscales) and attention problems.

Given the size of the total sample, it was not possible to form separate subgroups of reactive and proactive aggressive adolescents. Instead analyses were conducted by examining the unique connections between each type of aggression and the social cognitive measure, controlling for the influence of the nonfocal form of aggression (see, e.g., de Castro, Merk, Koops, Veerman, & Bosch, 2005; Smithmyer, Hubbard, & Simons, 2000). Controlling for proactive aggression, Arsenio et al. (2009) found that higher levels of adolescents' reactive aggression were associated with somewhat more hostile attributional biases, greater expected ease in enacting aggression, and lower verbal abilities. Proactive aggression, however, was uniquely related to greater expected happiness following both provoked and unprovoked immoral aggression, lower moral concerns regarding one's aggression (i.e., a focus on material gains rather than fairness), and higher verbal abilities. In other words, there was no overlap in the social cognitive variables uniquely related to adolescents' reactive and proactive aggression. Finally, mediation analyses revealed that adolescents' attention problems mediated the connection between reactive aggression and its related social cognitive correlates (e.g., hostile attributional bias), but not between proactive aggression and its correlates.

At one level, these findings fit with previous research (e.g., Dodge et al., 1997) indicating that reactive aggressive is more related to social cognitive deficits such as the hostile attributional bias, whereas proactive aggression is more related to social cognitive biases, such as outcome expectations for aggressive acts. The present results, however, also clarify the specifically moral aspects of these biases and deficits. It has been argued (Arsenio & Lemerise, 2001, 2004) that although reactively aggressive children have some problems in judging the moral intentions of others, they still focus on and care about whether any harmful act (theirs and others') was committed intentionally or not. Like their nonaggressive peers, reactively aggressive children share a core moral value that it not right/fair for someone to intentionally wrong another person. The issue for reactively aggressive children is more the accuracy of their reasoning involving harmful intentions than the moral permissibility of intentional harm, per se.

Consistent with these claims, reactive aggression in this study was not related to any moral deficits (e.g., a lack of empathy or increased concern with self-centered gains) or any expectations that one would feel happy following either provoked aggression or one's clearly unfair victimization of others. The observed connections between reactive aggression, hostile attributional biases, lower verbal abilities, and attentional problems paint a very different picture. It is not hard to imagine how these difficulties in attending to and understanding their social environments would lead such adolescents to feel frustrated, and in combination with lower verbal skills, cause many peer conflicts to escalate into what might seem like legitimate acts of aggression to these adolescents.

This description of reactive aggression is supported by results from several other studies. Hubbard et al. (2002), for example, found that when reactive aggressive children (second graders) played a "rigged" board game, they had higher levels and greater increases in their physiological reactivity and angry behavior than did proactively aggressive children. This pattern of emotion dysregulation might also help to explain why reactively aggressive children are so likely to reveal hostile attributional biases (de Castro et al., 2002). Interestingly, children's reactive aggression and problems with emotion regulation have both been linked with problems in attending to social cues, avoiding conflict, and coping effectively when conflicts do occur (see Saarni, Campos, Camras, & Witherington, 2006).

The results involving proactive aggression in this study were quite different. Proactive aggression was not connected with social cognitive deficits (e.g., hostile attributional biases) or problematic attentional or verbal skills but, as Sutton et al. (1999a) suggested, to a fundamentally different set of moral values regarding aggression than most peers. Specifically, proactive aggression was connected with expectations of greater happiness following both provoked acts of aggression as well as aggressive acts of unfair (and unprovoked) aggression. In addition, adolescents' rationales for their feelings following (unprovoked) moral transgression focused on the overt gains resulting from that victimization, even though they also realized that their victims' would be overwhelmingly angry because of the harm and unfairness of these acts (see also Menesini et al., 2003, for related results when children imagined themselves in the role of a bully). Overall, then, proactive aggression was related to the positive emotional and material gains expected for the self, without any obvious attempt to minimize the costs for one's victims.

Although there is some evidence (e.g., Dodge et al., 1997; Smithmyer et al., 2000) linking proactive aggression and positive emotion attributions in response to provoked aggression ("how would you feel if you pushed him back"), this study also shows that the happiness associated with unprovoked–immoral acts of victimization and a lack of remorse regarding this victimization are especially related to proactive aggression. Other studies have shown that expectations of happiness following immoral–unprovoked aggression are predictive of problematic behaviors in both school age children (see Chapter 9, this volume) and adolescents (Krettenauer & Eichler, 2006). The Arsenio et al. (2009) findings, however, are among the first to suggest that previous research linking happy victimizer attributions with broad measures of aggression and behavior problems may (a) stem from the overlap of general measures of aggressive–disruptive and proactive aggression (e.g., $r = .54$, $p < .001$, for the present link between overall externalizing tendencies and proactive aggression) and (b) that controlling for proactive aggression could largely eliminate the links between happy victimization and these broader measures of aggression. It will take additional research to confirm these claims, but if supported they would underscore the need to explain the emotional underpinnings of reactive and proactive aggression quite differently.

PROACTIVE AGGRESSION AND EMPATHIC DEFICITS

Are more proactively aggressive adolescents really "cold-blooded," with all that implies? Proactive aggression does seem to be linked with a belief that aggression "delivers the goods" and leads to positive emotions. Moreover, proactively aggressive adolescents appear to understand the negative consequences and losses (emotional and material) that their aggression causes in others and are apparently unmoved by those losses (see also Menesini & Camodeca, 2008, for recent findings that, compared with their peers, bullies expect to feel less guilt and shame following intentional aggressive acts). Taken together, it seems reasonable to argue that proactive aggression is related to potential flaws in children's and adolescents' empathic responsiveness, and to the kinds of callous emotional traits discussed by Marsee and Frick (see Chapter 7, this volume).

There are, however, several problems with accepting a preliminary "empathic deficit" explanation of proactive aggression too quickly. For example, there is evidence that proactive aggression is connected with fewer relationship problems (including peer rejection) than is reactive aggression (Schwartz et al., 1998). Furthermore, in some studies (Dodge & Coie, 1987; see also Little, Brauner, Jones, Nock, & Hawley, 2003) proactively aggressive children have been judged as more humorous and better leaders than their reactively aggressive peers. Another problem involves the complex interplay among the social cognitive mediators of aggression, children's aggression, and the larger social ecologies in which most studies on these topics get conducted. The participants in the Arsenio et al. (2009) study, like those in a number of other related SIP studies (see Dodge et al., 2006), were from economically disadvantaged racial groups living in a very low SES, high-risk, urban communities. Poverty, low educational and economic opportunities, and insufficient community resources are known predictors of elevated levels of aggression and behavior disorders in children and adolescents. Consequently, it is not entirely clear whether some adolescents end up using proactive aggression as a sensible (although troubling) strategy for negotiating socially toxic environmental contexts (Garbarino, 1997).

AGGRESSION, SOCIAL INEQUALITY, AND RELATED SOCIAL COGNITIONS

In an influential review of the research on aggression and conduct disorders, Dodge and Pettit (2003) argued that behaviorally disruptive children suffer from certain types of

> dispositions, contexts, and life experiences [that] lead children to develop
> idiosyncratic social knowledge about the world . . . [and] upon presentation

of a social stimulus (such as a peer interaction) that child, as an active agent, uses social knowledge to guide the processing of social information. (p. 361)

However, as Arsenio and Gold (2006) noted, it is not entirely clear how these atypical or idiosyncratic social cognitions, especially those related to proactive aggression, should be understood. Given what is known about the social realities of many aggressive children (e.g., harsh and/or erratic parenting, socioeconomic deprivation, and problematic peer relationships; Dodge & Pettit, 2003), the "atypical" social cognitions they form may have a coherent and rational basis in their social experiences. In other words, if some children's daily environment lacks basic emotional and moral reciprocity, and fundamental fairness, then what should we expect their emerging conscience and associated moral cognitions look like (see Chapter 1, this volume)?

Implicit in this discussion is the unexamined claim that there is a connection between how some aggressive children and adolescents view the moral status of their larger social environments and how they view aggression. As Arsenio and Gold (2006) proposed, the extent to which children view both their proximal (e.g., attachment relationships) and distal relationships (schools, neighborhoods, etc.) as governed by power and domination may have a significant effect on how they view the legitimacy and desirability of aggressive behavior. Related literature on procedural justice, for example, has already shown that "in the legal arena, people are found to believe authorities are more legitimate when they view their actions as consistent with fair procedures" such as avoiding racial profiling and unnecessary force (Tyler, 2006, p. 383). Similar types of research are needed to examine whether children's and adolescents' views of legal and social fairness are systematically related to their conceptions of interpersonal aggression.

SUMMARY AND IMPLICATIONS

This chapter focused on children's and adolescents' morally relevant emotion attributions and the connections of these attributions with aggressive externalizing tendencies. Some studies, for example, revealed that children with atypical emotion attributions and rationales regarding different sociomoral domains (including victimization and prosocial acts) have elevated levels of behavior problems. Much of the moral emotion attribution literature, and consequently a large part of this chapter, involves the happy victimizer attribution: children's and adolescents' expectation that victimizers will feel relatively happy following acts of victimization that produce material and psychological gains. Evidence was presented that individual differences in preschoolers' actual (observed) happy victimization are positively related to their aggressive tendencies, and that by adolescence, if not earlier (see Chapter 9, this volume), increased happy victimizer attributions are also related to increased aggressive tendencies.

Another important focus of this chapter was on the specific connection between happy victimization attributions and reasoning and adolescents' proactive aggression. Drawing on work by Sutton et al. (1999a, 1999b) and Crick and Dodge (1999; among others), my colleagues and I (Arsenio & Lemerise, 2001, 2004; Lemerise & Arsenio, 2000) have argued for a more integrative model for understanding how reactive and proactive aggression differ, a model that extends beyond the common focus on social information processing biases and deficits. And results from a recent study are broadly consistent with this integrative view in that (a) reactive aggression was associated with social cognitive, verbal, and attentional deficits, but also with an "intact" moral sensibility, whereas (b) proactive aggression was associated with expected emotional and material gains for the self-as-victimizer, moral disregard for victims, but no social cognitive, verbal, or attentional deficits.

Although these findings need to be replicated before their meaning for intervention and policy become clear, several tentative conclusions can be offered. At a clinical level, the recent Arsenio et al. (2009) findings are consistent with growing evidence that "reactive and proactive aggression . . . seem to represent distinct pathways to problem behaviors, which may require drastically different treatment approaches" (Chapter 7, this volume p. 150). As these authors note, there are already effective treatments for reactive aggression that include a significant focus on anger management and overall emotion regulation (Larson & Lochman, 2003). Treatments for proactive aggression, and the large group of mixed reactive and proactive aggressive children, are less clear. Frick's (2006) suggestion of treating proactive aggression by targeting empathic deficits and beliefs regarding the utility of aggression seems promising, especially in younger children. Moreover, these interventions could receive a boast if proactive aggressors really are characterized by higher verbal abilities and a lack of attention problems.

A less sanguine possibility is that proactive aggression, especially in high-risk adolescents, will be very difficult to treat using traditional interventions. For those children and adolescents who grow up in environments characterized by multiple layers of emotionally rejecting relationships (from family abuse to violent neighborhoods), there may be little basis for caring for others or refraining from using aggression to obtain whatever limited resources are available. In these circumstances, it may not be adequate to treat children's disrupted moral reasoning or empathic tendencies without also addressing the social and economic inequalities that often underlie aggression (Arsenio & Gold, 2006). Fortunately, some important intervention efforts, including the Fast Track program (Kupersmidt & Dodge, 2004), are already using a multisystem approach that targets both the negative environmental circumstances and social cognitions that are clear risk factors for childhood aggression.

Finally, it is important for future work to address the links between proactive aggression, bullying, and moral disengagement (Bandura, 1991). A number of European researchers (e.g., Perren & Gutzwiller-Helfenfinger, 2009) have already begun to examine some of the specific ways that bullies psychologically distance themselves from their victims and rationalize aggression. Additional research that examines the connections among moral disengagement, happy victimization, and proactive aggressive could prove especially revealing.

REFERENCES

Achenbach, T. (1991). *Integrative guide for the 1991 CBCL/4-18, YSR, and TRF profiles*. Burlington, VT: Department of Psychiatry, University of Vermont.

American Psychiatric Association. (1987). *Diagnostic and statistical manual of mental disorders* (3rd ed., rev.). Washington, DC: Author.

American Psychiatric Association. (1994). *Diagnostic and statistical manual of mental disorders* (4th ed.). Washington, DC: Author.

Arsenio, W. (1988). Children's conceptions of the situational affective consequences of sociomoral events. *Child Development, 59,* 1611–1622. Medline doi:10.2307/1130675

Arsenio, W. (2006). Happy victimization: Emotion dysregulation in the context of children's instrumental/proactive aggression. In D. Snyder, J. Simpson, & J. Hughes (Eds.), *Emotion regulation in families: Pathways to dysfunction and health* (pp. 101–121). Washington, DC: American Psychological Association.

Arsenio, W., Adams, E., & Gold, J. (2009). Social information processing, moral reasoning, and emotion attributions: Relations with adolescents' reactive and proactive aggression. *Child Development, 80,* 1739–1755.

Arsenio, W., Cooperman, S., & Lover, A. (2000). Affective predictors of preschoolers' aggression and peer acceptance: Direct and indirect effects. *Developmental Psychology, 36,* 438–448. Medline doi:10.1037/0012-1649.36.4.438

Arsenio, W., & Fleiss, K. (1996). Behaviourally disruptive and typical children's conceptions of socio-moral affect. *The British Journal of Developmental Psychology, 14,* 173–186.

Arsenio, W., & Gold, J. (2006). The effects of social injustice and inequality on children's moral judgments and behavior: Towards a theoretical model. *Cognitive Development, 21,* 388–400. doi:10.1016/j.cogdev.2006.06.005

Arsenio, W., Gold, J., & Adams, E. (2004). Adolescents' emotion expectancies regarding aggressive and nonaggressive events: Connections with behavior problems. *Journal of Experimental Child Psychology, 89,* 338–355. Medline doi:10.1016/j.jecp.2004.08.001

Arsenio, W., Gold, J., & Adams, E. (2006). Children's conceptions and displays of moral emotions. In M. Killen & J. Smetana (Eds.), *Handbook of moral development* (pp. 581–608). Hillsdale, NJ: Erlbaum.

Arsenio, W., & Kramer, R. (1992). Victimizers and their victims: Children's conceptions of the mixed emotional consequences of victimization. *Child Development, 63*, 915–927. Medline doi:10.2307/1131243

Arsenio, W., & Lemerise, E. (2001). Varieties of childhood bullying: Values, emotion processes, and social competence. *Social Development, 10*, 59–73. doi:10.1111/1467-9507.00148

Arsenio, W., & Lemerise, E. (2004). Aggression and moral development: Integrating the social information processing and moral domain models. *Child Development, 75*, 987–1002. Medline doi:10.1111/j.1467-8624.2004.00720.x

Arsenio, W., & Lover, A. (1995). Children's conceptions of sociomoral affect: Happy victimizers, mixed emotions and other expectancies. In M. Killen & D. Hart (Eds.), *Morality in everyday life: Developmental perspectives* (pp. 87–128). Cambridge, England: Cambridge University Press.

Arsenio, W., Shea, T., & Sacks, B. (1995). *Moral emotion judgments.* Unpublished manuscript.

Astor, R. (1994). Children's moral reasoning about family and peer violence: The role of provocation and retribution. *Child Development, 65*, 1054–1067. doi:10.2307/1131304

Bandura, A. (1991). Social cognitive theory of moral thought and action. In W. Kurtines & J. Gewirtz (Eds.), *Handbook of moral behavior and development* (pp. 45–103). Hillsdale, NJ: Erlbaum.

Barden, R. C., Zelko, F., Duncan, S., & Masters, J. (1980). Children's consensual knowledge about the experiential determinants of emotion. *Journal of Personality and Social Psychology, 39*, 968–976. Medline doi:10.1037/0022-3514.39.5.968

Crick, N., & Dodge, K. (1994). A review and reformulation of social-information-processing mechanisms in children's social adjustment. *Psychological Bulletin, 115*, 74–101. doi:10.1037/0033-2909.115.1.74

Crick, N., & Dodge, K. (1996). Social-information-processing mechanisms in reactive and proactive aggression. *Child Development, 64*, 783–790.

Crick, N., & Dodge, K. (1999). "Superiority" is in the eye of the beholder. *Social Development, 8*, 128–131. doi:10.1111/1467-9507.00084

Damasio, A. (1994). *Descartes error: Emotion, reason, and the human brain.* New York, NY: Avon.

Damasio, A. (2003). *Looking for Spinoza: Joy, sorrow, and the feeling brain.* New York, NY: Harcourt.

de Castro, B. O., Merk, W., Koops, W., Veerman, J., & Bosch, J. (2005). Emotions in social information processing and their relations with reactive and proactive aggression in referred aggressive boys. *Journal of Clinical Child and Adolescent Psychology, 34*, 105–116. Medline doi:10.1207/s15374424jccp3401_10 de Castro, B. O., Veerman, J., Koops, W., Bosch, J., & Monshouwer, H. (2002). Hostile attribution of intent and aggressive behavior: A meta-analysis. *Child Development, 73*, 916–934. Medline doi:10.1111/1467-8624.00447

Dodge, K. A., & Coie, J. (1987). Social-information-processing factors in reactive and proactive aggression in children's peer groups. *Journal of Personality and Social Psychology, 53*, 1146–1158. Medline doi:10.1037/0022-3514.53.6.1146

Dodge, K. A., Coie, J., & Lynam, D. (2006). Aggression and antisocial behavior in youth. In W. Damon & R. Lerner (Series Eds.) and N. Eisenberg (Vol. Ed.), *Handbook of child psychology: Vol. 3. Social, emotional, and personality development* (6th ed., pp. 719–788). New York, NY: Wiley.

Dodge, K. A., Lochman, J., Harnish, J., Bates, J., & Pettit, G. (1997). Reactive and proactive aggression in school children and psychiatrically impaired chronically assaultive youth. *Journal of Abnormal Psychology, 106*, 37–51. Medline doi:10.1037/0021-843X.106.1.37

Dodge, K. A., & Pettit, G. (2003). A biopsychosocial mode of chronic conduct disorders in adolescence. *Developmental Psychology, 39*, 349–371. Medline doi:10.1037/0012-1649.39.2.349

Dunn, L., & Dunn, L. (2001). *Peabody Picture Vocabulary Test* (3rd ed.). Circle Pines, MN: American Guidance Service.

Dunn, J., & Hughes, C. (2001). "I got some swords and you're dead!" Violent fantasy, antisocial behavior, friendship, and moral sensibility in young children. *Child Development, 72*, 491–505. Medline doi:10.1111/1467-8624.00292

Frick, P. (2006). Developmental pathways to conduct disorder. *Child Psychiatric Clinics of North America, 15*, 311–332. doi:10.1016/j.chc.2005.11.003

Garbarino, J. (1997). Growing up in a socially toxic environment. In D. Cicchetti, & S. Toth (Eds.), *Developmental perspectives on trauma: Theory, research, and intervention* (pp. 141–154). Rochester NY: University of Rochester Press.

Hollingshead, A. (1975). *Four factor index of social status*. Unpublished instrument, Yale University, New Haven, CT.

Hubbard, J., Smithmyer, C., Ramsden, S., Parker, E., Flanagan, K., Dearing, K., . . . Simons, R. F. (2002). Observational, physiological, and self-report measures of children's anger: Relations to reactive vs. proactive aggression. *Child Development, 73*, 1101–1118. Medline doi:10.1111/1467-8624.00460

Krettenauer, T., & Eichler, D. (2006). Adolescents' self-attributed moral emotions following a moral transgression: Relations with delinquency, confidence in moral judgments and age. *The British Journal of Developmental Psychology, 24*, 489–506. doi:10.1348/026151005X50825

Kupersmidt, J., & Dodge, K. (2004). *Children's peer relations: From development to intervention*. Washington, DC: American Psychological Association.

Lagattuta, K. H. (2005). When you shouldn't do what you want to do: Young children's understanding of desires, rules, and emotions. *Child Development, 76*, 713–733. Medline doi:10.1111/j.1467-8624.2005.00873.x

Larson, J., & Lochman, J. (2003). *Helping schoolchildren cope with anger*. New York, NY: Guilford.

Lemerise, E. A., & Arsenio, W. (2000). An integrated model of emotion processes and cognition in social information processing. *Child Development, 71*, 107–118. Medline doi:10.1111/1467-8624.00124

Little, T., Brauner, J., Jones, S., Nock, M., & Hawley, P. (2003). Rethinking aggression: A typological examination of the functions of aggression. *Merrill-Palmer Quarterly, 49*, 343–369. doi:10.1353/mpq.2003.0014

Miller, A. L., & Olson, S. (2000). Emotional expressiveness during peer conflicts: A predictor of social maladjustment among high-risk preschoolers. *Journal of Abnormal Child Psychology, 28*, 339–352. Medline doi:10.1023/A:1005117009370

Menesini, E., & Camodeca, M. (2008). Shame and guilt as behavior regulators: Relationships with bullying, victimization, and prosocial behavior. *The British Journal of Developmental Psychology, 26*, 183–196. doi:10.1348/026151007X205281

Menesini, F., Sanchez, V., Fonzi, A., Ortega, R., Costabile, A., & Lo Feudo, G. (2003). Moral emotions and bullying: A cross-national comparison of differences between bullies, victims, and outsiders. *Aggressive Behavior, 29*, 515–530. doi:10.1002/ab.10060

Nunner-Winkler, G., & Sodian, B. (1988). Children's understanding of moral emotions. *Child Development, 59*, 1323–1338. Medline doi:10.2307/1130495

Perren, S., & Gutzwiller-Helfenfinger, E. (2009, April). *Bully/victim problems in children and adolescents: Associations with moral disengagement and moral values.* Symposium presented at the biennial meeting of the Society for Research in Child Development, Denver, CO.

Piaget, J. (1981). *Intelligence and affectivity: Their relationship during child development* (T. Brown & C. Kaegi, Trans.). Palo Alto, CA: Annual Reviews Monograph. (Original work published 1954)

Saarni, C., Campos, J., Camras, L., & Witherington, D. (2006). Emotional development: Action, communication, and understanding. In W. Damon & R. Lerner (Series Eds.) and N. Eisenberg (Vol. Ed.), *Handbook of child psychology: Vol. 3. Social, emotional, and personality development* (6th ed., pp. 226–299). New York, NY: Wiley.

Schwartz, D., Dodge, K., Coie, J., Hubbard, J., Cillessen, A., Lemerise, E., & Bateman, H. (1998). Social-cognitive and behavioral correlates of aggression and victimization in boys' play groups. *Journal of Abnormal Child Psychology, 26*, 431–440. Medline doi:10.1023/A:1022695601088

Smithmyer, C. M., Hubbard, J., & Simons, R. (2000). Proactive and reactive aggression in delinquent adolescents: Relations to aggression outcome expectancies. *Journal of Clinical Child Psychology, 29*, 86–93. Medline doi:10.1207/S15374424jccp2901_9

Sutton, J., Smith, P., & Swettenham, J. (1999a). Bullying and "theory of mind": A critique of the "social skills deficit" view of antisocial behavior. *Social Development, 8*, 117–127. doi:10.1111/1467-9507.00083

Sutton, J., Smith, P., & Swettenham, J. (1999b). Socially desirable need not be incompetent: A reply to Crick and Dodge. *Social Development, 8,* 132–134. doi:10.1111/1467-9507.00085

Tisak, M., Tisak, J., & Goldstein, S. (2006). Aggression, delinquency, and morality: A social-cognitive perspective. In M. Killen & J. Smetana (Eds.), *Handbook of moral development* (pp. 611–629). Hillsdale, NJ: Erlbaum.

Turiel, E. (2006). The development of morality. In W. Damon & R. Lerner (Series Eds.) and N. Eisenberg (Vol. Ed.), *Handbook of Child Psychology: Vol. 3. Social, emotional, and personality development* (6th ed., pp. 789–857). New York, NY: Wiley.

Tyler, T. (2006). Psychological perspectives on legitimacy and legitimation. *Annual Review of Psychology, 57,* 375–400. Medline doi:10.1146/annurev.psych. 57.102904.190038

Wainryb, C., Brehl, B., & Matwin, S. (2005). Being hurt and hurting others: Children's narrative accounts and moral judgments of their own interpersonal conflicts. *Monographs of the Society for Research in Child Development, 70*(3, Serial No. 281).

II

FROM NEUROSCIENCE TO CULTURE: FACTORS INFLUENCING AGGRESSION AND MORALITY

5

EMPATHY, MORAL DEVELOPMENT, AND AGGRESSION: A COGNITIVE NEUROSCIENCE PERSPECTIVE

R. J. R. BLAIR

The goal of this chapter is to consider the relationship between empathy, moral development, and some aspects of aggression. I specify in relative detail the computational processes that underlie different manifestations of these constructs. It is important that if one can understand these details, one can potentially develop treatment strategies that are targeted toward the specific impairments shown by particular clinical populations at risk for heightened levels of aggression.

The chapter begins by considering how to conceptualize empathy, arguing that several dissociable neurocognitive processes can be considered empathy and that several of these are critically important to specific aspects of moral development. The chapter continues by considering how to conceptualize morality, arguing that there are several different forms of moral reasoning and that these different forms relate to different types of empathic response. The chapter ends by considering how specific types of empathic dysfunction might give rise to selective impairments for specific forms of moral reasoning and increase the risk for specific forms of antisocial behavior.

EMPATHY

The term empathy has many definitions. It is broadly applied to processes in which an observer uses information about the internal state of another. However, although some consider cognitive perspective taking (also known as theory of mind) as empathy (Decety & Moriguchi, 2007), the definition used by others is far narrower and requires an emotional reaction to another individual that is isomorphic to that other's affective state (de Vignemont & Singer, 2006). My purpose in this chapter is not to suggest that there is a correct definition. Rather, I argue that *empathy* should be considered to subsume a variety of dissociable neurocognitive processes. Three main divisions, each reliant on at least partially dissociable neural systems, can be identified: motor, emotional, and cognitive empathy (Blair, 2005). Motor empathy occurs when the individual mirrors the motor responses of an observed actor. Emotional empathy reflects an emotional response to another individual's emotional state. Cognitive empathy is effectively theory of mind (ToM) and involves the representation of the mental state of another individual. The neurocognitive bases of each of these forms of empathy are reviewed in the following sections.

Motor Empathy and Mirror Neurons

There has been considerable recent interest among some empathy researchers in "mirror neurons" (de Vignemont & Singer, 2006; Decety & Moriguchi, 2007; Iacoboni & Mazziotta, 2007; Rizzolatti, Fogassi, & Gallese, 2001). These neurons, originally identified in work on nonhuman primates, show activity both when a monkey performs a particular goal-directed action and when it observes another individual performing a similar action (e.g., Rizzolatti et al., 2001). The concept of mirror neurons has been extended by several researchers using functional magnetic resonance imaging (fMRI). These authors have argued that because there is a degree of overlap in the regions recruited when an individual moves and when the individual watches these movements (inferior frontal and posterior parietal cortex), there is a human mirror neuron system (Iacoboni & Mazziotta, 2007). The action of these neurons and this system can be considered to be the basis of motor empathy, the mimicry of another individual's motor actions by the self. However, currently there are no reasons to believe that motor empathy is necessary for moral development or that motor empathy dysfunction is associated with an increased risk for aggression. For these reasons, motor empathy is not considered further in this chapter.

Emotional Empathy and Mirror Neurons

Several accounts have suggested that mirror neurons are the basis of emotional empathy (Decety & Moriguchi, 2007; Preston & de Waal, 2002). These accounts suggested that the perception of another individual's emotional displays activates mechanisms in the observer that typically generate the same emotion. For example, "while watching someone smile, the observer activates the same facial muscles involved in producing a smile at a subthreshold level and this would create the corresponding feeling of happiness in the observer" (Decety & Moriguchi, 2007, p. 6).

There are several difficulties for perception–action accounts of emotional empathy, however (cf. Blair, 2005). In particular, a perception–action based account of emotional empathy should predict that the emotional reaction to the observed emotion is congruent with the emotional reaction. Indeed, the suggestion is that the "perception of a given behavior in another individual automatically activates one's own representations of that behavior" (Decety & Jackson, 2004, p. 75). A pained grimace in another should activate similar responses as pain experienced by the self. However, this is not always the case. In one recent study, empathic neural responses to another's pain were seen only if the observed individuals in pain had previously interacted with the subjects fairly in an economic game (Singer et al., 2006). If the individuals observed to be in pain had previously acted unfairly, there were no empathic responses to the observed individuals. In short, perception–action accounts of empathy cannot explain how the context (whether the observed individual is fair or unfair) determines whether the emotion experienced is congruent (pain in the observed and the observer) or incongruent (pain in the observed and pleasure in the observer). As such, mirror neuron based accounts of emotional empathy appear to be inadequate.

Emotional Empathy as an Emotional Response

The emotion-based view of empathy considers that the empathic reaction is simply one form of emotional response; that is, that an emotional expression is just another elicitor of an emotional reaction (Blair, 2003, 2005). An individual can experience fear because he or she has been exposed to a tiger, a blue square previously associated with electric shock, or another individual's fearful expression at the sight of the tiger/blue square. The suggestion is that the neurocognitive architecture initiating the emotional response in all three cases is identical (LeDoux, 2007). There would be differences in the observer's emotional experience of each of these events. However, it is argued here that such differences would be a product of the causal reasoning that is part of conscious experience and, in the absence of an adequate model of consciousness, will not be considered further here.

Emotions have been defined as "states elicited by rewards and punishers, including changes in rewards and punishments" (Rolls, 1999, p. 60). Within this view, *emotional expressions* are "reinforcers that modulate the probability that a particular behavior will be performed in the future" (Blair, 2003, p. 564).

The basic suggestion is that individuals show emotional reactions to stimuli, represented in the temporal cortex, which are either reinforcers themselves or have been previously associated with reinforcement. Such stimuli can be nonsocial (e.g., the large teeth of the tiger or the blue square) or social (e.g., the fearful expression of another or the description of a frightening event suffered by another). If they are social, the activation of the consequent emotional response can be considered to be empathic. It is important that the response to emotional stimuli is not automatic but under considerable top-down attentional control. This was seen clearly in de Vignemont and Singer's (2006) elegant study showing that a pain response was only shown to observed individuals in pain if they had been fair partners in the previous economic game (if they were unfair partners, their apparent pain activated regions implicated in reward processing in male participants). Moreover, it has also been seen with respect to the response to fearful expressions. Attentional manipulations that reduce the processing of fearful expressions reduce the response of the amygdala to these expressions (Mitchell et al., 2007; Pessoa, 2005).

The argument here is that emotional expressions are reinforcers that have specific communicatory functions and that they impart specific information to the observer (Blair, 2003, 2005). Therefore, emotional empathy is effectively the translation of the communication by the observer.

Different brain regions respond to different types of reinforcers. For example, the amygdala is critical for fear-based conditioning (LeDoux, 2000). It shows activation to fear-inducing threat and associates this information with the stimuli that were associated with these threats. The amygdala is preferentially activated by fearful expressions relative to other expressions (for a meta-analytic review, see Murphy, Nimmo-Smith, & Lawrence, 2003). This is because a main role of fearful expressions may be to rapidly convey information to others that a stimulus is aversive and should be avoided (Mineka & Cook, 1993). Indeed, it is notable that if a fearful expression is shown looking toward an object (i.e., both the reinforcement of the expression and a stimulus to associate with this reinforcement is provided), the amygdala shows significantly increased activation relative to situations in which a stimulus is not displayed (Hooker, Germine, Knight, & D'Esposito, 2006).

The insula, similarly, is critical for taste-aversion learning (e.g., Cubero, Thiele, & Bernstein, 1999). Disgusted expressions are reinforcers that most frequently provide valence information about foods (Rozin, Haidt, & McCauley, 1993). Disgusted expressions preferentially activate the insula, arguably readying it to show taste-aversion learning to whatever stimulus the disgusted expression is shown toward (Phillips et al., 1998).

Angry expressions are used to curtail the behavior of others when social rules or expectations have been violated (Averill, 1982). They appear to serve to inform the observer to stop the current behavioral action rather than necessarily conveying any information as to whether that action should be initiated in the future. In other words, angry expressions can be seen as triggers for response reversal (Blair, 2003; Blair, Morris, Frith, Perrett, & Dolan, 1999). Inferior frontal cortex is important for response reversal (Budhani, Marsh, Pine, & Blair, 2007; Cools, Clark, Owen, & Robbins, 2002). Interestingly, similar areas of inferior frontal cortex are activated by angry expressions and by response reversal as a function of contingency change (Blair et al., 1999).

Finally, individuals exposed to painful stimulation demonstrate activity in dorsal anterior cingulate cortex (dACC), the insula and primary somatosensory cortex (Rainville, 2002). Exposure to another in pain, whether viewing another's hand being pricked by a needle (Singer et al., 2004) or a pained facial expression (Botvinick et al., 2005), is also associated with activity in dACC and the insula.

EMOTIONAL EMPATHY AND MORAL DEVELOPMENT

Several authors have suggested that there are at least four forms of moral reasoning that can be distinguished at the cognitive, neural (Blair, 2007), and evolutionary psychology levels (Haidt, 2007). These have been termed *care based, fairness, social convention*, and *disgust based* (Blair, 2007). Haidt terms his roughly equivalent forms *harm, reciprocity, hierarchy*, and *purity* (Haidt, 2007). It seems reasonable, given recent fMRI data (Moll et al., 2006), that altruism should be added to this list (see the work of Batson; e.g., Batson, 1988).

Much work has focused on the distinction between moral (care based and fairness) and conventional transgressions (Arsenio & Ford, 1985; Smetana, 1993; Turiel, Killen, & Helwig, 1987). Within this work, moral transgressions (e.g., murder, theft) were defined by their consequences for the rights and welfare of others. In contrast, social conventional transgressions (e.g., talking in class, dressing in opposite gender clothing) were defined as violations of the behavioral uniformities that structure social interactions within social systems (Smetana, 1993; Turiel et al., 1987). These authors noted that typically developing individuals distinguished moral and conventional transgressions from the age of 39 months (Smetana, 1981) and across cultures (Song, Smetana, & Kim, 1987). In particular, the distinction is made in three main ways. First, children and adults usually judge moral transgressions as more serious than conventional transgressions (Nucci, 1981; Smetana, 1985). Second, moral transgressions are judged differently from conventional transgressions. For example, moral transgressions are judged less rule contingent than conventional transgressions; that is, individuals are less likely to state that moral, rather than conventional, transgressions are permissible in the absence of prohibiting rules (Nucci, 1981; Smetana, 1985). Third, individuals justify the wrongness of moral and conventional transgressions differently. When asked why it is wrong to hit another or damage their property, participants are significantly more likely to make reference to the suffering of a victim (Smetana, 1993; Turiel et al., 1987). In contrast, when asked why it is wrong to talk in class or wear opposite gender clothes (conventional transgressions), participants will make reference to established rules that can be either explicit (that action is prohibited in this school) or implicit (that action is "not the done thing").

Nucci and Turiel, in seminal work, have demonstrated that the social reactions to the breaking of what they termed *moral* and *conventional transgressions* were significantly different (Nucci & Nucci, 1982; Nucci & Turiel, 1978). Nucci, Turiel, and Smetana observed that the breaking of moral transgressions leads to the distress (fear/sadness) of the victim and was more likely to elicit empathy induction by caregivers. In contrast, conventional transgressions were more likely to lead to power assertive techniques by caregivers, including anger (Nucci & Nucci, 1982; Nucci & Turiel, 1978). The argument here is that this difference in the emotional reactions of observers of care-based and conventional transgressions is the basis of the difference in reasoning between these forms of transgression.

It is not only fearful but also sad expressions that rapidly convey information to others that stimuli associated with these expressions should be avoided (Blair et al., 1999). The basic suggestion is thus that moral socialization involves associating the victim's distress (their fear and sadness) with the action that caused this distress. On this basis, it is argued that empathy induction techniques, shown to be particularly effective in moral socialization (Hoffman, 1988), work because they focus the individual's attention on the distress of the victim. As shown in considerable work, increasing attention on an emotional stimulus increases the emotional response to this stimulus (Mitchell et al., 2007). It is important, and in line with this position, that it is the presence of victims that distinguishes moral transgressions (Smetana, 1985). If a participant believes that a transgression will result in a victim, he or she will process that transgression as moral. For example, Smetana (1985) found that unknown transgressions (specified by a nonsense word; i.e., X has done *dool*) were processed as moral if the specified consequence of the act involved the sadness of another (e.g., "X has done dool and made Y cry").

With respect to conventional transgressions, the focus is on displays of anger. This is the emotion most often displayed by observers of conventional transgressions (Nucci & Nucci, 1982; Nucci & Turiel, 1978). Smetana (1985) demonstrated that an unknown transgression was processed as conventional if the specified consequence of the act was the anger of a teacher. Moreover, it has been noted that angry expressions are used to curtail the behavior of others when social rules or expectations have been violated; they inform their intended recipient to stop their current behavioral action or face the consequences (Averill, 1982). People judge conventional transgressions to be bad because they disrupt the social order (Smetana, 1993; Turiel et al., 1987). Societal rules concerning conventional transgressions function to allow higher status individuals to constrain the behavior of lower status individuals. Indeed, Haidt refers to this type of morality as hierarchy (Haidt, 2007). They may also, by their operation, serve to reduce within-species hierarchy conflict. Angry expressions are triggers for response reversal (Blair, 2003; Blair et al., 1999), initiating the modification of behavior through the recruitment of ventrolateral prefrontal cortex (Blair et al., 1999; Budhani et al., 2007). Interestingly, high-status, nonverbal cues also activate this region (Marsh et al., 2008).

I argue that aversive social cues (particularly angry expressions) or expectations of such cues activate ventrolateral prefrontal cortex. By doing so, they (a) guide the individual away from committing conventional transgressions (particularly in the presence of higher status individuals) and (b) orchestrate a response to witnessed conventional transgressions (particularly when these are committed by lower status individuals), that is, to submit or become angry in turn (see Blair, 2003). In short, reasoning about social conventions should and does activate ventrolateral prefrontal cortex (Berthoz, Armony, Blair, & Dolan, 2002).

Finally, it is worth considering disgusted expressions. Although the use of disgusted expressions may have evolved to allow the rapid communication of information regarding foods that were unsafe to consume (Rozin et al., 1993), a strong argument can be made that disgust can be associated with behaviors potentially leading to these behaviors becoming regarded as immoral (Haidt, 2001). The same argument can be followed with respect to fearful/sad expressions. The individual sees another individual showing disgust in response to a particular behavior and thus learns to associate disgust with that behavior and regard it as bad to do (Blair, 2003).

EMOTIONAL EMPATHY AND ANTISOCIAL BEHAVIOR

This section considers the impact of dysfunction within the empathic emotional reactions described previously. In particular, the developmental consequences of dysfunction in the empathic response to the sadness and fear of others as well as the developmental consequences of dysfunction in the empathic response to the anger of others is considered.

Dysfunctional Empathic Responses to Others' Sadness and Fear and Moral Development

If moral socialization involves associating the victim's distress (their fear and sadness) with the action that caused this distress, then a population who is significantly less emotionally responsive to the distress of others should show difficulties in moral socialization. Individuals with psychopathy represent such a population.

Psychopathy is a developmental disorder that involves two core components: emotional dysfunction in the form of callous-unemotional (CU) traits (reduced guilt, empathy, and attachment to significant others) and antisocial behavior (Frick, 1995; Harpur, Hakstian, & Hare, 1988). Recent work has confirmed the stability of CU traits in particular and the disorder more generally from childhood into adulthood. Thus, CU traits have been shown to be relatively stable from late childhood to early adolescence (Frick, Kimonis, Dandreaux, & Farell, 2003). Moreover, CU traits indexed in clinic-referred boys ages 7 to 12 years have been shown to predict adult measures of psychopathy at ages 18 to 19 years (Burke, Loeber, & Lahey, 2007). Similarly, Lynam and colleagues reported that early measures of CU-related traits at age 13 predicted adult measures of psychopathy at age 24 (Lynam, Caspi, Moffitt, Loeber, & Stouthamer-Loeber, 2007).

Considerable data have demonstrated that individuals with psychopathy show clear impairment in processing the fearfulness and sadness of others. Thus, children and adults with psychopathy typically show impairment in the recognition of fearful and to a lesser extent sad facial and vocal expressions (see, for a revent meta-analytic review, Marsh & Blair, 2007). In addition, individuals with psychopathy show reduced autonomic responses to the distress of others (Aniskiewicz, 1979; Blair, Jones, Clark, & Smith, 1997) and reduced attention to the distress of others (Kimonis, Frick, Fazekas, & Loney, 2006).

If an appropriate emotional empathic response to the distress of others is crucial for moral socialization, then children and adults with psychopathy should show impaired care-based moral reasoning. This impairment can be seen in their performance on the moral–conventional distinction task. In particular, adults with psychopathy show significantly less of a differentiation between moral and conventional transgressions on this task relative to comparison individuals (Blair, 1995). Interestingly, work with other instrumentally aggressive populations shows reduced representation of the distress of victims in the context of care-based moral transgressions (e.g., behaviorally disruptive 6- to 12-year-olds; Arsenio & Fleiss, 1996). Moreover, adults with psychopathy at least fail to show appropriate associations of negative affect with moral transgressions when these are examined using morality implicit association task paradigms (Gray, MacCulloch, Smith, Morris, & Snowden, 2003). Work has clearly shown that 6- to 13-year-old children who show high levels of callous and unemotional traits are less responsive to socialization techniques; that is, the emotion dysfunction directly interferes with moral socialization (Wootton, Frick, Shelton, & Silverthorn, 1997).

Through the empathic process, the typically developing individual learns to avoid the action that has caused the other harm. The amygdala is critical for stimulus-reinforcement learning (LeDoux, 2000). Considerable data has indicated that psychopathy is marked by amygdala dysfunction (for a review, see Blair, Mitchell, & Blair, 2005). For example, some of the earliest findings in psychopathy were demonstrations of the impairment in aversive conditioning (Lykken, 1957), a function reliant on the amygdala. Moreover, recent fMRI work has shown that individuals with psychopathy show reduced amygdala activity during aversive conditioning (Birbaumer et al., 2005). Related to this function, the amygdala allows conditioned stimuli to prime brainstem threat circuits mediating the startle reflex such that a startle probe elicits greater startle after a threatening prime relative to a neutral prime (Davis, 2000). Individuals with psychopathy do not show appropriate augmentation of the startle reflex following a negative prime (Levenston, Patrick, Bradley, & Lang, 2000). Moreover, studies examining expression processing in both adults with psychopathy (Deeley et al., 2006) and children with psychopathic traits (Marsh et al., 2008) have shown a reduced differential response within fusiform cortex to fearful relative to neutral expressions. These data are consistent with reduced priming of emotion-relevant representations in temporal cortex by reciprocal amygdala activation in individuals with psychopathy (though only Marsh et al. [2008] observed reduced amygdala activity).

In conclusion, the amygdala is crucial for stimulus-reinforcement learning and responding to emotional expressions, particularly fearful expressions that, as reinforcers, are important initiators of stimulus-reinforcement learning. Moreover, the amygdala is involved in the formation of both stimulus-punishment and stimulus-reward associations. Individuals with psychopathy show impairment in stimulus-reinforcement learning (whether punishment or reward based) and responding to fearful and sad expressions. Stimulus-reinforcement learning is crucial for socialization, for learning that some things are bad to do, and individuals with psychopathy fail to take advantage of standard socialization techniques (Wootton et al., 1997). As such, they are more likely to learn to use antisocial strategies to achieve their goals. The reduced amygdala responding also diminishes empathy-based learning following the witnessing of another's distress and leads to reduced empathy generally.

Dysfunctional Empathic Responses to Others' Anger

Because part of the role of conventional rules is to maintain social order and facilitate hierarchy interactions, an individual engaging in conventional transgressions is going to elicit anger that may itself elicit reactive aggression in the transgressor. This position predicts that individuals with impairment to ventrolateral prefrontal cortex will show impairment when reasoning about conventional transgressions. They may also show an increased risk for reactive aggression. Two patient populations allow this prediction to be tested. The first are neurological patients with lesions of orbital/ventrolateral frontal cortex. Such patients show difficulties with expression recognition and an increased risk for reactive aggression (Blair & Cipolotti, 2000; Hornak, Rolls, & Wade, 1996). In line with the prediction, patients with such lesions show difficulties processing conventional transgressions as indexed by performance on the social contexts task (Dewey, 1991).

The second population is children with bipolar disorder. Childhood bipolar disorder is marked by emotional lability and irritability (Leibenluft, Blair, Charney, & Pine, 2003). Neuropsychological and neuroimaging data have suggested that at least part of the pathology seen in these children is related to ventrolateral prefrontal cortex dysfunction (Gorrindo et al., 2005). In line with this, children with bipolar disorder show impairment in expression recognition (McClure, Pope, Hoberman, Pine, & Leibenluft, 2003). Moreover, they show impairment on social cognition tasks in which the processing of conventional rules is important (McClure et al., 2005).

COGNITIVE EMPATHY

Cognitive empathy refers to the process by which an individual represents the internal mental state of another individual. This is also the definition of what many researchers refer to as ToM (Leslie, 1987; Premack & Woodruff, 1978). In concept, ToM is important because the attribution of mental states can be used to explain and predict behavior. At the neural level, fMRI work has implicated the medial prefrontal cortex (especially the anterior paracingulate cortex), the temporal-parietal junction, and the temporal poles in this ability (for a review, see Frith & Frith, 2006).

There have been various claims with respect to the importance of cognitive empathy for moral development. At first, it was assumed that emotional empathic responses required the ability to represent the mental states of others (Feshbach, 1978). This would predict that a population with impairment in the ability to represent the mental states of others (ToM) should show impairment in empathy and, by inference, moral reasoning. There is a patient population that allows these predictions to be tested: individuals with autism.

Autism is a severe developmental disorder described by the *Diagnostic and Statistical Manual of Mental Disorders* (4th ed.; *DSM–IV*; American Psychiatric Association, 1994) as "the presence of markedly abnormal or impaired development in social interaction and communication and a markedly restricted repertoire of activities and interests" (p. 66). The main criteria for the diagnosis in the *DSM–IV* can be summarized as qualitative impairment in social communication and restricted and repetitive patterns of behavior and interests.

Considerable data have suggested that individuals with autism are impaired in the representation of the mental states of others (for a review, see

Hill & Frith, 2003). Moreover, neuroimaging work has reported reduced activation in individuals with autism spectrum disorders in those brain regions critical to the representation of the mental states of others (i.e., medial prefrontal cortex, temporal-parietal junction, and the temporal poles; for a review, see Frith & Frith, 2006).

With respect to the issue of emotional empathy in autism, there is some confusion in the literature. It remains uncertain whether individuals with autism have difficulty recognizing the emotional expressions of others (Adolphs, Sears, & Piven, 2001; Humphreys, Minshew, Leonard, & Behrmann, 2007). However, it does appear that children with autism show autonomic responses to the distress of others (Blair, 1999) and that at least those who are more cognitively able are appropriately emotionally responsive to the distress of others (Corona, Dissanayake, Arbelle, Wellington, & Sigman, 1998). In short there are reasons to believe that the basic emotional empathic response is intact in individuals with autism. In line with this, individuals with autism appear to have basic moral intuitions, and they show no significant impairment on the moral–conventional distinction test (Blair, 1996).

More subtle positions made reference to the importance of intent information in moral reasoning, something first documented by Piaget. Piaget began a considerable literature indicating the importance of information on the perpetrator's intent when assigning moral blame or praise (Piaget, 1932). The individual who intentionally swings a baseball bat into another individual's face has behaved far more "morally wrongly" than the individual who accidentally swings a baseball bat into another individual's face (cf. Zelazo, Helwig, & Lau, 1996). This suggests that a population with ToM impairment should not use intent information appropriately in their moral reasoning. In line with this prediction, individuals with autism show reduced integration of such information into their moral reasoning (Steele, Joseph, & Tager-Flusberg, 2003).

CONCLUSION

There are four main conclusions from this chapter. First, many processes that are distinct at the cognitive and neural levels subserve empathy. Motor, emotional, and cognitive empathy can be distinguished. Within emotional empathy, there are at least partially separable neurocognitive systems that mediate the response to sad/fearful expressions, angry expressions, and disgusted expressions. Computationally, the basic suggestion is that sad/fearful and disgusted expressions initiate specific forms of stimulus-reinforcement learning. Sad and fearful expressions associated with objects and actions initiate aversive conditioning; the individual regards the associated object or action as aversive. Disgusted expressions associated with objects and actions initiate a form of taste aversion learning; the individual regards the associated object or action as disgusting. Angry expressions initiate reversal learning; the individual is predisposed to stop the current behavior in response to the expression and may avoid the behavior in future in the presence of the angered individual.

The second is that there are at least four partially distinct forms of process that can be referred to as moral reasoning: care based, justice, conventional, and hierarchy. With the exception of justice reasoning on which very little work has been done, the others are based on the three forms of emotional empathic response previously mentioned . The individual cares about care-based transgressions because the representation of these transgressions is associated with the aversive reinforcement of the victim's distress. The individual cares about disgust-based transgressions because they have been exposed to caregivers or peers showing disgusted reactions to others engaged in the proscribed behaviors. The individual cares about conventional transgressions because he or she has experienced or can anticipate the angry responses of other individuals in the environment if the conventional proscriptions are violated.

The third is that the distinct forms of empathic process can be selectively disrupted. In particular, patients with psychopathy appear to show relatively selective impairment for responding to the fear and sadness of other individuals. In line with the proposals previously discussed, this is accompanied by profound impairment in care-based moral reasoning. Patients with childhood bipolar disorder and acquired lesions of frontal cortex show more general expression recognition deficits and reduced behavioral modulation in response to expressions. This appears to be accompanied by impairment in conventional reasoning.

The fourth is that although ToM, or cognitive empathy, is not necessary for the formation of basic moral intuitions pushing the individual away from care-based, disgust-based, or conventional transgressions, it appears to exert a modulatory influence. Intentional transgressions, in which the intent of the transgressor can be represented as malevolent, are considered significantly more serious than unintentional transgressions. Interestingly, individuals impaired for this form of empathic process, individuals with autism, show a reduction in this modulation by intent information.

REFERENCES

Adolphs, R., Sears, L., & Piven, J. (2001). Abnormal processing of social information from faces in autism. *Journal of Cognitive Neuroscience, 13,* 232–240. Medline doi:10.1162/089892901564289

American Psychiatric Association. (1994). *Diagnostic and statistical manual of mental disorders* (4th ed.). Washington, DC: Author.

Aniskiewicz, A. S. (1979). Autonomic components of vicarious conditioning and psychopathy. *Journal of Clinical Psychology, 35*, 60–67. Medline doi:10.1002/1097-4679(197901)35:1<60::AID-JCLP2270350106>3.0.CO;2-R

Arsenio, W. F., & Fleiss, K. (1996). Typical and behaviourally disruptive children's understanding of the emotion consequences of socio-moral events. *The British Journal of Developmental Psychology, 14*, 173–186.

Arsenio, W. F., & Ford, M. E. (1985). The role of affective information in social-cognitive development: Children's differentiation of moral and conventional events. *Merrill-Palmer Quarterly, 31*, 1–17.

Averill, J. R. (1982). *Anger and aggression: An essay on emotion.* New York, NY: Springer-Verlag.

Batson, C. D. (1988). Prosocial motivation: Is it ever truly altruistic? In L. Berkowitz (Ed.), *Advances in experimental social psychology* (pp. 65–122). New York, NY: Academic Press.

Berthoz, S., Armony, J., Blair, R. J. R., & Dolan, R. (2002). Neural correlates of violation of social norms and embarrassment. *Brain, 125*, 1696–1708. Medline doi:10.1093/brain/awf190

Birbaumer, N., Veit, R., Lotze, M., Erb, M., Hermann, C., Grodd, W., & Flor, H. (2005). Deficient fear conditioning in psychopathy: A functional magnetic resonance imaging study. *Archives of General Psychiatry, 62*, 799–805. Medline doi:10.1001/archpsyc.62.7.799

Blair, R. J. R. (1995). A cognitive developmental approach to morality: Investigating the psychopath. *Cognition, 57*, 1–29. Medline doi:10.1016/0010-0277(95)00676-P

Blair, R. J. R. (1996). Brief report: Morality in the autistic child. *Journal of Autism and Developmental Disorders, 26*, 571–579. Medline doi:10.1007/BF02172277

Blair, R. J. R. (1999). Psycho-physiological responsiveness to the distress of others in children with autism. *Personality and Individual Differences, 26*, 477–485. doi:10.1016/S0191-8869(98)00154-8

Blair, R. J. R. (2003). Facial expressions, their communicatory functions and neuro-cognitive substrates. *Philosophical Transactions of the Royal Society of London. Series B, Biological Sciences, 358*(1431), 561–572. Medline doi:10.1098/rstb.2002.1220

Blair, R. J. R. (2005). Responding to the emotions of others: Dissociating forms of empathy through the study of typical and psychiatric populations. *Consciousness and Cognition, 14*, 698–718. Medline doi:10.1016/j.concog.2005.06.004

Blair, R. J. R. (2007). The amygdala and ventromedial prefrontal cortex in morality and psychopathy. *Trends in Cognitive Sciences, 11*, 387–392. Medline doi:10.1016/j.tics.2007.07.003

Blair, R. J. R., & Cipolotti, L. (2000). Impaired social response reversal: A case of "acquired sociopathy." *Brain, 123*, 1122–1141. Medline doi:10.1093/brain/123.6.1122

Blair, R. J. R., Jones, L., Clark, F., & Smith, M. (1997). The psychopathic individual: A lack of responsiveness to distress cues? *Psychophysiology, 34,* 192–198. Medline doi:10.1111/j.1469-8986.1997.tb02131.x

Blair, R. J. R., Mitchell, D. G. V., & Blair, K. S. (2005). *The psychopath: Emotion and the brain.* Oxford, England: Blackwell.

Blair, R. J. R., Morris, J. S., Frith, C. D., Perrett, D. I., & Dolan, R. (1999). Dissociable neural responses to facial expressions of sadness and anger. *Brain, 122,* 883–893. Medline doi:10.1093/brain/122.5.883

Botvinick, M., Jha, A. P., Bylsma, L. M., Fabian, S. A., Solomon, P. E., & Prkachin, K. M. (2005). Viewing facial expressions of pain engages cortical areas involved in the direct experience of pain. *NeuroImage, 25,* 312–319. Medline doi:10.1016/j.neuroimage.2004.11.043

Budhani, S., Marsh, A. A., Pine, D. S., & Blair, R. J. R. (2007). Neural correlates of response reversal: Considering acquisition. *NeuroImage, 34,* 1754–1765. Medline doi:10.1016/j.neuroimage.2006.08.060

Burke, J. D., Loeber, R., & Lahey, B. B. (2007). Adolescent conduct disorder and interpersonal callousness as predictors of psychopathy in young adults. *Journal of Clinical Child and Adolescent Psychology, 36,* 334–346.

Cools, R., Clark, L., Owen, A. M., & Robbins, T. W. (2002). Defining the neural mechanisms of probabilistic reversal learning using event-related functional magnetic resonance imaging. *The Journal of Neuroscience, 22,* 4563–4567.

Corona, R., Dissanayake, C., Arbelle, A., Wellington, P., & Sigman, M. (1998). Is affect aversive to young children with autism? Behavioural and cardiac responses to experimenter distress. *Child Development, 69,* 1494–1502.

Cubero, I., Thiele, T. E., & Bernstein, I. L. (1999). Insular cortex lesions and taste aversion learning: Effects of conditioning method and timing of lesion. *Brain Research, 839,* 323–330. Medline doi:10.1016/S0006-8993(99)01745-X

Davis, M. (2000). The role of the amygdala in conditioned and unconditioned fear and anxiety. In J. P. Aggleton (Ed.), *The amygdala: A functional analysis* (pp. 289–310). Oxford, England: Oxford University Press.

de Vignemont, F., & Singer, T. (2006). The empathic brain: How, when and why? *Trends in Cognitive Sciences, 10,* 435–441. Medline doi:10.1016/j.tics.2006.08.008

Decety, J., & Jackson, P. L. (2004). The functional architecture of human empathy. *Behavioral and Cognitive Neuroscience Reviews, 3,* 71–100. Medline doi:10.1177/1534582304267187

Decety, J., & Moriguchi, Y. (2007). The empathic brain and its dysfunction in psychiatric populations: Implications for intervention across different clinical conditions. *BioPsychoSocial Medicine, 1,* 22–65.

Deeley, Q., Daly, E., Surguladze, S., Tunstall, N., Mezey, G., Beer, D., . . . Murphy, D. G. (2006). Facial emotion processing in criminal psychopathy. Preliminary functional magnetic resonance imaging study. *The British Journal of Psychiatry, 189,* 533–539. Medline doi:10.1192/bjp.bp.106.021410

Dewey, M. (1991). Living with Asperger's syndrome. In U. Frith (Ed.), *Autism and Asperger's syndrome* (pp. 184–206). Cambridge, England: Cambridge University Press.

Feshbach, N. D. (1978). Studies of empathic behavior in children. In B. A. Maher (Ed.), *Progress in Experimental Personality Research* (pp. 1–47). New York, NY: Academic Press.

Frick, P. J. (1995). Callous-unemotional traits and conduct problems: A two-factor model of psychopathy in children. *Issues in Criminological and Legal Psychology, 24*, 47–51.

Frick, P. J., Kimonis, E. R., Dandreaux, D. M., & Farell, J. M. (2003). The 4-year stability of psychopathic traits in non-referred youth. *Behavioral Sciences & the Law, 21*, 713–736. Medline doi:10.1002/bsl.568

Frith, C. D., & Frith, U. (2006). The neural basis of mentalizing. *Neuron, 50*, 531–534. Medline doi:10.1016/j.neuron.2006.05.001

Gorrindo, T., Blair, R. J., Budhani, S., Dickstein, D. P., Pine, D. S., & Leibenluft, E. (2005). Deficits on a probabilistic response-reversal task in patients with pediatric bipolar disorder. *The American Journal of Psychiatry, 162*, 1975–1977. Medline doi:10.1176/appi.ajp.162.10.1975

Gray, N. S., MacCulloch, M. J., Smith, J., Morris, M., & Snowden, R. J. (2003, May 29). Forensic psychology: Violence viewed by psychopathic murderers. *Nature, 423*(6939), 497–498. Medline doi:10.1038/423497a

Haidt, J. (2001). The emotional dog and its rational tail: A social intuitionist approach to moral judgment. *Psychological Review, 108*, 814–834. Medline doi:10.1037/0033-295X.108.4.814

Haidt, J. (2007, May 18). The new synthesis in moral psychology. *Science, 316*(5827), 998–1002. Medline doi:10.1126/science.1137651

Harpur, T. J., Hakstian, A. R., & Hare, R. D. (1988). The factor structure of the Psychopathy Checklist. *Journal of Consulting and Clinical Psychology, 56*, 741–747. Medline doi:10.1037/0022-006X.56.5.741

Hill, E. L., & Frith, U. (2003). Understanding autism: Insights from mind and brain. *Philosophical Transactions of the Royal Society of London. Series B, Biological Sciences, 358*(1430), 281–289. Medline doi:10.1098/rstb.2002.1209

Hoffman, M. L. (1988). Moral development. In M. Bornstein & M. Lamb (Eds.), *Developmental psychology: An advanced textbook* (pp. 497–548). Hillsdale, NJ: Erlbaum.

Hooker, C. I., Germine, L. T., Knight, R. T., & D'Esposito, M. (2006). Amygdala response to facial expressions reflects emotional learning. *The Journal of Neuroscience, 26*, 8915–8922. Medline doi:10.1523/JNEUROSCI.3048-05.2006

Hornak, J., Rolls, E. T., & Wade, D. (1996). Face and voice expression identification in patients with emotional and behavioural changes following ventral frontal damage. *Neuropsychologia, 34*, 247–261. Medline doi:10.1016/0028-3932(95)00106-9

Humphreys, K., Minshew, N., Leonard, G. L., & Behrmann, M. (2007). A fine-grained analysis of facial expression processing in high-functioning adults with autism. *Neuropsychologia, 45,* 685–695. Medline doi:10.1016/j.neuropsychologia. 2006.08.003

Iacoboni, M., & Mazziotta, J. C. (2007). Mirror neuron system: Basic findings and clinical applications. *Annals of Neurology, 62,* 213–218. Medline doi:10.1002/ana.21198

Kimonis, E. R., Frick, P. J., Fazekas, H., & Loney, B. R. (2006). Psychopathy, aggression, and the processing of emotional stimuli in non-referred girls and boys. *Behavioral Sciences & the Law, 24,* 21–37. Medline doi:10.1002/bsl.668

LeDoux, J. E. (2000). The amygdala and emotion: A view through fear. In J. P. Aggleton (Ed.), *The Amygdala: A functional analysis* (pp. 289–310). Oxford, England: Oxford University Press.

LeDoux, J. E. (2007). The amygdala. *Current Biology, 17,* R868–R874. Medline doi:10.1016/j.cub.2007.08.005

Leibenluft, E., Blair, R. J., Charney, D. S., & Pine, D. S. (2003). Irritability in pediatric mania and other childhood psychopathology. *Annals of the New York Academy of Sciences, 1008,* 201–218. Medline doi:10.1196/annals.1301.022

Leslie, A. M. (1987). Pretense and representation: The origins of "theory of mind" *Psychological Review, 94,* 412–426. doi:10.1037/0033-295X.94.4.412

Levenston, G. K., Patrick, C. J., Bradley, M. M., & Lang, P. J. (2000). The psychopath as observer: Emotion and attention in picture processing. *Journal of Abnormal Psychology, 109,* 373–386. Medline doi:10.1037/0021-843X.109.3.373

Lykken, D. T. (1957). A study of anxiety in the sociopathic personality. *Journal of Abnormal and Social Psychology, 55,* 6–10. doi:10.1037/h0047232

Lynam, D. R., Caspi, A., Moffitt, T. E., Loeber, R., & Stouthamer-Loeber, M. (2007). Longitudinal evidence that psychopathy scores in early adolescence predict adult psychopathy. *Journal of Abnormal Psychology, 116,* 155–165. Medline doi:10.1037/0021-843X.116.1.155

Marsh, A. A., & Blair, R. J. (2007). Deficits in facial affect recognition among antisocial populations: A meta-analysis. *Neuroscience and Biobehavioral Reviews, 32,* 454–465.

Marsh, A. A., Finger, E. C., Mitchell, D. G. V., Reid, M. E., Sims, C., Kosson, D. S., . . . Blair, R. J. R. (2008). Reduced amygdala response to fearful expressions in children and adolescents with callous-unemotional traits and disruptive behavior disorders. *The American Journal of Psychiatry, 165,* 712–720. Medline doi:10.1176/appi.ajp.2007.07071145

McClure, E. B., Pope, K., Hoberman, A. J., Pine, D. S., & Leibenluft, E. (2003). Facial expression recognition in adolescents with mood and anxiety disorders. *The American Journal of Psychiatry, 160,* 1172–1174. Medline doi:10.1176/appi.ajp.160.6.1172

McClure, E. B., Treland, J. E., Snow, J., Schmajuk, M., Dickstein, D. P., Towbin, K. E., . . . Leibenluft, E. (2005). Deficits in social cognition and response flexibility in pediatric bipolar disorder. *The American Journal of Psychiatry, 162,* 1644–1651. Medline doi:10.1176/appi.ajp.162.9.1644

Mineka, S., & Cook, M. (1993). Mechanisms involved in the observational conditioning of fear. *Journal of Experimental Psychology: General, 122,* 23–38. Medline doi:10.1037/0096-3445.122.1.23

Mitchell, D. G., Nakic, M., Fridberg, D., Kamel, N., Pine, D. S., & Blair, R. J. (2007). The impact of processing load on emotion. *NeuroImage, 34,* 1299–1309. Medline doi:10.1016/j.neuroimage.2006.10.012

Moll, J., Krueger, F., Zahn, R., Pardini, M., de Oliveira-Souza, R., & Grafman, J. (2006). Human fronto-mesolimbic networks guide decisions about charitable donation. *Proceedings of the National Academy of Sciences, USA, 103,* 15623–15628. Medline doi:10.1073/pnas.0604475103

Murphy, F. C., Nimmo-Smith, I., & Lawrence, A. D. (2003). Functional neuroanatomy of emotions: A meta-analysis. *Cognitive, Affective & Behavioral Neuroscience, 3,* 207–233. Medline doi:10.3758/CABN.3.3.207

Nucci, L. P. (1981). Conceptions of personal issues: A domain distinct from moral or societal concepts. *Child Development, 52,* 114–121. doi:10.2307/1129220

Nucci, L. P., & Nucci, M. (1982). Children's social interactions in the context of moral and conventional transgressions. *Child Development, 53,* 403–412. doi:10.2307/1128983

Nucci, L. P., & Turiel, E. (1978). Social interactions and the development of social concepts in preschool children. *Child Development, 49,* 400–407. doi:10.2307/1128704

Pessoa, L. (2005). To what extent are emotional visual stimuli processed without attention and awareness? *Current Opinion in Neurobiology, 15,* 188–196. Medline doi:10.1016/j.conb.2005.03.002

Phillips, M. L., Young, A. W., Scott, S. K., Calder, A. J., Andrew, C., Giampietro, V., . . . Gray, J. A. (1998). Neural responses to facial and vocal expressions of fear and disgust. *Philosophical Transactions of the Royal Society of London. Series B, Biological Sciences, 265*(1408), 1809–1817. doi:10.1098/rspb.1998.0506

Piaget, J. (1932). *The Moral Development of the Child.* London, England: Routledge.

Premack, D., & Woodruff, G. (1978). Does the chimpanzee have a theory of mind? *The Behavioral and Brain Sciences, 1,* 515–526.

Preston, S. D., & de Waal, F. B. (2002). Empathy: Its ultimate and proximate bases. *The Behavioral and Brain Sciences, 25,* 1–20.

Rainville, P. (2002). Brain mechanisms of pain affect and pain modulation. *Current Opinion in Neurobiology, 12,* 195–204. Medline doi:10.1016/S0959-4388(02)00313-6

Rizzolatti, G., Fogassi, L., & Gallese, V. (2001, September). Neurophysiological mechanisms underlying the understanding and imitation of action. *Nature Reviews Neuroscience, 2,* 661–670. Medline doi:10.1038/35090060

Rolls, E. T. (1999). *The brain and emotion.* Oxford, England: Oxford University Press.

Rozin, P., Haidt, J., & McCauley, C. R. (1993). Disgust. In M. Lewis & J. M. Haviland (Eds.), *Handbook of emotions* (pp. 575–594). New York, NY: Guilford Press.

Singer, T., Seymour, B., O'Doherty, J., Kaube, H., Dolan, R. J., & Frith, C. D. (2004, February 20). Empathy for pain involves the affective but not sensory components of pain. *Science, 303*(5661), 1157–1162. Medline doi:10.1126/science.1093535

Singer, T., Seymour, B., O'Doherty, J. P., Stephan, K. E., Dolan, R. J., & Frith, C. D. (2006, January 18). Empathic neural responses are modulated by the perceived fairness of others. *Nature, 439*(7075), 466–469. Medline doi:10.1038/nature04271

Smetana, J. G. (1981). Preschool children's conceptions of moral and social rules. *Child Development, 52*, 1333–1336. doi:10.2307/1129527

Smetana, J. G. (1985). Preschool children's conceptions of transgressions: The effects of varying moral and conventional domain-related attributes. *Developmental Psychology, 21*, 18–29. doi:10.1037/0012-1649.21.1.18

Smetana, J. G. (1993). Understanding of social rules. In M. Bennett (Ed.), *The child as psychologist: An introduction to the development of social cognition* (pp. 111–141). New York, NY: Harvester Wheatsheaf.

Song, M., Smetana, J. G., & Kim, S. Y. (1987). Korean children's conceptions of moral and conventional transgressions. *Developmental Psychology, 23*, 577–582. doi:10.1037/0012-1649.23.4.577

Steele, S., Joseph, R. M., & Tager-Flusberg, H. (2003). Brief report: developmental change in theory of mind abilities in children with autism. *Journal of Autism and Developmental Disorders, 33*, 461–467. Medline doi:10.1023/A:1025075115100

Turiel, E., Killen, M., & Helwig, C. C. (1987). Morality: Its structure, functions, and vagaries. In J. Kagan & S. Lamb (Eds.), *The emergence of morality in young children* (pp. 155–245). Chicago, IL: University of Chicago Press.

Wootton, J. M., Frick, P. J., Shelton, K. K., & Silverthorn, P. (1997). Ineffective parenting and childhood conduct problems: The moderating role of callous-unemotional traits. *Journal of Consulting and Clinical Psychology, 65*, 301–308. Medline doi:10.1037/0022-006X.65.2.292.b

Zelazo, P. D., Helwig, C. C., & Lau, A. (1996). Intention, act, and outcome in behavioural prediction and moral judgment. *Child Development, 67*, 2478–2492. doi:10.2307/1131635

6

EMPATHY-RELATED RESPONDING AND MORAL DEVELOPMENT

NANCY EISENBERG, NATALIE D. EGGUM, AND ALISON EDWARDS

The topic of empathy and its role in moral development is not new. Over a century ago, philosophers were arguing about the role of empathy and sympathy in moral functioning (e.g., Hume, 1751/1966). In psychology, although the topic was discussed occasionally, programmatic work on the topic of emotional empathy was hardly evident until the late 1960s and 1970s (Batson, 1991; Feshbach & Feshbach, 1982; Hoffman, 2000). Part of the growth in interest in empathy-related responding is its purported role in many aspects of moral functioning.

Empathy has been defined in numerous ways; in this chapter, we define it as having an emotional component rather than being purely a cognitive process akin to perspective taking. Specifically, *empathy* is defined as an affective response stemming from the apprehension or comprehension of another's emotional state or condition; thus, it is a response that is identical, or very similar, to what the other person is feeling or might be expected to be feeling. For example, if a girl views a sad friend and consequently feels sad herself, she is experiencing empathy. We differentiate empathy from two related responses: sympathy and personal distress. We define *sympathy* as feelings of sorrow or concern for another; in contrast to empathy, it does not involve feeling the same emotion as another. Sympathy often may stem from empathy, but it also can occur solely as a consequence of perspective taking or other cognitive processing, including retrieval of information from memory. For example, a person may hear or read about someone who has suffered tragedy and feel concern for that person without experiencing the other's distress or sadness. Batson (1991), Hoffman (2000), Eisenberg et al. (1989), and others have argued that sympathetic concern is often the basis of altruistic responding.

Personal distress is another response involving emotion that can stem from exposure to another's state or condition, but it is conceptualized as a self-focused, aversive emotional reaction to the vicarious experiencing of another's emotion (e.g., as discomfort or anxiety; see Batson, 1991; Eisenberg, Shea, Carlo, & Knight, 1991). Thus, for example, if an adolescent experiences anxiety or discomfort that is based on self-focused cognitions (e.g., thinking of similar past upsetting events) and/or emotional overarousal when a friend is discussing a personal problem, the adolescent likely is experiencing personal distress. Batson (1991) argued that personal distress is associated with the egoistic motivation of making oneself, not necessarily the other person, feel better.

We have argued that empathy is basically morally neutral, whereas sympathy involves other-oriented feelings, cognitions, and motivation, and personal distress involves self-oriented motivation and behaviors. However, it is quite possible that empathy sometimes motivates action that is typically viewed as moral, even if the behavior is not motivated by moral concerns or other-oriented feelings and motivations (see the following section for examples). Thus, the distinctions among empathy, sympathy, and personal distress can be very useful for conceptual frameworks regarding moral development and behavior.

In this chapter, we review representative theory and research on the role of empathy-related responding (henceforth we use this term to refer to all the aforementioned reactions) in several areas of functioning relevant to morality: prosocial behavior, aggression and antisocial or externalizing behavior, and moral judgment. It is our view that empathy-related responding plays a fundamental role in moral development and in some morally relevant actions. We also discuss a related moral emotion, guilt, which often may stem from empathy and its role in moral behavior.

PROSOCIAL BEHAVIOR

Prosocial behavior typically has been defined as voluntary behavior intended to benefit another and includes behaviors such as helping, sharing, and communications of caring. Although all prosocial behavior is intentional and voluntary, it is not necessarily moral. People sometimes assist others, for example, to obtain reciprocal benefits or social approval. Altruism is a subset of prosocial behaviors motivated by moral concerns, including values or emotions such as sympathy, rather than by egoistic or pragmatic concerns or the desire for approval (see Eisenberg, Fabes, & Spinrad, 2006).

Batson (1991) argued that altruistic behavior is often motivated by sympathetic concern, which engenders the other-oriented motivation to reduce another's emotional distress or need. In contrast, he argued that personal distress should motivate prosocial actions only when doing so is the easiest way to alleviate one's own negative emotional state. For example, the aforementioned adolescent who is experiencing personal distress while with a friend may try to comfort the friend so that the friend will exhibit fewer cues that are distressing to the adolescent.

In a series of studies with adults, Batson (1991) obtained evidence that individuals induced to experience sympathy (e.g., through perspective-taking manipulations) were more likely to assist another person than were people in conditions designed to evoke personal distress when it was easy to escape from the distressed or needy person. In contexts in which escape was not easy, both groups tended to assist, but likely for different reasons. In addition, numerous investigators have demonstrated that adults high in the tendency to experience sympathy (i.e., dispositional sympathy) tend to be more helpful and caring than individuals who are less sympathetic (e.g., Davis, 1994; Eisenberg et al., 2002).

Hoffman (2000) has discussed in depth the emergence of empathy-related responding in the early years of life. In brief, Hoffman argued that empathy has a biological basis and that children experience rudimentary empathic reactions in the first year of life. He further suggested that the young child does not clearly differentiate another's distress from his or her own, and thus experiences self-related distress as part of empathy. Moreover, the young child has limited perspective taking and does not clearly understand what makes others as opposed to the self feel better, so early attempts to assist another with whom the child has empathized often are egocentric (e.g., the child may bring her own mother to assist another child who is upset even if the other child's mother is available). With improvements in the abilities to understand the difference between one's own and others' feelings and in the ability to take the perspective of others, children are increasing likely to experience sympathy and to help in nonegocentric ways (see Hoffman's writings for more detail on the developmental sequence).

Developmental scientists have attempted to document the emergence of empathy-related reactions in children and their relations to prosocial (and other morally relevant) behaviors. Batson's experimental procedures generally were not easily translated into research with children. However, many developmental scientists have studied relations of empathy-related responding to prosocial behavior in children (see Eisenberg et al., 2006, for a review). For example, in a series of studies, Zahn-Waxler, Radke-Yarrow, and their colleagues (e.g., Zahn-Waxler, Radke-Yarrow, & King, 1979; Zahn-Waxler, Radke-Yarrow, Wagner, & Chapman, 1992) demonstrated that even 1- to 2-year-olds sometimes exhibit behaviors that seem to reflect empathy, sympathy, and personal distress, and their displays of concern are sometimes related to attempts to assist another. In addition, there is evidence across studies that children's empathy-related responding and prosocial behavior generally increase with age across childhood (Eisenberg & Fabes, 1998); it is quite possible that some of the increase in prosocial behavior is due to changes in empathy-related responding.

To test the relations of preschool- and school-age children's sympathy and personal distress to prosocial behavior, we conducted a series of studies in which sympathy and personal distress were measured with self-reports, facial reactions, and physiological measures. A first step in this program of research was to validate the various markers of sympathy and personal distress, especially the facial and physiological measures. In a typical study, children viewed tapes selected to induce sympathy or distress. In one other study, children discussed past events in which they felt concern for someone else or felt distressed. While viewing the tapes or discussing the events, their facial reactions were taped and their physiological responding (heart rate [HR] and/or skin conductance [SC]) were monitored; immediately afterward, they reported on their emotions during the film or recall procedure by rating how much they felt a number of adjectives, including ones pertaining to sympathy (e.g., concerned for another) or personal distress (e.g., distressed).

We expected that when children experienced sympathy, they would show intense interest (and not distress) at the most evocative moments (e.g., eyebrows pulled toward the nose and down, often head slightly forward) and perhaps empathic sadness. In contrast, children experiencing personal distress were expected to exhibit facial distress (e.g., scrunching eyes with furrowed brows, biting lips or pressing and moving them). Because SC tends to be associated with relatively intense emotional arousal, it was expected to index a reaction akin to personal distress. High SC is more likely to accompany anxiety than sadness (which is involved in empathic feelings) and therefore was expected to reflect emotional arousal that is aversive (e.g., personal distress; see Eisenberg & Fabes, 1990; Fabes, Eisenberg, Karbon, Troyer, & Switzer, 1994). We also hypothesized that HR acceleration in our studies would reflect distress whereas HR deceleration would be a marker of interest in, and processing of, information coming from external stimuli—in this case, the sympathy-inducing stimulus. HR acceleration has been linked to the processing of information that is internal rather than outside of the self and, consequently, might tap a self-focus, whereas HR deceleration has been associated with attention to a stimulus (see Cacioppo, & Sandman, 1978; Lazarus, 1975).

In general, we found that children (and adults in some studies) tended to exhibit more facial concerned attention in sympathy-inducing contexts and distress in situations believed to elicit personal distress (see Eisenberg & Fabes, 1990, for a review; Eisenberg, Fabes, et al., 1988; Eisenberg, Fabes, Schaller, Miller, et al., 1991; Eisenberg, Schaller, et al., 1988). Younger children's self-reports of sympathy and personal distress were less contextually appropriate than those of older children and adults, although in general, their self-reports were consistent with the context (i.e., sympathy or distress inducing) at all ages (Eisenberg, Fabes, et al., 1988; Eisenberg, Schaller, et al. 1988). Moreover, study participants exhibited higher HR and SC in the distressing situations (see Eisenberg & Fabes, 1990; Eisenberg, Fabes, et al., 1988; Eisenberg, Fabes, Schaller, Carlo, et al., 1991; Eisenberg, Fabes, Schaller, Miller, et al., 1991; Eisenberg, Schaller, et al., 1988; Fabes, Eisenberg, Karbon, Troyer, & Switzer, 1994).

In a related set of studies, we examined the relations of facial, physiological, and self-reported reactions to empathy-inducing films to children's (and sometimes adults') prosocial behaviors (sometimes actual behavior, sometimes offers to help in the future) when it was easy to avoid contact with the person needing assistance. In a typical study, children would view a film of injured children who were talking about their experiences in the hospital. We would assess children's HR and/or SC while they watched the film; tape and later code their facial reactions to the film; and immediately after the film, ask the children to rate how they felt during the film (using simple adjectives and visual response scales for children). A short time later, the children had an opportunity to assist the person(s) in the film or similar individuals by, for example, donating part of a payment or doing a boring but helpful activity rather than playing with attractive toys. Using this multimethod approach, we have found, as predicted by many theorists, links between empathy-related responding and prosocial behavior.

In studies of this sort, HR deceleration was found to be positively related with elementary-school children's and adults' helping behavior (Eisenberg et al., 1989), children's donating (Eisenberg & Fabes, 1990), and preschoolers' helping (Eisenberg et al., 1990). Using a more life-like paradigm, HR acceleration (vs. deceleration) in response to a crying baby was negatively related to young elementary school children's quality (but not quantity) of comforting behavior (Fabes, Eisenberg, Karbon, Troyer, et al., 1994) but was unrelated to helping behavior in another study (Eisenberg et al., 1993). Moreover, consistent with the argument that SC reflects personal distress, in a study of young elementary school children, SC was inversely related to helping behavior and positively correlated with facial distress. SC reactivity also accounted for significant variance in helping behavior, above and beyond all other predictors (i.e., facial indexes; Fabes, Eisenberg, Karbon, Bernzweig, et al., 1994). In another study with young school children, SC assessed during a section of a film expected to elicit personal distress was related to teachers' reports of low levels of prosocial behavior (Holmgren, Eisenberg, & Fabes, 1998). Similarly, Fabes, Eisenberg, and Eisenbud (1993) found that third- and sixth-grade girls' (but not boys') high SC in response to an empathy-inducing film was related to mothers' ratings of daughters as relatively low in helpfulness.

Facial reactions also predicted prosocial responding in the predicted ways, although more so for boys than for girls (Eisenberg & Fabes, 1990). In a study with 4- and 5-year-olds, boys' facial sadness was positively related to helping, whereas their facial distress was negatively correlated; no findings were obtained for girls (Eisenberg et al., 1990). Similarly, boys' (but not girls') facial concerned attention and sadness were positively related to helping in a study of second and fifth graders (Fabes, Eisenberg, & Miller, 1990). However, sex differences have not always been reported (e.g., Fabes, Eisenberg, Karbon, Bernzweig, et al., 1994), and sometimes findings have held for both sexes (Eisenberg et al., 1989). Facial distress has sometimes (Eisenberg et al., 1993) but not always (Fabes, Eisenberg, Karbon, Troyer, et al., 1994) been negatively related to young children's helping of a crying infant or an adult. Moreover, facial measures of sympathy or distress in response to a specific film sometimes have not been related to measures of dispositional prosocial behavior outside of the empathy-inducing setting (e.g., Eisenberg et al., 1990; Fabes et al., 1993; contrast with Miller, Eisenberg, Fabes, & Shell, 1996).

Finally, self-reports of empathy-related emotions have sometimes been related to children's prosocial behavior, although this appears to be more likely for older children and adults than for younger children. In general, reports of positive mood when watching an empathy-inducing film have been related with low levels of prosocial behavior, whereas reports of negative emotion, including sympathy and sometimes distress, have been positively related to prosocial behavior (Eisenberg et al., 1989; Fabes et al., 1990; Miller et al., 1996). The finding that personal distress has sometimes been positively related to prosocial behavior may be due to the difficulty in differentiating between distress for others or self-related distress with self-report measures (Batson et al., 1988; Eisenberg et al., 1989). Moreover, relations between self-reported sympathy and helping have not always been found (e.g., Fabes, Eisenberg, Karbon, Bernzweig, et al., 1994; also see Eisenberg et al., 1990).

In summary, the bulk of the literature supports the common view that empathy-related emotional reactions, especially sympathy, often motivate prosocial behavior and that personal distress reactions can undermine helping (if escape is easy). However, findings for personal distress are not consistent with self-report measures of emotional responding. Moreover, most of the findings reviewed previously pertain to associations of empathy-related responding in a given setting and helping of people in that situation (or similar individuals). It should be noted, however, that there is a relatively consistent pattern of positive relations between measures of children's dispositional empathy-related responding (i.e., responding across contexts, often self-reported or reported by parents, teachers, or peers) and children's prosocial behavior (measured in specific situations or with ratings of dispositional tendencies; see Eisenberg et al., 2006, and Eisenberg & Miller, 1987, for reviews). Thus, in general, it appears that empathy-related responding does provide a basis for prosocial actions, at least in some situations.

EMPATHY-RELATED BEHAVIOR AND NEGATIVE BEHAVIOR

Although sympathy and personal distress often have been found to relate in different ways to prosocial behavior, both of these reactions, as well as empathy, are thought to inhibit aggression, albeit perhaps for different (e.g., other- vs. self-oriented) reasons. Experiencing what the victim is expected to feel (i.e., empathy) or feeling sorrow or concern for the victim (i.e., sympathy) should lead the perpetrator to want to assist the victim, cease causing harm to a victim, and alleviate any inflicted harm (Miller & Eisenberg, 1988). In terms of personal distress, Feshbach and Feshbach (1969) argued that one would be expected to feel distress when observing the outcomes of aggression regardless of whether the observer is the perpetrator or not, as long as the individual is empathic. The distress experienced by the observer should inhibit future acts of aggression and, furthermore, the relief of negative arousal when ceasing aggression may be reinforcing. In contrast, individuals with empathy deficits who exhibit aggressive behavior toward a victim would not be expected to feel empathic arousal when witnessing the victim's distress. Dispositional as well as situationally induced empathy-related reactions would be expected to relate to relatively low aggression because individuals tending to experience empathy (dispositional) should be inclined to experience empathy in a variety of contexts (Miller & Eisenberg, 1988).

Empathy-Related Responding and Externalizing Problems

Consistent with theory, empathic responding has been negatively related to children's aggressive behavior. For example, Strayer and Roberts (2004) found that 5-year-olds' empathy (a composite of parent-reported, teacher-reported, and observed [which tapped affective and cognitive] empathy) was negatively related to observed physical and verbal aggression. In a study of kindergarteners through second graders, Eisenberg et al. (1996) found that teacher-reported dispositional sympathy was positively related to teachers' reports of nonaggressive-socially appropriate behavior and negatively related to mothers' reports of problem behavior, which included aggression, although relations were stronger for boys. In addition, children's self-reported dispositional sympathy was negatively related to boys' mother-reported problem behavior. Similarly, in a study of young adolescents in the Netherlands, self-reported dispositional empathy was related negatively with self-reported aggressive behavior and delinquent behavior (de Kemp, Overbeek, de Wied, Engels, & Scholte, 2007).

Some support for the inverse association between empathy and aggression or externalizing has been obtained using measures tapping situational empathy; however, the relation is sometimes positive at young ages. The positive relation may be due to empathy and aggression having common links to general arousability/emotionality or extraversion (e.g., Feshbach & Feshbach, 1969; Gill & Calkins, 2003). For example, Gill and Calkins (2003) found that maternally rated aggressive/destructive 2-year-olds displayed more situational empathy than did nonaggressive toddlers. In addition, children's self-reported situational empathy to short vignettes (a method that seems to be problematic for assessing empathy; see Eisenberg & Lennon, 1983; Eisenberg & Miller, 1987) was positively related to teacher-reported aggression for 4- and 5-year-old boys, whereas the reverse was true for 6- and 7-year-olds (no significant difference for girls in either age group; Feshbach & Feshbach, 1969). Feshbach and Feshbach (1969) theorized that the age difference was due to maturation of the child, and that the sex difference might have been due to different meanings of aggression or ranges of aggression scores for each sex.

Indeed, the negative association between situational empathy and aggression appears to become more consistent with age. For example, in a longitudinal study, children who were rated as at high risk for behavior problems did not differ from children who were rated as at moderate or low risk for behavior problems in concern for others at 4 to 5 years of age. However, children at high risk for behavior problems exhibited a decline in concern for others from 4 to 5 and 6 to 7 years of age, whereas children at low or moderate risk remained stable in concern for others from 4 to 5 and 6 to 7 years of age (Hastings, Zahn-Waxler, Robinson, Usher, & Bridges, 2000). In another study, second through fifth graders who exhibited less negative expressivity while viewing slides depicting pictures of sad people or people in negative situations were rated as having a greater degree of externalizing problems, particularly for boys, whereas positive expressivity in response to slides with positive images was unrelated to externalizing problems (Eisenberg, Losoya, et al., 2001). Two years later, negative expressivity to negative slides continued to be negatively related to concurrent externalizing; however, positive expressivity to positive slides also was negatively related to concurrent externalizing (although empathy with negative emotion appeared to be the stronger predictor; Zhou et al., 2002). In addition, empathy (facial and reported combined on a latent construct) with negative, but not positive, emotions using the same task related negatively to concurrent externalizing problems, even when externalizing measured 2 years prior was controlled (Zhou et al., 2002). Facial responding to evocative images may reflect an emotional and somewhat reflexive form of empathic arousal, which may foster the experience or comprehension of how the other likely feels (affective and cognitive empathy, respectively; Hoffman, 2000). Results from these and other studies (e.g., see Blair, 2005) have supported the notion that deficits in empathic responding to negative images often are related to externalizing problems, but deficits in empathic responding to positive images are less consistently related to externalizing problems.

In sum, dispositional empathy and, particularly for older children, situational empathy have been negatively related to aggression and, more broadly, externalizing. Indeed, in a meta-analysis, Miller and Eisenberg (1988) concluded that empathy was negatively related to aggression, externalizing, and antisocial behaviors, although the degree of association ranged from low to moderate. Associations tended to be significant when questionnaires, but not other methods (e.g., facial affect), were used to measure empathy; thus, dispositional empathy may offer greater predictive power for externalizing behaviors than situational empathy.

Empathy-Related Responding and Severe Problem Behavior

A related body of research has supported an association between lack of empathy and more severe problems, such as conduct disorder and psychopathy. In a model somewhat similar to that of Feshbach and Feshbach (e.g., 1982), Blair (1995) asserted that deficits in emotion recognition and processing cause an aggression-suppressing mechanism to malfunction. To elaborate, social animals normally will cease attack when they perceive signs of submission. Individuals with psychopathic tendencies are less adept at detecting these cues (e.g., sadness) and, thus, do not withdraw their aggression. Consistent with this model, individuals with psychopathic tendencies possess deficits in recognizing or processing others' emotional expressions of fear and sadness, but not of happy, angry, surprised, or disgusted expressions (Blair & Coles, 2000; for a review, see Blair, 2005).

Moreover, individuals with more severe behavior problems, including criminal offenders, have been found to have deficits in empathy. For example, Cohen and Strayer (1996) found that adolescents with conduct disorder scored significantly lower on self-reported measures of situational empathy and dispositional empathic concern, as well as higher in dispositional personal distress, than did normal controls. Conduct-disordered youths were also significantly lower in cognitive empathy measures, such as perspective taking, than were normal controls. Findings were interpreted as suggesting that conduct disorder was associated with deficits in other-focused, but not self-focused, emotion (Cohen & Strayer, 1996). In a meta-analysis, Jolliffe and Farrington (2004) found that empathy/sympathy, as measured with questionnaires, was negatively related to criminal offending, but the relation was greater for adolescents than adults. Furthermore, the strength of the significant negative relation was stronger for cognitive empathy than affective empathy/sympathy, although the difference may have been a function of measurement (in contrast, Shechtman [2002] found that aggressive boys demonstrated less affective empathy but not cognitive empathy than did nonaggressive boys in Israel).

Differences in situational empathy also have been found for incarcerated and nonincarcerated individuals. For example, Robinson, Roberts, Strayer, and Koopman (2007) found that incarcerated adolescent boys, 81% of whom were diagnosed with conduct disorder, demonstrated less situational empathy in response to vignettes than did community adolescent boys (girls were not included in the sample). In addition, the offenders' responses were more egocentric than the community youths' responses.

Consistent with results suggesting deficits in situational empathy with negative, but not positive, evocative stimuli (e.g., Eisenberg, Losoya, et al., 2001), boys with disruptive behavior disorders (i.e., conduct disorder or oppositional defiant disorder) have been found to report less situational empathy as well as dispositional empathy in response to vignettes portraying anger and sadness, but not happiness, than normal controls (girls were not included in the sample; de Wied, Goudena, & Matthys, 2005). Furthermore, boys with disruptive behavior disorders exhibited less facial mimicry than normal control boys when viewing video in which a model displayed angry facial expressions; however, facial mimicry responses when viewing expressions of happiness did not significantly differ between disordered and control boys (de Wied, van Boxtel, Zaalberg, Goudena, & Matthys, 2006).

A lack of empathy has been identified as one of several (e.g., lack of empathy, lack of guilt, callous use of others for one's own gain) callous-unemotional traits identified as being associated with conduct problems, aggression, and delinquency. These traits assist in distinguishing among types of antisocial behavior, in that youths with these traits seem at higher risk for more severe antisocial behavior (e.g., aggressive, early onset, greater persistence; see Frick & White, 2008). Results from a large sample of twins suggested that 7-year-olds' callous-unemotional traits are genetically influenced, and that antisocial behavior may be influenced by genetics to a greater degree for children with high rather than low callous-unemotional traits (Viding, Blair, Moffitt, & Plomin, 2005).

SELF-CONSCIOUS MORAL EMOTIONS

Whereas the lack of empathy has been associated with aggression and other externalizing problems, the presence of guilt has been associated with moral development and empathy. Shame, guilt, embarrassment, and pride are considered "self-conscious" moral emotions because the individual's own appraisal of a situation or behavior is central to these emotions (Tangney, Stuewig, & Mashek, 2007). These moral emotions provide individuals with feedback about their behavior and the self. The majority of research on moral emotions has focused on shame and guilt. We briefly describe the differences between the two before reviewing guilt and its correlates. Pride and embarrassment are not discussed in this chapter because those emotions are likely to be less important in moral development than is guilt and are less related to empathy (Eisenberg, 2000).

Shame and Guilt

Shame and guilt have often been treated as synonymous moral emotions, but recently some researchers have differentiated the two emotions (see Tangney et al., 2007). These two emotions may occur in similar situations (Tangney, 1992), but a major factor that separates them is the focus of the transgressor. Guilt appears to be the more moral of the two emotions because individuals experiencing guilt tend to focus on their transgression (i.e., their particular behavior in a given situation), which may prompt attempts to provide restitution, reparation, or apology to the victim. In contrast, individuals experiencing shame tend to focus on the self, that is, the core of their identity. Shamed individuals tend to feel exposed and inferior, and these feelings may prompt behavior to avoid the victim. Shamed individuals are likely to focus on their own personal distress when faced with transgressions, which interferes with their ability to experience other-oriented empathy (Lindsay-Hartz, 1984; Niedenthal, Tangney, & Gavanski, 1994; Tangney, 1991, 1992, 1998; Tangney et al., 2007).

Proneness to shame and proneness to guilt have been differentially related to a range of psychological and social characteristics (Ferguson, Stegge, Miller, & Olsen, 1999; Tangney, 1991; Tangney, Wagner, Fletcher, & Gramzow, 1992). Proneness to shame has been linked to more severe psychological symptoms (such as anxiety and depression), impaired empathy, and high levels of anger and aggression. In contrast, guilt has been linked to constructive anger management and is generally unrelated to severe psychological symptoms (e.g., Tangney, Wagner, & Gramzow, 1992; Tangney, Wagner, Hill-Barlow, Marschall, & Gramzow, 1996). However, too much guilt may engender feelings of shame, which causes negativity about the self (Eisenberg, 2000; Tangney et al., 2007). Also, if the guilt is based on irrational, unresolved interpretations of responsibility, it can lead to maladaptive views about the self over time. For example, children (especially girls) of depressed mothers may have guilt that is chronic, unjustified, and maladaptive (Zahn-Waxler, Kochanska, Krupnick, & McKnew, 1990). These children may also have muted responses of tension and frustration in response to mishaps because they do not want to arouse maternal negative emotion, or they may have learned such expressions do not elicit responses from their mothers (Cole, Barrett, & Zahn-Waxler, 1992).

Guilt and Empathy-Related Responding

The experience of guilt has been repeatedly linked to other dimensions of morality, such as empathy, sympathy, and prosocial behavior (e.g., Aksan & Kochanska, 2005; Cornell & Frick, 2007; Tangney, 1991; Tangney et al., 1996). Empathic arousal has been shown to be related to children's and adults' guilt over transgressions (Okel & Mosher, 1968; Thompson & Hoffman, 1980). Moreover, theorists point to empathy as a contributor to the development of guilt (e.g., Kochanska, 1993). Hoffman (2000) described the development of guilt in "stages" in which guilt moves from an egocentric, self-orientation to a more other-focused, mature level as experienced by adults, much like empathy-related responding. Tangney (1991) linked the development of guilt and empathy with children's capacity for differentiation: To experience guilt, the child must differentiate the self from the behavior, whereas to experience empathy, the child must distinguish the self from the other. It is likely that these capacities for differentiation emerge during the same time frame.

In studies by Zahn-Waxler and her colleagues (Zahn-Waxler et al., 1979, 1992), similarities have been found in the development of empathy in a bystander situation (in which the child witnesses someone else's distress) and the development of guilt-like behavior when the child causes another's distress. Zahn-Waxler and colleagues, as well as other researchers (Hoffman, 1975; Yarrow, Scott, & Waxler, 1973; Zahn-Waxler, Radke-Yarrow, & King, 1983), link the development of empathy-related responding to the development of guilt because issues of wrongfulness, harming others, and discipline are becoming important issues in parent–child interactions during the child's first 18 months of life. Dealing with such issues may promote the development of empathy and related reactions as well as guilt over transgressions in young children. Parents who are responsive and authoritative, and who use inductions (i.e., reasoning with the child about his or her misbehavior) in discipline encounters, are more likely to have children who are empathic and show guilt over their transgressions. It may be that the emphasis on the child's accountability and responsibility for their transgressions helps foster empathy as well as guilt (Cornell & Frick, 2007; Kochanska, Forman, Aksan, & Dunbar, 2005; Kochanska, Gross, Lin, & Nichols, 2002; Krevans & Gibbs, 1996; Zahn-Waxler et al., 1979). That is, empathy and guilt seem to have similarities in the way that parents socialize these responses.

Guilt and Prosocial Behavior

Empathy-based guilt appears to be an effective motivator of prosocial and reparative actions, such as apologizing (Baumeister, Stillwell, & Heatherton, 1994; Estrada-Hollenbeck & Heatherton, 1998; Roseman, Wiest, & Swartz, 1994). Guilt appears to be especially likely to lead to prosocial behaviors for highly empathic children (Krevans & Gibbs, 1996). Guilt over inaction as well as over transgressions functions as a prosocial motivator (see Hoffman, 1987, 2000). Chapman, Zahn-Waxler, Cooperman, and Iannotti (1987) found that preschoolers and grade school children who attributed guilt to the child in stories about transgressions were more likely to help during observational distress tasks than were children who did not attribute guilt to the story child. Consistent with this evidence, Zahn-Waxler et al. (1990) found a positive correlation between guilt and empathy/prosocial themes in 5- to 9-year-old children's interpretations of narrative stories. The link between guilt and prosocial behavior appears to be through their shared relation with empathy, as well as their role in interpersonal functioning. Empathy and guilt are both linked to increased social contact with others because of attempts to improve or maintain relationships (Baumeister et al., 1994; Estrada-Hollenbeck & Heatherton, 1998).

EMPATHY-RELATED RESPONDING AND MORAL REASONING

Centuries ago, Hume (1751/1966) argued that people use empathy to evaluate the morality of actions. More recently, Hoffman (2000) argued that many moral dilemmas elicit empathy for others, and that empathy activates moral cognitions and principles; thus, moral judgments can be directly affected by the elicited empathy or indirectly affected through the application of elicited moral principles (see Eisenberg, 1986, for a similar priming argument). Moreover, Eisenberg (1986) suggested that beliefs and motives that guide moral decisions are reflected in the level of moral reasoning that a person expresses and that empathy and sympathy contribute to the development of the moral values and principles reflected in moral judgments.

In a typical moral judgment task, children (or adults) are presented with moral dilemmas and asked what the actor should do and why. Even if children are not capable of understanding or expressing higher levels of moral judgment, we might expect children prone to empathy and sympathy (especially the latter) to verbalize more rudimentary other-oriented concerns (e.g., note another's need) and fewer hedonistic, egoistic concerns than their less sympathetic peers (Eisenberg, 1986). In fact, there is considerable support for this argument. In a study of adults, Skoe, Eisenberg, and Cumberland (2002) found relations between adults' reports of experiencing sympathy when resolving moral conflicts and both their care-related moral reasoning (especially when discussing real-life dilemmas) and the importance they assigned to a real-life or hypothetical moral dilemma. Moreover, in their studies of prosocial moral reasoning (i.e., dilemmas in which one person's needs conflict with those of another in a situation in which the role of rules, laws, authorities' dictates, or formal obligations is minimal), Eisenberg and colleagues (e.g., 1995, 2002; Eisenberg, Miller, Shell, McNalley, & Shea, 1991) have often found associations between children's, adolescents', and adults' reported sympathy and the greater use of empathy-related types of moral reasoning or lesser use of hedonistic reasoning. Furthermore, preschoolers' spontaneous sharing has been related to rudimentary other-oriented moral reasoning (Eisenberg-Berg & Hand, 1979).

In a study of adolescents in Brazil, Eisenberg, Zhou, and Koller (2001) obtained empirical support for the argument that prosocial moral reasoning mediates the relation of sympathy to prosocial behavior. They found that sympathy (as well as cognitive perspective taking) predicted adolescents' level of prosocial moral reasoning, which in turn predicted their prosocial responding (sympathy also had a direct path to prosocial responding). Moreover, cognitive perspective taking was related to prosocial tendencies only indirectly through its relations with sympathy and moral reasoning. Thus, sympathy, often derived from empathy, may contribute to prosocial behavior directly, as well as through its effects on prosocial moral reasoning.

CONCLUSION

Empathy and related sympathetic responding appear to play a major role in moral cognitions and behavior. Sympathy in particular has been related to prosocial responding, both in specific situations and as a behavioral tendency. Moreover, empathic responding and sympathy have been associated with low levels of aggression, externalizing problems, and delinquent/ criminal behavior, and with higher levels of moral reasoning (or more other-oriented reasoning). In addition, guilt appears to be associated with empathy, both developmentally and in terms of its relation to moral behavior.

Given the importance of empathy and sympathy for moral behavior, it is important to identify whether empathy alone or only sympathy is related to moral outcomes. Sympathy appears to be especially related to altruism, whereas either empathy or sympathy may be sufficient to inhibit harm-doing toward others. Moreover, relations of empathy-related reactions with moral cognitions or behaviors may change with age. For example, empathy may be linked to the early development of guilt, whereas sympathy may be more closely linked to its elicitation in older children and adults.

Nearly all of the research on the role of empathy-related responding in moral behavior and cognitions has been correlational. Experimental studies and experimental interventions are needed to examine the causal relations between empathy/sympathy and moral behavior/cognition. Moreover, it is likely that part of the associations among empathy-related responding, guilt, and prosocial behavior is due to genetic factors. Research on how genetically based biases and tendencies interact with socialization and other environmental factors in the development of empathy and its relations to moral behavior and cognitions is needed to clarify developmental pathways for empathy-related responding and its role in moral development.

REFERENCES

Aksan, N., & Kochanska, G. (2005). Conscience in childhood: Old questions, new answers. *Developmental Psychology, 41*, 506–516. Medline doi:10.1037/0012-1649.41.3.506

Batson, C. D. (1991). *The altruism question: Toward a social-psychological answer.* Hillsdale, NJ: Erlbaum.

Batson, C. D., Dyck, J. L., Brandt, J. R., Batson, J. G., Powell, A. L., McMaster, M. R., . . . Griffit, C. (1988). Five studies testing two new egoistic alternatives to the empathy-altruism hypothesis. *Journal of Personality and Social Psychology, 55*, 52–77. Medline doi:10.1037/0022-3514.55.1.52

Baumeister, R. F., Stillwell, A. M., & Heatherton, T. F. (1994). Guilt: An interpersonal approach. *Psychological Bulletin, 115*, 243–267. Medline doi:10.1037/0033-2909.115.2.243

Blair, R. J. R. (1995). A cognitive developmental approach to morality: Investigating the psychopath. *Cognition, 57*, 1–29. Medline doi:10.1016/0010-0277(95)00676-P

Blair, R. J. R. (2005). Responding to the emotions of others: Dissociating forms of empathy through the study of typical and psychiatric populations. *Consciousness and Cognition, 14*, 698–718. Medline doi:10.1016/j.concog.2005.06.004

Blair, R. J. R., & Coles, M. (2000). Expression recognition and behavioral problems in early adolescence. *Cognitive Development, 15*, 421–434. doi:10.1016/S0885-2014(01)00039-9

Cacioppo, J. T., & Sandman, C. A. (1978). Physiological differentiation of sensory and cognitive tasks as a function of warning processing demands and reported unpleasantness. *Biological Psychology, 6*, 181–192. Medline doi:10.1016/0301-0511(78)90020-0

Chapman, M., Zahn-Waxler, C., Cooperman, G., & Iannotti, R. (1987). Empathy and responsibility in the motivation of children's helping. *Developmental Psychology, 23*, 140–145. doi:10.1037/0012-1649.23.1.140

Cohen, D., & Strayer, J. (1996). Empathy in conduct-disordered and comparison youth. *Developmental Psychology, 32,* 988–998. doi:10.1037/0012-1649.32.6.988

Cole, P. M., Barrett, K. C., & Zahn-Waxler, C. (1992). Emotion displays in two-year-olds during mishaps. *Child Development, 63,* 314–324. Medline doi:10.2307/1131481

Cornell, A. H., & Frick, P. J. (2007). The moderating effects of parenting styles in the association between behavioral inhibition and parent-reported guilt and empathy in preschool children. *Journal of Clinical Child and Adolescent Psychology, 36,* 305–318.

Davis, M. H. (1994). *Empathy: A social psychological approach.* Madison, WI: Brown & Benchmark.

de Kemp, R. A. T., Overbeek, G., de Wied, M., Engels, R. C. M. E., & Scholte, R. H. J. (2007). Early adolescent empathy, parental support, and antisocial behavior. *The Journal of Genetic Psychology, 168,* 5–18. Medline doi:10.3200/GNTP.168.1.5-18

de Wied, M., van Boxtel, A., Zaalberg, R., Goudena, P. P., & Matthys, W. (2006). Facial EMG responses to dynamic emotional facial expressions in boys with disruptive behavior disorders. *Journal of Psychiatric Research, 40,* 112–121. Medline doi:10.1016/j.jpsychires.2005.08.003

de Wied, M., Goudena, P. P., & Matthys, W. (2005). Empathy in boys with disruptive behavior disorders. *Journal of Child Psychology and Psychiatry, and Allied Disciplines, 46,* 867–880. Medline doi:10.1111/j.1469-7610.2004.00389.x

Eisenberg, N. (1986). *Altruistic emotion, cognition, and behavior.* Hillsdale, NJ: Erlbaum.

Eisenberg, N. (2000). Emotion, regulation, and moral development. *Annual Review of Psychology, 51,* 665–697. Medline doi:10.1146/annurev.psych.51.1.665

Eisenberg, N., Carlo, G., Murphy, B., & Van Court, P. (1995). Prosocial development in late adolescence: A longitudinal study. *Child Development, 66,* 1179–1197. Medline doi:10.2307/1131806

Eisenberg, N., & Fabes, R. A. (1990). Empathy: Conceptualization, assessment, and relation to prosocial behavior. *Motivation and Emotion, 14,* 131–149. doi:10.1007/BF00991640

Eisenberg, N., & Fabes, R. A. (1998). Prosocial development. In W. Damon (Series Ed.) & N. Eisenberg (Vol. Ed.), *Handbook of child psychology: Vol. 3. Social, emotional, and personality development* (5th ed., pp. 701–778). New York, NY: Wiley.

Eisenberg, N., Fabes, R. A., Bustamante, D., Mathy, R. M., Miller, P. A., & Lindholm, E. (1988). Differentiation of vicariously induced emotional reactions in children. *Developmental Psychology, 24,* 237–246. doi:10.1037/0012-1649.24.2.237

Eisenberg, N., Fabes, R. A., Carlo, G., Speer, A. L., Switzer, G., Karbon, M., . . . Troyer, D. (1993). The relations of empathy-related emotions and maternal practices to children's comforting behavior. *Journal of Experimental Child Psychology, 55,* 131–150. Medline doi:10.1006/jecp.1993.1007

Eisenberg, N., Fabes, R. A., Miller, P. A., Fultz, J., Mathy, R. M., Shell, R., . . . Reno, R. R. (1989). The relations of sympathy and personal distress to prosocial behavior: A multimethod study. *Journal of Personality and Social Psychology, 57*, 55–66. Medline doi:10.1037/0022-3514.57.1.55

Eisenberg, N., Fabes, R. A., Miller, P. A., Shell, C., Shea, R., & May-Plumlee, T. (1990). Preschoolers' vicarious emotional responding and their situational and dispositional prosocial behavior. *Merrill-Palmer Quarterly, 36*, 507–529.

Eisenberg, N., Fabes, R. A., Murphy, B., Karbon, M., Smith, M., & Maszk, P. (1996). The relations of children's dispositional empathy-related responding to their emotionality, regulation, and social functioning. *Developmental Psychology, 32*, 195–209. doi:10.1037/0012-1649.32.2.195

Eisenberg, N., Fabes, R. A., Schaller, M., Carlo, G., & Miller, P. A. (1991). The relations of parental characteristics and practices to children's vicarious emotional responding. *Child Development, 62*, 1393–1408. Medline doi:10.2307/1130814

Eisenberg, N., Fabes, R. A., Schaller, M., Miller, P., Carlo, G., Poulin, R., . . . Shell, R. (1991). Personality and socialization correlates of vicarious emotional responding. *Journal of Personality and Social Psychology, 61*, 459–470. Medline doi:10.1037/0022-3514.61.3.459

Eisenberg, N., Fabes, R. A., & Spinrad, T. L. (2006). Prosocial behavior. In N. Eisenberg (Vol. Ed.) and W. Damon & R. M. Lerner (Series Eds.), *Handbook of child psychology: Vol. 3. Social, emotional, and personality development* (6th ed., pp. 646–718). New York, NY: Wiley.

Eisenberg, N., Guthrie, I., Cumberland, A., Murphy, B. C., Shepard, S. A., Zhou, Q., . . . Carlo, G. (2002). Prosocial development in early adulthood: A longitudinal study. *Journal of Personality and Social Psychology, 82*, 993–1006. Medline doi:10.1037/0022-3514.82.6.993

Eisenberg, N., & Lennon, R. (1983). Gender differences in empathy and related capacities. *Psychological Bulletin, 94*, 100–131. doi:10.1037/0033-2909.94.1.100

Eisenberg, N., Losoya, S., Fabes, R. A., Guthrie, I. K., Reiser, M., Murphy, B., . . . Padgett, S. J. (2001). Parental socialization of children's dysregulated expression of emotion and externalizing problems. *Journal of Family Psychology, 15*, 183–205. Medline doi:10.1037/0893-3200.15.2.183

Eisenberg, N., & Miller, P. (1987). The relation of empathy to prosocial and related behaviors. *Psychological Bulletin, 101*, 91–119. Medline doi:10.1037/0033-2909.101.1.91

Eisenberg, N., Miller, P. A., Shell, R., McNalley, S., & Shea, C. (1991). Prosocial development in adolescence: A longitudinal study. *Developmental Psychology, 27*, 849–857.

Eisenberg, N., Schaller, M., Fabes, R. A., Bustamante, D., Mathy, R. M., Shell, R., . . . Rhodes, K. (1988). Differentiation of personal distress and sympathy in children and adults. *Developmental Psychology, 24*, 766–775. doi:10.1037/0012-1649.24.6.766

Eisenberg, N., Shea, C. L., Carlo, G., & Knight, G. (1991). Empathy-related responding and cognition: A "chicken and the egg" dilemma. In W. Kurtines & J. Gewirtz

(Eds.), *Handbook of moral behavior and development: Vol. 2. Research* (pp. 63–88). Hillsdale, NJ: Erlbaum.

Eisenberg, N., Zhou, Q., & Koller, S. (2001). Brazilian adolescents' prosocial moral judgment and behavior: Relations to sympathy, perspective taking, gender-role orientation, and demographic characteristics. *Child Development, 72*, 518–534. Medline doi:10.1111/1467-8624.00294

Eisenberg-Berg, N., & Hand, M. (1979). The relationship of preschooler's reasoning about prosocial moral conflicts to prosocial behavior. *Child Development, 50*, 356–363. doi:10.2307/1129410

Estrada-Hollenbeck, M., & Heatherton, T. F. (1998). Avoiding and alleviating guilt through prosocial behavior. In J. Bybee (Ed.), *Guilt and children* (pp. 215–231). San Diego, CA: Academic Press.

Fabes, R. A., Eisenberg, N., & Eisenbud, L. (1993). Behavioral and physiological correlates of children's reactions to others in distress. *Developmental Psychology, 29*, 655–663. doi:10.1037/0012-1649.29.4.655

Fabes, R. A., Eisenberg, N., Karbon, M., Troyer, D., & Switzer, G. (1994). The relations of children's emotion regulation to their vicarious emotional responses and comforting behavior. *Child Development, 65*, 1678–1693. Medline doi:10.2307/1131287

Fabes, R. A., Eisenberg, N., Karbon, M., Bernzweig, J., Speer, A. L., & Carlo, G. (1994). Socialization of children's vicarious emotional responding and prosocial behavior: Relations with mothers' perceptions of children's emotional reactivity. *Developmental Psychology, 30*, 44–55. doi:10.1037/0012-1649.30.1.44

Fabes, R. A., Eisenberg, N., & Miller, P. A. (1990). Maternal correlates of children's vicarious emotional responsiveness. *Developmental Psychology, 26*, 639–648. doi:10.1037/0012-1649.26.4.639

Ferguson, T. J., Stegge, H., Miller, E. R., & Olsen, M. E. (1999). Guilt, shame, and symptoms in children. *Developmental Psychology, 35*, 347–357. Medline doi:10.1037/0012-1649.35.2.347

Feshbach, N. D., & Feshbach, S. (1969). The relationship between empathy and aggression in two age groups. *Developmental Psychology, 1*, 102–107. doi:10.1037/h0027016

Feshbach, N. D., & Feshbach, S. (1982). Empathy training and the regulation of aggression: Potentialities and limitations. *Academic Psychology Bulletin, 4*, 399–413.

Frick, P. J., & White, S. F. (2008). Research review: The importance of callous-unemotional traits for developmental models of aggressive and antisocial behavior. *Journal of Child Psychology and Psychiatry, and Allied Disciplines, 49*, 359–375. Medline doi:10.1111/j.1469-7610.2007.01862.x

Gill, K. L., & Calkins, S. D. (2003). Do aggressive/destructive toddlers lack concern for others? Behavioral and physiological indicators of empathic responding in 2-year-old children. *Development and Psychopathology, 15*, 55–71. Medline doi:10.1017/S095457940300004X

Hastings, P. D., Zahn-Waxler, C., Robinson, J., Usher, B., & Bridges, D. (2000). The development of concern for others in children with behavior problems. *Developmental Psychology, 36*, 531–546. Medline doi:10.1037/0012-1649.36.5.531

Hoffman, M. L. (1975). Developmental synthesis of affect and cognition and its implication for altruistic motivation. *Developmental Psychology, 11*, 607–622. doi:10.1037/0012-1649.11.5.607

Hoffman, M. L. (1987). The contribution of empathy to justice and moral judgment. In N. Eisenberg & J. Strayer (Eds.), *Empathy and its development* (pp. 47–80). New York, NY: Cambridge University Press.

Hoffman, M. L. (2000). *Empathy and moral development: Implications for caring and justice.* Cambridge, England: Cambridge University Press.

Holmgren, R. A., Eisenberg, N., & Fabes, R. A. (1998). The relations of children's situational empathy-related emotional to dispositional prosocial behaviour. *International Journal of Behavioral Development, 22*, 169–193. doi:10.1080/016502598384568

Hume, D. (1966). *An enquiry concerning the principle of morals.* Oxford, England. Clarendon Press. (Original work published 1751)

Jolliffe, D., & Farrington, D. P. (2004). Empathy and offending: A systematic review and meta-analysis. *Aggression and Violent Behavior, 9*, 441–476. doi:10.1016/j.avb.2003.03.001

Kochanska, G. (1993). Toward a synthesis of parental socialization and child temperament in early development of conscience. *Child Development, 64*, 325–347. doi:10.2307/1131254

Kochanska, G., Forman, D. R., Aksan, N., & Dunbar, S. B. (2005). Pathways to conscience: Early mother–child mutually responsive orientation and children's moral emotion, conduct, and cognition. *Journal of Child Psychology and Psychiatry, and Allied Disciplines, 46*, 19–34. Medline doi:10.1111/j.1469-7610.2004.00348.x

Kochanska, G., Gross, J. N., Lin, M., & Nichols, K. E. (2002). Guilt in young children: Development, determinants, and relations with a broader system of standards. *Child Development, 73*, 461–482. doi:10.1111/1467-8624.00418

Krevans, J., & Gibbs, J. C. (1996). Parents' use of inductive discipline: Relations to children's empathy and prosocial behavior. *Child Development, 67*, 3263–3277. Medline doi:10.2307/1131778

Lazarus, R. S. (1975). A cognitively oriented psychologist looks at biofeedback. *The American Psychologist, 30*, 553–561. doi:10.1037/h0076649

Lindsay-Hartz, J. (1984). Contrasting experiences of shame and guilt. *The American Behavioral Scientist, 27*, 689–704. doi:10.1177/000276484027006003

Miller, P. A., & Eisenberg, N. (1988). The relation of empathy to aggressive and externalizing/antisocial behavior. *Psychological Bulletin, 103*, 324–344. Medline doi:10.1037/0033-2909.103.3.324

Miller, P. A., Eisenberg, N., Fabes, R. A., & Shell, R. (1996). Relations of moral reasoning and vicarious emotion to young children's prosocial behavior toward peers and adults. *Developmental Psychology, 32,* 210–219. doi:10.1037/0012-1649.32.2.210

Niedenthal, P. M., Tangney, J. P., & Gavanski, I. (1994). "If only I weren't" versus "If only I hadn't": Distinguishing shame and guilt in counterfactual thinking. *Journal of Personality and Social Psychology, 67,* 585–595. Medline doi:10.1037/0022-3514.67.4.585

Okel, E., & Mosher, D. (1968). Changes in affective states as a function of guilt over aggressive behavior. *Journal of Consulting and Clinical Psychology, 32,* 265–270. doi:10.1037/h0025917

Robinson, R., Roberts, W. L., Strayer, J., & Koopman, R. (2007). Empathy and emotional responsiveness in delinquent and non-delinquent adolescents. *Social Development, 16,* 555–579. doi:10.1111/j.1467-9507.2007.00396.x

Roseman, I. J., Wiest, C., & Swartz, T. S. (1994). Phenomenology, behaviors, and goals differentiate discrete emotions. *Journal of Personality and Social Psychology, 67,* 206–221. doi:10.1037/0022-3514.67.2.206

Shechtman, Z. (2002). Cognitive and affective empathy in aggressive boys: Implications for counseling. *International Journal for the Advancement of Counseling, 24,* 211–222. doi:10.1023/A:1023316712331

Skoe, E., Eisenberg, N., & Cumberland, A. (2002). The role of reported emotion in real-life and hypothetical moral dilemmas. *Personality and Social Psychology Bulletin, 28,* 962–973.

Strayer, J., & Roberts, W. (2004). Empathy and observed anger and aggression in five-year-olds. *Social Development, 13,* 1–13. doi:10.1111/j.1467-9507.2004.00254.x

Tangney, J. P. (1991). Moral affect: The good, the bad, and the ugly. *Journal of Personality and Social Psychology, 61,* 598–607. Medline doi:10.1037/0022-3514.61.4.598

Tangney, J. P. (1992). Situational determinants of shame and guilt in young adulthood. *Personality and Social Psychology Bulletin, 18,* 199–206. doi:10.1177/0146167292182011

Tangney, J. P. (1998). How does guilt differ from shame? In J. Bybee (Ed.), *Guilt and children* (pp. 1–17). San Diego, CA: Academic Press.

Tangney, J. P., Stuewig, J., & Mashek, D. J. (2007). Moral emotions and moral behavior. *Annual Review of Psychology, 58,* 345–372. Medline doi:10.1146/annurev.psych.56.091103.070145

Tangney, J. P., Wagner, P., Fletcher, C., & Gramzow, R. (1992). Shamed into anger? The relation of shame and guilt to anger and self-reported aggression. *Journal of Personality and Social Psychology, 62,* 669–675. Medline doi:10.1037/0022-3514.62.4.669

Tangney, J. P., Wagner, P., & Gramzow, R. (1992). Proneness to shame, proneness to guilt, and psychopathology. *Journal of Abnormal Psychology, 101,* 469–478. Medline doi:10.1037/0021-843X.101.3.469

Tangney, J. P., Wagner, P. E., Hill-Barlow, D., Marschall, D. E., & Gramzow, R. (1996). Relation of shame and guilt to constructive versus destructive responses to anger across the lifespan. *Journal of Personality and Social Psychology, 70,* 797–809. Medline doi:10.1037/0022-3514.70.4.797

Thompson, R., & Hoffman, M. L. (1980). Empathy and the development of guilt in children. *Developmental Psychology, 16,* 155–156. doi:10.1037/0012-1649.16.2.155

Viding, E., Blair, R. J. R., Moffitt, T. E., & Plomin, R. (2005). Evidence for substantial genetic risk for psychopathy in 7-year-olds. *Journal of Child Psychology and Psychiatry, and Allied Disciplines, 46,* 592–597. Medline doi:10.1111/j.1469-7610.2004.00393.x

Yarrow, M. R., Scott, P. M., & Waxler, C. Z. (1973). Learning concern for others. *Developmental Psychology, 8,* 240–260. doi:10.1037/h0034159

Zahn-Waxler, C., Kochanska, G., Krupnick, J., & McKnew, D. (1990). Patterns of guilt in children of depressed and well mothers. *Developmental Psychology, 26,* 51–59. doi:10.1037/0012-1649.26.1.51

Zahn-Waxler, C., Radke-Yarrow, M., & King, R. (1979). Child rearing and children's prosocial initiations toward victims of distress. *Child Development, 50,* 319–330. Medline doi:10.2307/1129406

Zahn-Waxler, C., Radke-Yarrow, M., & King, R. (1983). Early altruism and guilt. *Academic Psychology Bulletin, 5,* 247–259.

Zahn-Waxler, C., Radke-Yarrow, M., Wagner, E., & Chapman, M. (1992). Development of concern for others. *Developmental Psychology, 28,* 126–136. doi:10.1037/0012-1649.28.1.126

Zhou, Q., Eisenberg, N., Losoya, S. H., Fabes, R. A., Reiser, M., Guthrie, I. K., . . . Shepard, S. (2002). The relations of parental warmth and positive expressiveness to children's empathy-related responding and social functioning: A longitudinal study. *Child Development, 73,* 893–915. Medline doi:10.1111/1467-8624.00446

7

CALLOUS-UNEMOTIONAL TRAITS AND AGGRESSION IN YOUTH

MONICA A. MARSEE AND PAUL J. FRICK

Researchers attempting to explain the development of antisocial and aggressive behavior in youth generally agree that such behaviors are heterogeneous and may result from a number of different causal mechanisms (Frick & Marsee, 2006). Theoretical models resulting from this body of work suggest that within aggressive and antisocial youth, specific subgroups may exist that can be differentiated on the basis of the types of problem behavior that they show, the age at which it begins, and the course of such behavior in terms of risk for later negative outcomes (Frick & Marsee, 2006; Moffitt & Caspi, 2001). Additionally, youth in these subgroups may show unique cognitive and emotional correlates to their problem behavior that have important implications for designing effective interventions (Frick, 2006). The purpose of this chapter is to review recent research on the emotional and cognitive components of antisocial and aggressive behavior that may provide important insight into its causes and consequences. We focus on two lines of research relevant to defining and understanding distinct subgroups of antisocial youth. First, we review research on the presence of callous-unemotional (CU) traits (e.g., poverty of emotions, lack of empathy and guilt, callous use of others for one's own gain), a constellation of characteristics that designates a more severe group of antisocial youth (see Frick & Dickens, 2006). Second, we focus on subtypes of aggression that have proven useful for describing antisocial youth with regard to their development, peer relationships, and psychosocial adjustment. Finally, we discuss implications of this research for assessing and treating aggressive and antisocial youth.

CU TRAITS AND THE DEVELOPMENT
OF AGGRESSIVE AND ANTISOCIAL BEHAVIOR

Individuals with CU traits show an aberrant affective and interpersonal style that is the hallmark of the construct of psychopathy (Cleckley, 1976). Psychopathy refers to a cluster of affective (e.g., lack of guilt and remorse), interpersonal (e.g., manipulative), and behavioral (e.g., impulsivity, irresponsibility) traits that have proven to be quite important for designating a distinct group of antisocial adults. Although there is some debate over the number of dimensions that make up the construct of psychopathy (see Cooke, Michie, & Hart, 2006), much research supports the existence of at least three components: CU traits, narcissistic traits (e.g., thinks he or she is more important than others; brags excessively), and impulsive behaviors (e.g., acts without thinking, does not plan ahead). Research has consistently shown that incarcerated adults who also exhibit psychopathic traits engage in a more severe and violent pattern of antisocial behavior, both within the institution and after release (Gendreau, Goggin, & Smith, 2002). In addition, these individuals display a number of distinct cognitive, affective, and neurological correlates, suggesting that different causal processes may be involved in the development of their antisocial behavior compared with incarcerated adults without psychopathic traits.

Similar to the findings for adults, research has demonstrated that psychopathic traits also seem to designate a distinct subgroup of antisocial and aggressive youth (see Frick & Dickens, 2006). Further, the three dimensions that characterize these traits are very similar in community samples of youth using both teacher and parent ratings (Frick, Bodin, & Barry, 2000), as well as in incarcerated samples of youth using self-report or clinical ratings (Neumann, Kosson, Forth, & Hare, 2006). However, some studies have suggested that it may be the CU dimension that is most important for differentiating an important subgroup within antisocial youth (Caputo, Frick, & Brodsky, 1999; Christian, Frick, Hill, Tyler, & Frazer, 1997). Specifically, Christian et al. (1997) conducted a cluster analysis of psychopathic traits and conduct problems in a clinic-referred sample of children ages 6 to 13 years and found two distinct conduct problem clusters. Although these clusters did not differ on levels of impulsivity and narcissism, they did differ on levels of CU traits, with the group high on CU traits showing more severe patterns of antisocial behavior. Similarly, in a sample of adjudicated adolescents, narcissistic and impulsive traits did not differentiate among nonviolent offenders, violent offenders, and violent sex offenders, but the violent sex offenders showed significantly higher levels of CU traits (Caputo et al, 1999). Across both studies, children who were high in CU traits also tended to be high in narcissistic traits and impulsivity. However, there were children with childhood-onset conduct problems and serious adolescent offenders who showed high levels of impulsive and narcissistic traits without CU traits (see Frick et al., 2000, for similar findings in a community sample).

Relevant to research on the importance of CU traits in grouping antisocial youth is the issue of whether these traits are stable across development. Several studies have supported the stability of these traits from late childhood to early adolescence as assessed by self- (Muñoz & Frick, 2007), parent (Frick, Kimonis, Dandreaux, & Farrell, 2003), and teacher reports (Obradovic, Pardini, Long, & Loeber, 2007). For example, Frick, Kimonis, et al. (2003) reported an intraclass correlation coefficient of .71 across a 4-year period for parent report, whereas Obradovic et al. (2007) reported a correlation of .50 for parents and .27 for teachers across a 9-year period. Research also supports the stability of CU traits from childhood into adulthood (Lynam, Caspi, Moffitt, Loeber, & Stouthamer-Loeber, 2007). Although these results indicate a substantial degree of stability in ratings of CU traits, it is important to note that a number of youth in these studies showed a decrease in their level of CU traits over time (e.g., Frick, Kimonis, et al., 2003; Lynam et al., 2007). Interestingly, Frick, Kimonis, et al. (2003) found that this decrease in CU traits was consistently related to contextual factors affecting the child (i.e., socioeconomic status and quality of parenting), suggesting that these traits may be influenced by the child's social environment. These findings suggest that the quality of a child's socialization may play an important role in the development of empathy and guilt (see also Frick & Morris, 2004) and could have significance for intervention with youth with CU traits. Because these contextual factors seem to affect the continuity of CU traits, new interventions may need to focus on promoting quality parenting and prosocial environments in order to reduce the risk of these traits increasing over time.

USING CU TRAITS TO IDENTIFY SUBGROUPS OF ANTISOCIAL YOUTH

Numerous studies have supported the utility of CU traits in designating a distinct group of antisocial youth who show more severe aggression, conduct problems, and/or delinquent behavior (see Frick & Dickens, 2006, for a review). Studies of youth in juvenile forensic facilities (e.g., Caputo et al., 1999), outpatient mental health clinics (e.g., Christian et al., 1997), and school-based samples (Frick, Cornell, Barry, Bodin, & Dane, 2003; Frick, Stickle, Dandreaux, Farrell, & Kimonis, 2005), have indicated that youth with CU traits seem to show an especially severe, aggressive, and stable pattern of conduct problems. For example, clinic-referred youth who met criteria for a conduct problem diagnosis showed a more severe and varied pattern of conduct problems and were more likely to have contact with the police prior to adolescence if they were also high in CU traits (Christian et al., 1997). Similar results were found in a sample of nonreferred community youth in which children who showed both conduct problems and CU traits exhibited more aggression overall and were more likely to show proactive and instrumental patterns of aggression than were children with conduct problems but not CU traits (Frick, Cornell, Barry, et al., 2003).

Research on the predictive utility of CU traits (and psychopathic traits in general) has shown that psychopathic features predict subsequent delinquency, aggression, number of violent offenses, and a shorter length of time to violent reoffending in antisocial youth (Brandt, Kennedy, Patrick, & Curtin, 1997). In one of the only studies to test the predictive utility of CU traits in a nonreferred sample of children, Frick et al. (2005) reported that children with conduct problems who also showed CU traits exhibited the highest rates of conduct problems, self-reported delinquency, and police contacts across a 4-year period. In fact, the group with CU traits accounted for at least half of all of the police contacts reported in the sample across the last three waves of data collection. In contrast, children with conduct problems who were low on CU traits did not report higher rates of self-reported delinquency than did nonconduct problem children. In fact, the second highest rate of self-reported delinquency in the sample was found for the group of children who were high on CU traits but without conduct problems at the start of the study. This latter finding suggests that CU traits may designate a group of children at risk for delinquency, even in the absence of significant conduct problems.

In addition to showing a more severe, aggressive, and stable pattern of conduct problems, there is also evidence to suggest that the antisocial behavior of youth with CU traits may result from different causal processes compared with other antisocial youth. This is perhaps most clearly demonstrated by results from two recent twin studies in which children with conduct problems with and without CU traits were compared (Viding, Blair, Moffitt, & Plomin, 2005; Viding, Jones, Frick, Moffitt, & Plomin, 2008). Viding et al. (2005) collected teacher reports of antisocial behavior and CU traits for 3,687 twin pairs (average age 7 years) and divided the children with the highest levels of conduct problems into those who were high and low on CU traits. Results indicated that the heritability estimate for the group high on both conduct problems and CU traits (.81) was substantially higher than that for the group low on

CU traits (.30). Using a subsample of same-sex twin pairs ($n = 1,865$) from the original sample, Viding et al. (2008) replicated this finding when the youth were age 9 years, with the heritability estimate for the conduct problem/CU group (.75) being higher than that of the conduct problem only group (.53). It is important that the differences in heritability in the groups high and low on CU traits could not be attributed to greater severity of conduct problems (Viding et al., 2005) or greater levels of impulsivity and hyperactivity (Viding et al., 2008).

DISTINCT COGNITIVE AND EMOTIONAL CHARACTERISTICS OF YOUTH WITH CU TRAITS

Although heritability studies have suggested that genetic factors may play a significant role in the development of problem behavior for children with CU traits, other studies have examined specific cognitive and emotional correlates of CU traits in order to better determine how these factors may exert their influence (see Frick & White, 2008, for a review). One of the most consistent findings with regard to emotional correlates is that youth with CU traits show particular deficits in their ability to process emotional information. Researchers have measured these deficits by presenting emotional stimuli (e.g., words, pictures, facial expressions, vocal tones) to participants and assessing response times and emotion recognition as indices of emotional processing. For example, Loney, Frick, Clements, Ellis, and Kerlin (2003) found that antisocial adolescents who were high on CU traits showed reduced emotional reactivity to negative emotional words compared with emotionally neutral words. In contrast, youth who were high on impulsivity but not CU traits showed evidence of faster recognition times for negative emotional words, suggesting heightened emotional reactivity. In a similar study of nonreferred children, Kimonis, Frick, Fazekas, and Loney (2006) found that those children with conduct problems and CU traits showed reduced reactivity to pictures involving distressing content (e.g., a child in pain) using a dot-probe paradigm, whereas children high on a measure of conduct problems but low on CU traits showed a heightened level of reactivity to these stimuli.

Along with these deficits in emotional reactivity, youth with CU traits often show impairments in emotion recognition, particularly when asked to identify sad or fearful facial expressions (Blair & Coles, 2000; Dadds et al., 2006; Stevens, Charman, & Blair, 2001). For example, Blair and Coles (2000) presented 11- to 14-year-old school children with images of six different facial expressions (sadness, fearfulness, surprise, happiness, anger, and disgust) and asked the participants to name the expression being displayed. Overall, children with higher levels of CU traits showed reduced ability to recognize sad and fearful expressions but showed no impairments in the recognition of happiness, surprise, disgust, or anger. Similar results were found in a sample of boys (ages 9–15 years) attending a school for children with emotional and behavioral difficulties (Stevens et al., 2001). In this study, participants were grouped according to their psychopathy scores and were then asked to look at a photo album and identify the emotions of 24 different individuals. Results indicated that boys who scored high on a psychopathy measure were significantly less likely to accurately name the sad and fearful facial expressions than were those with low psychopathy scores. Interestingly, Dadds et al. (2006) found that this deficit is related to a failure on the part of youth with psychopathic traits to attend to the eye region of other people's faces, lending support to the idea that these emotion-recognition problems may result from a lack of attention to emotionally relevant aspects of the environment.

Research on emotion recognition in youth with psychopathic traits has also documented abnormalities in how these youth process vocal affect. In two experimental studies, boys identified as having general emotional and behavioral problems were divided into those with and without psychopathic traits and asked to categorize words (Blair, Budhani, Colledge, & Scott, 2005) or phrases (Stevens et al., 2001) on the basis of emotional intonation. Blair et al. (2005) found that boys with psychopathic traits made more errors in recognition than did comparison boys, specifically for fearful vocal intonation. In contrast, results from Stevens et al. (2001) indicated that boys high in psychopathic traits were significantly less able to recognize sad vocal tones but showed no differences in recognition of fearful, happy, and angry tones. Blair et al. (2005) suggested that this discrepancy in results may be due to differences in sample size or failure to control for IQ scores in the Stevens et al. (2001) study.

On the basis of their research, Blair, Colledge, Murray, and Mitchell (2001) and others (e.g., Kochanska, 1991) have proposed theories of moral socialization that focus on the experience of negative emotional arousal in response to distress from others or when faced with a forbidden activity. These theories suggest that children become conditioned to avoid certain harmful activities (e.g., causing distress in others) in order to reduce negative arousal and therefore learn to inhibit certain behaviors that may be morally questionable. Much of this work centers on explaining the link between fearful inhibitions and conscience development (see Frick & Morris, 2004, for a review) and suggests children with conduct problems who show low levels of fearful inhibitions and are impaired on measures of guilt, empathy, and conscience development may be those who show the most severe and persistent forms of antisocial behavior. These emotional deficits are consistent with those seen in children with CU traits and may represent a potential pathway by which these traits develop.

Several authors have suggested that the emotional impairments associated with CU traits in youth may reflect an underlying amygdala dysfunction (e.g., Blair, 2007). This has been largely based on indirect evidence from research showing that damage to the amygdala affects the processing of sad and fearful affect (Blair, Morris, Frith, Perrett, & Dolan, 1999). However, in one of the few direct tests of this link between the functioning of the amygdala and CU traits, Marsh et al. (2008) used functional MRI to assess amygdala activity while youth (ages 10–17 years) processed emotional facial expressions. Youth with CU traits showed reduced amygdala functioning while processing fearful facial expressions but not neutral or angry expressions. Also, youth with CU traits showed reduced connectivity between the amygdala and the ventromedial prefrontal cortex. Blair (2007) argued that such connectivity is necessary for moral decision making, in that the amygdala is responsible for stimulus-reinforcement learning (and thus learning which actions are harmful), whereas the ventromedial prefrontal cortex is responsible for using the information provided by the amygdala to select an appropriate moral response.

In addition to these emotional deficits, antisocial youth with CU traits also show a number of distinct cognitive characteristics (see Frick & White, 2008, for a review). In particular, children with CU traits and conduct problems show response perseveration on computer tasks in which a reward-oriented response set is primed (Frick, Cornell, Bodin, et al., 2003). That is, on tasks in which responding leads to a high rate of rewards initially but then leads to a high rate of punishment (e.g., loss of points) later in the task, children with conduct problems and CU traits continue to respond despite the increasing rate of punishment. It is important that this reward-oriented response set appears not only in computerized laboratory tasks but also in social situations. For example, in a sample of adjudicated adolescents, CU traits were related to a tendency to emphasize the positive aspects (e.g., obtaining rewards, gaining dominance) of solving peer conflicts with aggression and to deemphasize the negative aspects (e.g., getting punished; Pardini, Lochman, & Frick, 2003).

Overall, research on the emotional and cognitive characteristics of youth with CU traits has suggested that they exhibit impairments in several areas, including emotional reactivity, emotion recognition, and moral/emotional socialization. Youth with the low levels of guilt and empathy characteristic of psychopathy seem to have particular difficulty in recognizing and responding to others' distress and thus may not have the capacity to inhibit behaviors that cause such distress. These emotional impairments may be associated with a lack of connectivity between brain areas that regulate the recognition of distress signals and moral decision making (Blair, 2007). Such deficits, when paired with the cognitive tendency to focus on reward to the exclusion of punishment, have important implications as to the severity of youths' antisocial behavior.

AGGRESSIVE SUBTYPES, ANTISOCIAL BEHAVIOR, AND YOUTH DEVELOPMENT

Examining the type of aggressive behavior that children and adolescents engage in also has important implications for grouping antisocial youth (Frick & Marsee, 2006; Muñoz, Frick, Kimonis, & Aucoin, 2008). The distinction between youth with aggressive and nonaggressive forms of antisocial behavior is important in that aggression in children is often quite stable across the life-span (Huesmann, Eron, Lefkowitz, & Walder, 1984) and is very difficult to treat (Quay, 1987). Additionally, different types of aggressive behavior may develop differently and may require unique intervention strategies, especially as certain subtypes have unique cognitive and emotional correlates (Marsee & Frick, 2007; Muñoz et al., 2008).

The Reactive–Proactive Aggression Distinction

Aggression is generally considered to be multidimensional, and one distinction frequently examined in research is between reactive and proactive aggression (Dodge & Coie, 1987). Reactive aggression is defined as aggression that occurs as an angry response to a perceived provocation or threat (e.g., Berkowitz, 1993). Aggressive acts of this type often occur in the context of high emotional arousal, such as in an argument or fight, and they are typically unplanned. In contrast, proactive aggression, also referred to as instrumental or premeditated aggression, is generally defined as aggression that is unprovoked and involves planning and forethought. Most important, however, this form of aggression is often used for some sort of instrumental gain, such as to obtain goods or services, to obtain dominance over others, or to enhance one's social status (Dodge & Pettit, 2003).

Because of the high level of overlap between reactive and proactive aggression (see Card & Little, 2006), there has been some discussion of whether these subtypes are unique enough to provide useful scientific and clinical information (Bushman & Anderson, 2001). Two recent meta-analyses provide evidence for the substantial correlation among reactive and proactive aggression, both finding similar effect sizes ($r = .68$, Card & Little, 2006; $r = .64$, Polman, Orobio de Castro, Koops, van Boxtel, & Merk, 2007). Although these large correlations suggest that a significant number of aggressive children show both types of aggression, research has indicated that there is some asymmetry in the high degree of association between the two types of aggression. Specifically, there seems to be a significant number of children who only show reactive forms of aggression, whereas most children who show high levels of proactive aggression also show high rates of reactive aggression (Brown, Atkins, Osborne, & Milnamow, 1996). Therefore, there appears to be a group of highly aggressive children who show both types of aggressive behavior and another group of children who are less aggressive overall and who show only reactive types of aggression (Frick, Cornell, Barry, et al., 2003). Despite the significant overlap, however, factor analyses have consistently identified separate dimensions of aggressive behavior related to these two categories in samples of children and adolescents (e.g., Brown et al., 1996; Poulin & Boivin, 2000), leading researchers to conclude that they are distinct and useful behavioral subtypes (Card & Little, 2006; Polman et al., 2007).

Unique Cognitive and Emotional Correlates of Reactive and Proactive Aggression in Youth

The utility of the reactive–proactive distinction becomes especially clear when considering the growing evidence of distinct characteristics between youth in these aggressive subgroups. In terms of later problem behavior, youth who show proactive aggression are at higher risk for delinquency and alcohol abuse in adolescence, as well as criminality in adulthood (Vitaro, Brendgen, & Tremblay, 2002). However, meta-analytic results indicated that youth who exhibit reactive aggression (controlling for proactive aggression) also show high rates of delinquency and low rates of prosocial behavior (Card & Little, 2006). When considering social adjustment, findings indicate that reactively aggressive children show greater school adjustment problems, higher rates of peer rejection, and more peer victimization than proactively aggressive children (Dodge, Lochman, Harnish, Bates, & Pettit, 1997). These social problems may be related to deficits in social cognition that have been linked to reactive aggression, such as a tendency to attribute hostile intent to ambiguous provocations by peers and difficulty developing nonaggressive solutions to problems in social encounters (Crick & Dodge, 1996). In contrast, children who show proactive aggression are less rejected and victimized, have more friends, and are often perceived as leaders in social groups (Poulin & Boivin, 2000). However, proactively aggressive children overestimate the possible positive consequences of their aggressive behavior (e.g., the likelihood that it will produce tangible rewards and reduce adverse treatment from others) and are less likely to believe that they will be punished because of their behavior (Dodge et al., 1997). These findings are similar to findings for youth with CU traits, who show a reward-oriented response set (Frick, Cornell, Bodin, et al., 2003) and a tendency to emphasize the positive aspects of using aggression while ignoring the negative aspects (Pardini et al., 2003).

In addition to differences in antisocial behavior and social adjustment, the two patterns of aggressive behavior have been related to distinct emotional correlates. Evidence exists for a number of unique characteristics among youth who display reactive rather than proactive types of aggression, especially with regard to anger, emotional regulation, or emotional reactivity (Marsee & Frick, 2007; McAuliffe, Hubbard, Rubin, Morrow, & Dearing, 2006). For example, Marsee and Frick (2007) examined the differential correlates of reactive and proactive aggression in detained adolescent girls and found that self-reported reactive aggression was uniquely associated with measures of poorly regulated emotion and anger to perceived provocation after controlling for the variance accounted for by proactive aggression.

Other studies have documented differences in the expression of anger between reactively and proactively aggressive children that may reflect differences in their ability to regulate angry emotion (e.g., Hubbard et al., 2002; McAuliffe et al., 2006). These studies have shown that second-grade children's reactive (but not proactive) aggression is associated with observed angry nonverbal behavior (Hubbard et al., 2002) as well as with teacher, self-, and peer reports of expressions of anger (i.e., children's tendency to display overtly angry expressions; McAuliffe et al., 2006). Research has also shown that children who exhibit reactive aggression (as compared with proactive aggression only or no aggression) at ages 10 to 12 years are also those who are rated by their mothers as temperamentally more inattentive and reactive to aversive stimuli at age 6 years (Vitaro et al., 2002), which is in line with the theory that these temperamental processes may be related to emotional regulation abilities (see Frick & Morris, 2004).

In contrast, children who are high on proactive aggression often do not show these problems in emotional regulation (Dodge et al., 1997; Vitaro et al., 2002) and instead sometimes show reduced levels of emotional reactivity. For example, Pitts (1997) reported on a group of 103 boys (Grades 3–6) who were placed into three groups: nonaggressive ($n = 38$), reactive aggressive ($n = 19$), and reactive–proactive aggressive ($n = 38$). Both groups of aggressive children exhibited lower rates of resting heart rate than did the nonaggressive group. However, in response to a simulated provocation from peers, the heart rate of the reactive group increased significantly compared with control children, whereas the heart rate of the reactive–proactive group remained low. These results are consistent with findings from Muñoz et al. (2008), who found that detained boys high in reactive (but not proactive) aggression showed increased retaliatory aggressive responding to fictitious peers at low levels of provocation during a computer task.

In addition to variations in the regulation of angry emotion, differences have also been found in the display of positive emotions between reactively and proactively aggressive youth. Arsenio, Gold, and Adams (2004) compared 50 adolescents who met *Diagnostic and Statistical Manual of Mental Disorders* (4th ed.; American Psychiatric Association, 1994) criteria for either oppositional defiant disorder or conduct disorder with 50 comparison adolescents in order to assess their emotional expectations following aggressive situations.

Participants were presented with hypothetical vignettes in which they were asked to imagine committing an aggressive act resulting in a desired outcome (e.g., stealing a wanted item from a school locker). Results indicated that adolescents with conduct problems expected to feel happier following such acts of proactive aggression, even after controlling for their level of reactive aggression. These results support the contention that, along with negative emotions such as anger, youth's positive emotions also play an important role in their aggressive behavior (Arsenio, 2006).

A few studies also provide a link between proactive forms of aggression and CU traits in youth. For example, violent sex offenders, who tend to show more instrumental and premeditated violence, had higher rates of CU traits compared with other violent offenders and nonviolent juvenile offenders (Caputo et al., 1999). Similarly, in a sample of juvenile offenders incarcerated in adult prison, offenders who showed more severe, repeated, instrumental, and sadistic violence against their victims scored higher on a self-report measure of CU traits (Kruh, Frick, & Clements, 2005). Finally, in a nonreferred community sample of children, youth with conduct problems and CU traits exhibited more aggression overall, and more proactive aggression specifically, than did other children with conduct problems (Frick, Cornell, Bodin, et al., 2003).

This research demonstrating the association between CU traits and proactive aggression raises the question as to whether the distinct emotional and cognitive characteristics are more strongly related to the presence of CU traits or to the pattern of aggressive behavior. Muñoz et al. (2008) provided results suggesting that it may be the former, at least for measures of emotional reactivity. That is, in detained adolescent boys, those who showed high levels of proactive aggression showed reduced emotional reactivity to low levels of provocation but only if they were also high on CU traits.

The Relational–Physical Aggression Distinction

The reactive and proactive subtypes of aggressive behavior are generally defined in terms of the function that the aggression serves (e.g., as either an angry response to provocation or to reach a goal). However, much research has also centered on the forms that aggressive behavior takes, regardless of its function. Two major forms that have received attention in the clinical and developmental literature are physical and relational aggression (Crick & Grotpeter, 1995). Physical and relational forms of aggression can be descriptively distinguished by their method of harm and the goals they serve. Physical aggression harms others by damaging their physical well-being and includes physically and verbally aggressive behaviors such as hitting, pushing, and threatening (Coie & Dodge, 1998). In contrast, relational aggression harms others by damaging social relationships, friendships, or feelings of inclusion in the peer group (Crick, Ostrov, & Kawabata, 2007). Relational aggression consists of behaviors such as gossiping about others, excluding target children from a group, spreading rumors, or telling others not to be friends with a target child (Crick & Grotpeter, 1995). Relational aggression may be manifested both directly (e.g., withdrawing friendship) or covertly (e.g., spreading rumors), but regardless of the means, the underlying goal of such behavior is to harm another person's social relationships or social standing.

Physical and relational aggression have been found to be moderately correlated in past research, suggesting that they represent distinct yet related constructs. Although positive correlations (rs ranging from approximately .50 to .70) have been obtained in both normative and clinical samples (e.g., Crick, 1996; Moretti, Holland, & McKay, 2001), factor analyses of teacher (Crick, 1996), self- (Prinstein, Boergers, & Vernberg, 2001), and peer ratings (Crick & Grotpeter, 1995) have provided evidence for the distinctiveness of relational and physical aggression. Although results are mixed with regard to gender differences in overall rates of relational aggression (see Crick et al., 2007, for a review), many studies have found that relational aggression predicts social-psychological maladjustment above and beyond physical aggression consistently for girls but less consistently for boys (e.g., Crick & Grotpeter, 1995; Prinstein et al., 2001).

Unique Correlates of Relational and Physical Aggression in Youth

Overall, findings indicate that relational aggression is associated with social and psychological problems such as peer rejection (Crick, 1996), depression and anxiety (Marsee, Weems, & Taylor, 2008), and low self-esteem (Prinstein et al., 2001). Studies have also shown that similar to physically aggressive children, relationally aggressive children exhibit social-cognitive deficits that may cause them to respond to social situations with inappropriate aggression, thus increasing the likelihood of rejection by peers and other adjustment problems (Marsee et al., 2008).

In addition to these social-psychological correlates, relational aggression has also been found to be associated with a variety of more serious behavior problems and psychopathology, especially for girls. For example, Prinstein et al. (2001) found that self-reported relational aggression was significantly associated with conduct disorder and oppositional defiant disorder symptoms in adolescent girls, even after controlling for physical aggression. However, relational aggression was not associated with externalizing behavior for boys in this study. Further, Zalecki and Hinshaw (2004) found that girls who met criteria for a diagnosis of attention-deficit/hyperactivity disorder were rated by parents and teachers as significantly more relationally aggressive than comparison girls. Finally, Moretti et al. (2001) found that relational aggression was significantly correlated with serious violent behavior for girls but not for boys.

Research shows that relational aggression is also associated with serious personality pathology in girls and women. Werner and Crick (1999) found that peer-reported relational aggression was significantly associated with both borderline and antisocial personality disorder features in college women. Results of a similar study indicated that relational aggression was associated with borderline personality features in emerging adults, even after controlling for physical aggression (Ostrov & Houston, 2008). Crick, Murray-Close, and Woods (2005) obtained comparable results in a sample of fourth through sixth graders, finding that teacher-reported relational aggression was significantly associated with borderline personality features after controlling for physical aggression. Finally, a recent study of incarcerated adolescent girls found an association between borderline, histrionic, and narcissistic personality traits and self-reported relational aggression (Burnette, South, & Reppucci, 2007).

Similar to results for physical aggression, several studies have also found a link between relational aggression and CU traits in emerging adults and youth. Findings suggest that relational aggression in emerging adults is more associated with CU traits for women than for men (Miller & Lynam, 2003), especially for the proactive forms of relational aggression (Ostrov & Houston, 2008). Studies with younger samples have also supported this association. For example, Marsee and Frick (2007) found that CU traits were uniquely associated with proactive relational aggression in a sample of detained adolescent girls, even after controlling for physical aggression. Further, a study of 10- to 15-year-old nonreferred children found that teacher-reported relational aggression was associated with CU traits for girls but not for boys (Marsee, Silverthorn, & Frick, 2005). The results from these studies supported the idea that relational aggression is an important predictor of social-psychological adjustment, psychopathology, and personality disorder features, especially for girls and women.

CONCLUSION AND IMPLICATIONS FOR ASSESSMENT AND INTERVENTION

This chapter reviews two important lines of research relevant to the identification of subgroups of antisocial youth that differ in terms of the type, severity, and chronicity of their antisocial behavior, as well as in the causal processes presumed to underlie such behavior. In particular, CU traits seem to designate a distinct subgroup of antisocial youth and could be quite helpful in designing interventions and advancing causal models of antisocial and aggressive behavior. Specifically, CU traits show stability across childhood and adolescence and are associated with a more severe pattern of aggression and delinquency. Furthermore, youth with CU traits show a number of distinct emotional, cognitive, and personality characteristics that may have important implications for understanding distinct causes of their antisocial behavior and for designing intervention and prevention programs (Frick, 2006).

Research reviewed in this chapter also supports the need to consider aggressive subtypes when attempting to understand distinct subgroups of antisocial youth. Consideration of the reactive and proactive subtypes of aggression is critical in that they seem to represent distinct pathways to problem behavior, which may require drastically different treatment approaches (Frick & Morris, 2004). For example, interventions for youth who use reactive aggression often focus on developing better emotion regulation skills and may consist of strategies such as helping youth control aggressive responses when angry (Larson & Lochman, 2003). In contrast, youth who use proactive aggression may require a different treatment focus that addresses either their perceptions of the usefulness of aggression for obtaining social goals and/or their deficits in empathic concern toward others (Frick, 2006). Children who use both types of aggression typically show cognitive and emotional correlates consistent with children who only use proactive aggression (Pardini et al., 2003) and therefore might benefit most from the latter type of intervention.

For both reactive and proactive treatment approaches, however, most past interventions have focused largely on reducing physical aggression. Recent research has suggested that these programs need to be broadened to target relational forms of aggression, especially when intervening with antisocial girls (Moretti et al., 2001). A focus on relational aggression may allow for more prevention-centered efforts, given findings that relational aggression may precede more serious delinquent and aggressive behavior in girls (Moretti et al., 2001). Thus, attention to relational aggression, as well as reactive, proactive, and physical forms of aggression, may be important in the design and implementation of individualized approaches to treatment that consider both emotional and cognitive differences, as well as gender differences, in the manifestation of aggressive behavior.

REFERENCES

American Psychiatric Association. (1994). *The diagnostic and statistical manual of mental disorders* (4th ed.). Washington, DC: Author.

Arsenio, W. F. (2006). Happy victimization: Emotion dysregulation in the context of instrumental, proactive aggression. In D. K. Snyder, J. A. Simpson, & J. N. Hughes (Eds.), *Emotion regulation in couples and families: Pathways to dysfunction and health* (pp. 101–121). Washington, DC: American Psychological Association.

Arsenio, W. F., Gold, J., & Adams, E. (2004). Adolescents' emotion expectancies regarding aggressive and nonaggressive events: Connections with behavior problems. *Journal of Experimental Child Psychology, 89,* 338–355. Medline doi:10.1016/j.jecp.2004.08.001

Berkowitz, L. (1993). *Aggression: Its causes, consequences, and control.* New York, NY: Academic Press.

Blair, R. J. R. (2007). The amygdala and ventromedial prefrontal cortex in morality and psychopathy. *Trends in Cognitive Sciences, 11,* 387–392. Medline doi:10.1016/j.tics.2007.07.003

Blair, R. J. R., Budhani, S., Colledge, E., & Scott, S. (2005). Deafness to fear in boys with psychopathic tendencies. *Journal of Child Psychology and Psychiatry, and Allied Disciplines, 46,* 327–336. Medline doi:10.1111/j.1469-7610.2004.00356.x

Blair, R. J. R., & Coles, M. (2000). Expression recognition and behavioural problems in early adolescence. *Cognitive Development, 15,* 421–434. doi:10.1016/S0885-2014(01)00039-9

Blair, R. J. R., Colledge, E., Murray, L., & Mitchell, D. G. V. (2001). A selective impairment in the processing of sad and fearful expressions in children with psychopathic tendencies. *Journal of Abnormal Child Psychology, 29,* 491–498.

Blair, R. J. R., Morris, J. S., Frith, C. D., Perrett, D. I., & Dolan, R. (1999). Dissociable neural responses to facial expressions of sadness and anger. *Brain, 122,* 883–893. Medline doi:10.1093/brain/122.5.883

Brandt, J. R., Kennedy, W. A., Patrick, C. J., & Curtin, J. J. (1997). Assessment of psychopathy in a population of incarcerated adolescent offenders. *Psychological Assessment, 9,* 429–435. doi:10.1037/1040-3590.9.4.429

Brown, K., Atkins, M. S., Osborne, M. L., & Milnamow, M. (1996). A revised teacher rating scale for reactive and proactive aggression. *Journal of Abnormal Child Psychology, 24,* 473–480. Medline doi:10.1007/BF01441569

Burnette, M. L., South, S. C., & Reppucci, N. D. (2007). Cluster B personality pathology in incarcerated girls: Structure, comorbidity, and aggression. *Journal of Personality Disorders, 21,* 262–272. Medline doi:10.1521/pedi.2007.21.3.262

Bushman, B. J., & Anderson, C. A. (2001). Is it time to pull the plug on the hostile versus instrumental dichotomy? *Psychological Review, 108,* 273–279. Medline doi:10.1037/0033-295X.108.1.273

Caputo, A. A., Frick, P. J., & Brodsky, S. L. (1999). Family violence and juvenile sex offending: Potential mediating roles of psychopathic traits and negative attitudes toward women. *Criminal Justice and Behavior, 26,* 338–356. doi:10.1177/0093854899026003004

Card, N. A., & Little, T. D. (2006). Proactive and reactive aggression in childhood and adolescence: A meta-analysis of differential relations with psychosocial adjustment. *International Journal of Behavioral Development, 30,* 466–480. doi:10.1177/0165025406071904

Christian, R. E., Frick, P. J., Hill, N. L., Tyler, L., & Frazer, D. R. (1997). Psychopathy and conduct problems in children: II. Implications for subtyping children with conduct problems. *Journal of the American Academy of Child and Adolescent Psychiatry, 36,* 233–241.

Cleckley, H. (1976). *The mask of sanity* (5th ed.). St. Louis, MO: Mosby.

Coie, J. D., & Dodge, K. A. (1998). Aggression and antisocial behavior. In W. Damon & N. Eisenberg (Eds.), *Handbook of child psychology: Social, emotional, and personality development* (pp. 779–862). Toronto, Canada: Wiley.

Cooke, D. J., Michie, C., & Hart, S. (2006). Facets of clinical psychopathy: Toward clearer measurement. In C. J. Patrick (Ed.), *Handbook of psychopathy* (pp. 91–106). New York, NY: Guilford Press.

Crick, N. R. (1996). The role of overt aggression, relational aggression, and prosocial behavior in the prediction of children's future social adjustment. *Child Development, 67,* 2317–2327. Medline doi:10.2307/1131625

Crick, N. R., & Dodge, K. A. (1996). Social information-processing mechanisms in reactive and proactive aggression. *Child Development, 67,* 993–1002. Medline doi:10.2307/1131875

Crick, N. R., & Grotpeter, J. K. (1995). Relational aggression, gender, and social-psychological adjustment. *Child Development, 66,* 710–722. Medline doi:10.2307/1131945

Crick, N. R., Murray-Close, D., & Woods, K. (2005). Borderline personality features in childhood: A short-term longitudinal study. *Development and Psychopathology, 17,* 1051–1070. Medline doi:10.1017/S0954579405050492

Crick, N. R., Ostrov, J. M., & Kawabata, Y. (2007). Relational aggression and gender: An overview. In D. J. Flannery, A. T. Vazsonyi, & I. D. Waldman (Eds.), *The Cambridge handbook of violent behavior and aggression* (pp. 245–259). New York, NY: Cambridge University Press.

Dadds, M. R., Perry, Y., Hawes, D. J., Merz, S., Riddell, A. C., Haines, D. J., . . . Abeygunawardane, A. I. (2006). Attention to the eyes and fear-recognition deficits in child psychopathy. *The British Journal of Psychiatry, 189,* 280–281. Medline doi:10.1192/bjp.bp.105.018150

Dodge, K. A., & Coie, J. D. (1987). Social-information-processing factors in reactive and proactive aggression in children's peer groups. *Journal of Personality and Social Psychology, 53,* 1146–1158. Medline doi:10.1037/0022-3514.53.6.1146

Dodge, K. A., Lochman, J. E., Harnish, J. D., Bates, J. E., & Pettit, G. S. (1997). Reactive and proactive aggression in school children and psychiatrically impaired chronically assaultive youth. *Journal of Abnormal Psychology, 106,* 37–51. Medline doi:10.1037/0021-843X.106.1.37

Dodge, K. A., & Pettit, G. S. (2003). A biopsychosocial model of the development of chronic conduct problems in adolescence. *Developmental Psychology, 39,* 349–371. Medline doi:10.1037/0012-1649.39.2.349

Frick, P. J. (2006). Developmental pathways to conduct disorder. *Child Psychiatric Clinics of North America, 15,* 311–332. doi:10.1016/j.chc.2005.11.003

Frick, P. J., Bodin, S. D., & Barry, C. T. (2000). Psychopathic traits and conduct problems in community and clinic-referred samples of children: Further development of the Psychopathy Screening Device. *Psychological Assessment, 12,* 382–393. Medline doi:10.1037/1040-3590.12.4.382

Frick, P. J., Cornell, A. H., Barry, C. T., Bodin, S. D., & Dane, H. A. (2003). Callous-unemotional traits and conduct problems in the prediction of conduct problem severity, aggression, and self-report of delinquency. *Journal of Abnormal Child Psychology, 31,* 457–470. Medline doi:10.1023/A:1023899703866

Frick, P. J., Cornell, A. H., Bodin, S. D., Dane, H. A., Barry, C. T., & Loney, B. R. (2003). Callous-unemotional traits and developmental pathways to severe conduct problems. *Developmental Psychology, 39,* 246–260. Medline doi:10.1037/0012-1649.39.2.246

Frick, P. J., & Dickens, C. (2006). Current perspectives on conduct disorder. *Current Psychiatry Reports, 8,* 59–72. Medline doi:10.1007/s11920-006-0082-3

Frick, P. J., Kimonis, E. R., Dandreaux, D. M., & Farrell, J. M. (2003). The four-year stability of psychopathic traits in non-referred youth. *Behavioral Sciences & the Law, 21,* 713–736. Medline doi:10.1002/bsl.568

Frick, P. J., & Marsee, M. A. (2006). Psychopathy and developmental pathways to antisocial behavior in youth. In C. J. Patrick (Ed.), *Handbook of psychopathy* (pp. 355–374). New York: Guilford Press.

Frick, P. J., & Morris, A. S. (2004). Temperament and developmental pathways to conduct problems. *Journal of Clinical Child and Adolescent Psychology, 33,* 54–68. Medline doi:10.1207/S15374424JCCP3301_6

Frick, P. J., Stickle, T. R., Dandreaux, D. M., Farrell, J. M., & Kimonis, E. R. (2005). Callous-unemotional traits in predicting the severity and stability of conduct problems and delinquency. *Journal of Abnormal Child Psychology, 33,* 471–487. Medline doi:10.1007/s10648-005-5728-9

Frick, P. J., & White, S. F. (2008). Research review: The importance of callous-unemotional traits for developmental models of aggressive and antisocial behavior. *Journal of Child Psychology and Psychiatry, and Allied Disciplines, 49,* 359–375. Medline doi:10.1111/j.1469-7610.2007.01862.x

Gendreau, P., Goggin, C., & Smith, P. (2002). Is the PCL-R really the "unparalleled" measure of offender risk? A lesson in knowledge accumulation. *Criminal Justice and Behavior, 29,* 397–426. doi:10.1177/0093854802029004004

Hubbard, J. A., Smithmyer, C. M., Ramsden, S. R., Parker, E. H., Flanagan, K. D., Dearing, K. F., . . . Simons, R. F. (2002). Observational, physiological, and self-report measures of children's anger: Relations to reactive versus proactive aggression. *Child Development, 73,* 1101–1118. Medline doi:10.1111/1467-8624.00460

Huesmann, L. R., Eron, L. D., Lefkowitz, M. M., & Walder, L. O. (1984). Stability of aggression over time and generations. *Developmental Psychology, 20,* 1120–1134. doi:10.1037/0012-1649.20.6.1120

Kimonis, E. R., Frick, P. J., Fazekas, H., & Loney, B. R. (2006). Psychopathy, aggression, and the processing of emotional stimuli in non-referred girls and boys. *Behavioral Sciences & the Law, 24,* 21–37. Medline doi:10.1002/bsl.668

Kochanska, G. (1991). Socialization and temperament in the development of guilt and conscience. *Child Development, 62,* 1379–1392. Medline doi:10.2307/1130813

Kruh, I. P., Frick, P. J., & Clements, C. B. (2005). Historical and personality correlates to the violence patterns of juveniles tried as adults. *Criminal Justice and Behavior, 32,* 69–96. doi:10.1177/0093854804270629

Larson, J., & Lochman, J. E. (2003). *Helping schoolchildren cope with anger.* New York, NY: Guilford Press.

Loney, B. R., Frick, P. J., Clements, C. B., Ellis, M. L., & Kerlin, K. (2003). Callous-unemotional traits, impulsivity, and emotional processing in antisocial adolescents. *Journal of Clinical Child and Adolescent Psychology, 32,* 66–80.

Lynam, D. R., Caspi, A., Moffitt, T. E., Loeber, R., & Stouthamer-Loeber, M. (2007). Longitudinal evidence that psychopathy scores in early adolescence predict adult psychopathy. *Journal of Abnormal Psychology, 116,* 155–165. Medline doi:10.1037/0021-843X.116.1.155

Marsee, M. A., & Frick, P. J. (2007). Exploring the distinction between reactive and proactive aggression in sample of detained girls. *Journal of Abnormal Child Psychology, 35,* 969–981. Medline doi:10.1007/s10802-007-9147-y

Marsee, M. A., Silverthorn, P., & Frick, P. J. (2005). The association of psychopathic traits with aggression and delinquency in non-referred boys and girls. *Behavioral Sciences & the Law, 23,* 803–817. Medline doi:10.1002/bsl.662

Marsee, M. A., Weems, C. F., & Taylor, L. K. (2008). Exploring the association between aggression and anxiety in youth: A look at aggressive subtypes, gender, and social cognition. *Journal of Child and Family Studies, 17,* 154–168. doi:10.1007/s10826-007-9154-1

Marsh, A. A., Finger, E. C., Mitchell, D. G. V., Reid, M. E., Sims, C., Kosson, D. S., . . . Blair, R. J. (2008). Reduced amygdala response to fearful expressions in children and adolescents with callous-unemotional traits and disruptive behavior disorders. *The American Journal of Psychiatry, 165,* 712–720. Medline doi:10.1176/appi.ajp.2007.07071145

McAuliffe, M. D., Hubbard, J. A., Rubin, R. M., Morrow, M. T., & Dearing, K. F. (2006). Reactive and proactive aggression: Stability of constructs and relations to correlates. *The Journal of Genetic Psychology, 167,* 365–382. doi:10.3200/GNTP.167.4.365-382

Miller, J. D., & Lynam, D. R. (2003). Psychopathy and the five-factor model of personality: A replication and extension. *Journal of Personality Assessment, 81,* 168–178. Medline doi:10.1207/S15327752JPA8102_08

Moffitt, T. E., & Caspi, A. (2001). Childhood predictors differentiate life-course persistent and adolescent-limited antisocial pathways among males and females. *Development and Psychopathology, 13,* 355–375. Medline doi:10.1017/S095-4579401002097

Moretti, M. M., Holland, R., & McKay, S. (2001). Self-other representations and relational and overt aggression in adolescent girls and boys. *Behavioral Sciences & the Law, 19,* 109–126. Medline doi:10.1002/bsl.429

Muñoz, L. C., & Frick, P. J. (2007). The reliability, stability, and predictive utility of the self-report version of the Antisocial Process Screening Device. *Scandinavian*

Journal of Psychology, 48, 299–312. Medline doi:10.1111/j.1467-9450.2007.00560.x

Muñoz, L. C., Frick, P. J., Kimonis, E. R., & Aucoin, K. J. (2008). Types of aggression, responsiveness to provocation, and callous-unemotional traits in detained adolescents. Journal of Abnormal Child Psychology, 36, 15–28. Medline doi:10.1007/s10802-007-9137-0

Neumann, C. S., Kosson, D. S., Forth, A. E., & Hare, R. D. (2006). Factor structure of the Hare Psychopathy Checklist: Youth Version (PCL-YV) in incarcerated adolescents. Psychological Assessment, 18, 142–154. Medline doi:10.1037/1040-3590.18.2.142

Obradovic, J., Pardini, D. A., Long, J. D., & Loeber, R. (2007). Measuring interpersonal callousness in boys from childhood to adolescence: An examination of longitudinal invariance and temporal stability. Journal of Clinical Child and Adolescent Psychology, 36, 276–292.

Ostrov, J. M., & Houston, R. J. (2008). The utility of forms and functions of aggression in emerging adulthood: Association with personality disorder symptomatology. Journal of Youth and Adolescence, 37, 1147–1158. doi:10.1007/s10964-008-9289-4

Pardini, D. A., Lochman, J. E., & Frick, P. J. (2003). Callous/unemotional traits and social-cognitive processes in adjudicated youth. Journal of the American Academy of Child and Adolescent Psychiatry, 42, 364–371. Medline doi:10.1097/00004583-200303000-00018

Pitts, T. B. (1997). Reduced heart rate levels in aggressive children. In A. Raine, P. A. Brennan, D. P. Farrington, & S. A. Mednick (Eds.), Biosocial bases of violence (pp. 317–320). New York: Plenum.

Polman, H., Orobio de Castro, B., Koops, W., van Boxtel, H. W., & Merk, W. W. (2007). A meta-analysis of the distinction between reactive and proactive aggression in children and adolescents. Journal of Abnormal Child Psychology, 35, 522–535. Medline doi:10.1007/s10802-007-9109-4

Poulin, F., & Boivin, M. (2000). Reactive and proactive aggression: Evidence of a two-factor model. Psychological Assessment, 12, 115–122. Medline doi:10.1037/1040-3590.12.2.115

Prinstein, M. J., Boergers, J., & Vernberg, E. M. (2001). Overt and relational aggression in adolescents: Social-psychological adjustment of aggressors and victims. Journal of Clinical Child Psychology, 30, 479–491. Medline doi:10.1207/S15374424JCCP3004_05

Quay, H. C. (1987). Patterns of delinquent behavior. In H. C. Quay (Ed.), Handbook of juvenile delinquency (pp. 118–138). New York, NY: Wiley.

Stevens, D., Charman, T., & Blair, R. J. R. (2001). Recognition of emotion in facial expressions and vocal tones in children with psychopathic tendencies. The Journal of Genetic Psychology, 16, 201–211.

Viding, E., Blair, R. J. R., Moffitt, T. E., & Plomin, R. (2005). Evidence for substantial genetic risk for psychopathy in 7-year-olds. Journal of Child Psychology and

Psychiatry, and Allied Disciplines, 46, 592–597. Medline doi:10.1111/j.1469-7610. 2004.00393.x

Viding, E., Jones, A. P., Frick, P. J., Moffitt, T. E., & Plomin, R. (2008). Heritability of antisocial behavior at 9: Do callous-unemotional traits matter? *Developmental Science, 11*, 17–22.

Vitaro, F., Brendgen, M., & Tremblay, R. E. (2002). Reactively and proactively aggressive children: Antecedent and subsequent characteristics. *Journal of Child Psychology and Psychiatry, and Allied Disciplines, 43*, 495–506. Medline doi:10.1111/1469-7610.00040

Werner, N. E., & Crick, N. R. (1999). Relational aggression and social-psychological adjustment in a college sample. *Journal of Abnormal Psychology, 108*, 615–623. Medline doi:10.1037/0021-843X.108.4.615

Zalecki, C. A., & Hinshaw, S. P. (2004). Overt and relational aggression in girls with attention deficit hyperactivity disorder. *Journal of Clinical Child and Adolescent Psychology, 33*, 125–137. Medline doi:10.1207/S15374424JCCP3301_12

8

EMOTIONS AND SOCIAL INFORMATION PROCESSING: IMPLICATIONS FOR UNDERSTANDING AGGRESSIVE (AND NONAGGRESSIVE) CHILDREN

ELIZABETH A. LEMERISE AND JENNIFER MAULDEN

Social information processing (SIP) models of social behavior were originally proposed to explain individual differences in social behaviors ranging from social competence to aggression (e.g., Crick & Dodge, 1994; Dodge, 1986). These models describe how information is processed in social situations as well as the related decision-making processes. As described by Crick and Dodge (1994), a given child brings to each social situation a "database" of past experiences, social knowledge, and biological predispositions; this database can influence any of the following steps of SIP. The steps of SIP are hypothesized to occur relatively rapidly, in parallel, and with numerous feedback loops. To illustrate, imagine that "Fred" is walking down a crowded hallway at school. Suddenly he is bumped from behind with enough force that he stumbles and falls. Fred must first encode the various internal and external cues associated with the situation (SIP Step 1) and make an interpretation of their meaning (SIP Step 2, attribution of intent—was this an accident or an intentional act?). In the third SIP step, Fred clarifies his goals for the situation; the goal(s) chosen here exert a selective influence on the subsequent SIP Steps 4 to 6 of response generation, evaluation, and decision. For example, a revenge goal makes quite different potential responses accessible than do goals to maintain friendship or to avoid trouble. Possible responses are evaluated in terms of their likely consequences, and finally, a response is chosen and enacted.

Research testing the SIP model has shown that the model explains individual differences in aggression, including differences in various subtypes of aggression (e.g., Bailey & Ostrov, 2008; Dodge, Lochman, Harnish, Bates, & Pettit, 1997; Fontaine, 2008; Pettit, Polaha, & Mize, 2001). Although the model has primarily been applied to the study of aggressive children and adolescents, it also has been useful in studying depression (e.g., Quiggle, Garber, Panak, & Dodge, 1992), prosocial behavior (Nelson & Crick, 1999), and shy/withdrawn behavior (Burgess, Wojslawowicz, Rubin, Rose-Krasnor, & Booth-LaForce, 2006).

Despite the SIP model's clear utility, it has been criticized for failing to fully consider emotion-related processes (e.g., Gottman, 1986). In response to this criticism, Lemerise and Arsenio (2000) proposed a revised SIP model that integrated different kinds of emotion processes into the Crick and Dodge (1994) SIP model. Briefly, Lemerise and Arsenio argued that a variety of emotion-related processes can affect SIP, including temperamentally based differences in emotionality, emotion-regulation skills, affect-event links stored in memory, moods, briefly experienced emotions, emotion cues expressed by others, and the affective nature of the relationship that the "processor" has with the relevant peer(s). In this chapter, we review research that has tested hypotheses either derived from the Lemerise and Arsenio (2000) model or that is relevant to this model because a SIP-relevant emotion-related process was examined. This review is organized according to the methodological approach taken. Studies in which emotion-related processes are measured in conjunction with other SIP measures (e.g., correlational designs) are discussed first; studies in which some aspect of emotion was manipulated are reviewed subsequently.

EMOTIONALITY, EMOTION REGULATION, AND SIP

Lemerise and Arsenio (2000) proposed that poorly regulated emotionality may underlie the SIP processing errors and biases found in aggressive children. More specifically, Arsenio and Lemerise (2001) argued that poorly regulated, strong negative emotions (especially anger) may be an important contributor to the biases and distortions in early stage SIP that are associated with reactive aggression. Conversely, failures in empathy (i.e., not becoming emotionally aroused by another's plight) may enable proactive aggression or bullying (see also Chapters 7 and 10 this volume). In two different studies, Lengua and colleagues (Lengua & Long, 2002; Lengua, Sandler, West, Wolchik, & Curran, 1999) found that emotionality and self-regulation were important predictors of 8- to 12-year-old children's appraisals of threat and coping.

Children who were higher in negative emotionality were more likely to appraise situations as threatening, to use avoidant coping, and to have behavior or conduct problems. Children who were better regulated used more adaptive forms of coping and had fewer adjustment problems. Musher-Eizenman et al. (2004) reported for the same age group that poor control of anger was associated with beliefs that indirect and direct forms of aggression were appropriate when provoked. Such beliefs would be part of the database that is brought to bear in processing social information and would be particularly relevant in the response evaluation step of SIP.

In work that more explicitly examined the six SIP steps, Bauminger and Kimhi-Kind (2008) studied SIP, attachment security, and emotion regulation in fourth- to sixth-grade boys with and without learning disabilities (LD). For boys with and without LD, attachment security and emotion regulation were positively associated with more accurate encoding, benign attributions, positive social goals, and the generation and selection of competent responses to problems. Although non-LD boys were more likely to be securely attached and have better emotion regulation and more competent SIP, results showed that LD boys who were securely attached had better emotion regulation and more competent SIP (secure attachment and emotion regulation made independent contributions in explaining the variance in SIP even with LD status accounted for).

Finally, a study by Wilson (2003) offers some insight into how emotion regulation might impact SIP. In her study, groups of aggressive–rejected and nonaggressive–popular kindergarten and first-grade children were studied. A computer task was used to measure children's ability to shift attention from one affective event to another; this ability is considered to be an important component of emotion regulation (Eisenberg, Fabes, & Guthrie, 2000). Children also participated in an analogue peer-entry task; their latency to share was measured after experiencing failure in the peer-entry task. Aggressive–rejected children had more difficulty shifting attention from negative to positive events on the computer task and also exhibited longer latencies to share after entry failure as well as poorer behavior regulation in the analogue task.

Across these studies, negative emotionality and/or poor regulation of negative emotions were associated with biases toward perceiving situations as threatening, preferences for aggressive problem solving, and poorer adjustment. Interestingly, data from one study suggested that security of attachment and better emotion regulation reduce the risk for less competent SIP, even for children with LD (Bauminger & Kimhi-Kind, 2008). Finally, Wilson's (2003) results suggested that rejected–aggressive children's difficulties in shifting attention from negative to positive events may interfere with responding competently when situations are demanding or perceived as threatening. Overall, the results of these studies are consistent with predictions made by Lemerise and Arsenio (2000). However, there is a need for more research exploring the connections among emotionality, emotion regulation, and SIP.

EMOTION-RELATED ABILITIES AS CORRELATES OF SIP AND PREDICTORS OF AGGRESSION

A number of studies have measured the role of emotion-related processes by asking participants about their own and others' emotions in the context of SIP or other social cognitive tasks. Young children's difficulties with accurately recognizing emotions have been shown to be related to negative peer experiences and victimization in preschoolers (Garner & Lemerise, 2007) and in kindergartners and first graders (Miller et al., 2005). In first and second graders, multiple emotion processing deficits (emotion attribution accuracy, anger attribution bias, and failures in empathy) were associated with a higher risk for teacher-reported aggression (Schultz, Izard, & Bear, 2004). Anger perception biases made an independent contribution to the longitudinal prediction of aggression from the third to the fifth grade (Fine, Trentacosta, Izard, Mostow, & Campbell, 2004). Finally, for second, fourth, and sixth graders who were presented with hypothetical situations involving another person's emotionally laden experiences, children who dismissed others' emotions were rated by teachers as being higher in aggression (Bengtsson, 2003). In summary, both a failure to read emotion cues accurately and a bias to perceive anger enable aggression, as does a failure to empathize with others' emotions.

In a number of SIP studies, investigators have obtained self-reports of anger and other emotions in conjunction with the typical SIP measures. Across studies examining participants ranging in age from 7 to 8 years to adolescence and early adulthood, aggressive individuals reported experiencing more anger than did nonaggressive individuals (e.g., Arsenio, Gold, & Adams, 2004; Camodeca & Goosens, 2005; Camodeca, Goosens, Schuengel, & Terwogt, 2003; DiLiberto, Katz, Beauchamp, & Howells, 2002; Graham, Hudley, & Williams, 1992; de Castro, Merk, Koops, Veerman, & Bosch, 2005). Aggressive individuals also reported that they felt less able to control their anger than did their nonaggressive peers (DiLiberto et al., 2002; de Castro et al., 2005). When asked how they would regulate their emotions, aggressive individuals reported less adaptive emotion regulation strategies (Nas, de Castro, & Koops, 2005; Orobio de Castro et al., 2005). Aggressive individuals also made more hostile attributions of intent and generated more aggressive problem-solving responses (Camodeca & Goosens, 2005; Camodeca et al., 2003; DiLiberto et al., 2002; Graham et al., 1992; de Castro et al., 2005). Arsenio et al. (2004) found that, compared with normal controls, behaviorally disruptive adolescents expected to feel happier following acts of instrumental–proactive aggression, supporting the idea that expectancy of reward underlies proactive or bullying forms of aggression (Arsenio & Lemerise, 2001). Arsenio, Adams, and Gold (2009) similarly found proactive aggression to be associated with expectations of positive emotions for both provoked and unprovoked aggression, whereas reactive aggression was associated with hostile attributional biases and greater self-efficacy for enacting aggression.

Thus, across a number of studies, aggression has been associated with a variety of emotion-related processes. Aggressive children exhibit deficits in perceiving emotions accurately and in empathy, as well as a bias toward perceiving anger. Aggressive children and adolescents report experiencing more anger than do their nonaggressive peers, and they also report feeling less able to control their anger. These feelings of anger are associated with both hostile attributions of intent and hostile problem solving (see also Murphy & Eisenberg, 2002). Aggressive individuals also have expectancies that aggression will produce positive emotional outcomes for the self, and they are more likely to dismiss negative emotional outcomes for others. However, in all of these studies, the evidence is correlational. Although it seems reasonable to argue that emotion influences SIP on the basis of the evidence from these studies, it also is possible that the emotions themselves were the product of SIP. Thus, it is important to demonstrate that SIP is influenced by emotion-relevant processes in research designs in which emotion is manipulated. In the remaining sections, we review studies in which emotion is manipulated in the research design.

MANIPULATION OF EMOTION IN SIP STUDIES

Investigators have used a variety of techniques to manipulate some aspect of emotion in the context of SIP studies. Following, we review these studies, organized by the technique used to manipulate emotion.

Manipulation of Provocateurs' Emotions in Hypothetical Situation Methodology

Lemerise and Arsenio (2000) proposed that emotion cues in social situations were likely to influence SIP and that children who were rejected-aggressive were likely to be more affected by these emotion cues because of hypothesized difficulties in emotion regulation. In an early study, Keane and Parrish (1992) attempted to manipulate the emotion information provided to participants in a SIP task by randomly assigning popular and rejected fourth-grade children to conditions in which they were told that the provocateur in a videotaped ambiguous provocation was either happy or angry, or no information was provided. The actual video-taped stimulus, however, was neutral with respect to emotion cues. When children were told the provocateur was angry, there were no status group differences in attributions of intent, but when no information was provided and when children were told the provocateur was happy, rejected children had higher rates of hostile attributions than did popular children. Across conditions, rejected children had a high rate of hostile attributions, whereas popular children made more hostile attributions in the angry condition and more benign attributions in the happy condition. Keane and Parrish argued that the rejected children were less sensitive to the emotion information. However, it may have been that rejected children discounted the verbally provided information as it did not match the affectively neutral video-taped stimulus (Lemerise, Gregory, & Fredstrom, 2005).

In two different studies, Lemerise and colleagues (Lemerise, Fredstrom, Kelley, Bowersox, & Waford, 2006; Lemerise et al., 2005) used videotaped ambiguous provocation stimuli in which the affective displays of provocateurs were systematically manipulated (happy, angry, sad; order counterbalanced across stimulus versions). Thus, in these studies, the emotion cues were presented in a more ecologically valid way than in the Keane and Parrish (1992) study. Lemerise et al. (2005) studied first- to fourth-graders who varied in social adjustment (rejected–aggressive, rejected–nonaggressive, average–nonaggressive, popular–nonaggressive). Children were randomly assigned to be asked versus not asked about provocateurs' emotions; all children were asked to imagine that they were the victims in the provocation situations. Encoding of situational cues, attribution of intent, and problem-solving response decision were assessed with open-ended responses. When provocateurs were angry, children made more hostile attributions; asking about provocateurs' emotions produced lower rates of hostile attributions for happy and sad, but not angry, provocateurs. Children's open-ended problem-solving responses were rated for hostility/friendliness (e.g., Murphy & Eisenberg, 2002). Rejected–aggressive children who were not asked about provocateurs' emotions made problem-solving responses that were significantly less friendly (e.g., more hostile) than those of other children and significantly less friendly (more hostile) than those of rejected–aggressive children who were asked about provocateurs' emotions. Thus, asking about provocateurs' emotions was associated with more competent problem-solving for rejected-aggressive children, suggesting that under normal conditions, they may either not pay attention to or discount others' emotion cues.

In a second study, Lemerise et al. (2006) studied the goal clarification and response decision steps of SIP in a sample of first, third, and fifth graders using the same stimuli. The same social adjustment groups (rejected–aggressive, rejected–nonaggressive, average–nonaggressive, popular–nonaggressive) were compared. Children imagined that they were the victims of the provocations and were not asked about provocateurs' emotions. After viewing each video-taped vignette (two each of happy, angry, and sad, order counterbalanced across three versions), children were asked to rate the importance of six social goals (revenge, dominance, problem focus, remaining friends, avoid provocateur, avoid trouble) and provide an open-ended problem-solving response. When provocateurs were happy, there were few social adjustment group differences in SIP, but when provocateurs were angry or sad, rejected–aggressive children rated hostile/instrumental goals more positively, rated prosocial goals less positively, and made problem-solving responses that were less friendly than those of other children. Popular–nonaggressive children, on the other hand, showed no disruption of goals or problem solving across provocateur emotion conditions. In particular, they were successful in balancing other-oriented social relational goals (being friends) with the self-interested goals of solving the problem and avoiding trouble across provocateur emotion conditions. In contrast, when provocateurs were happy or angry, rejected–aggressive children rated the self-interested goals of solving the problem and avoiding trouble more positively than the social-relational goal of remaining friends with the provocateur. When provocateurs were angry or sad, rejected–aggressive children also made less friendly problem-solving responses than did other children, but when provocateurs were happy, rejected–aggressive children's problem-solving responses did not differ in friendliness from other groups.

Lemerise and Arsenio (2000) hypothesized that emotion cues in others could influence SIP, and that children who were rejected and/or aggressive would show more disruptions of SIP in response to these emotion cues. When information about provocateurs' emotions was provided verbally to participants (Keane & Parrish, 1992), results suggested that this information influenced the attributions of more competent children who made fewer hostile attributions when provocateurs were happy than when they were angry. In contrast, rejected children had high rates of hostile attributions regardless of the verbal information provided about emotions. However, when provocateur emotions were presented in the videotaped stimuli in a more ecologically valid way (Lemerise et al., 2006, 2005), results suggested that aggressive children's SIP was disrupted, especially in the context of negative emotion cues. Interestingly, in the context of positive emotions and when rejected–aggressive children were asked about provocateurs' emotions, their SIP was similar to that of non-aggressive children. These results lend support to interventions for aggressive children that focus on teaching children to recognize emotion in self and others and to learn ways to cope with one's own strong emotions (see Chapter 12, this volume).

Manipulating Emotion in the Social Information Processor: Situational Manipulations

Another approach to studying emotion and SIP has been to use structured laboratory situations to manipulate arousal in participants whose SIP is measured both before and after the arousal-eliciting event. For example, in Dodge and Somberg's (1987) classic study, under "relaxed" conditions, rejected–aggressive and adjusted–nonaggressive third- through fifth-grade boys' SIP did not differ. Boys then experienced a staged "threat" by overhearing a conversation (actually a tape recording) in which another boy did not want to play with them and threatened to hurt them. After hearing this threat, boys completed additional SIP tasks in which rejected–aggressive boys made more SIP errors of presumed hostility and hostile attributions than did adjusted–nonaggressive boys. In a different study, arousal was manipulated by having participants unjustly lose a computer game, with analogous results (de Castro, Slot, Bosch, Koops, & Veerman, 2003). In a study of adjusted– and rejected–aggressive first and second graders that used a more intense staged provocation, the SIP (attributions and social problem solving) of both adjusted and rejected–aggressive first and second graders was disrupted, especially when assessed immediately after the provocation (Vitaro, Pelletier, & Coutu, 1989). Similarly, both peer-rejected and accepted third graders made more hostile attributions after experiencing failure in a math problem-solving game; peer-rejected children made more aggressive problem-solving responses than did accepted children in three out of four conditions: failure–competitive, failure–cooperative, and success–cooperative versus success–competitive (Dorsch & Keane, 1994).

The situational manipulations reviewed previously have been shown to influence SIP, particularly in children who are rejected and/or aggressive. However, when participants were asked how "bothered" they were in response to the manipulation, there were no adjustment group differences in arousal as might be expected (Dodge & Somberg, 1987; de Castro et al., 2003; Vitaro et al., 1989), but these studies did not use very sensitive or "online" measures of arousal. In a study that used more sensitive measures of online arousal, Hubbard et al. (2002) assessed nonverbal behavior and physiological reactivity in the context of a manipulation in which second graders lost a board game to a confederate who obviously cheated. They found that children's reactive aggression was positively related to the nonverbal (but not facial) expression of anger and to physiological reactivity, both of which increased throughout the course of the game for those high in reactive aggression. Children who were low in reactive aggression displayed low and steady levels of both nonverbal expressions of anger and physiological reactivity throughout the game. These results suggested that some children are more reactive than others to the kinds of experimental manipulations reviewed here (see also Waschbusch et al., 2002).

An unresolved issue involves the nature of the negative arousal induced by situational manipulations. For example, in the case of losing a game unjustly or to a "cheater," anger, sadness, and/or disappointment are all likely emotional reactions. Overhearing a threat that is directed toward the self may make some children feel angry, but others may feel sad or fearful. This is an important point because the effects of different emotions on SIP may not be equivalent. Research with adults has demonstrated that the effects of induced anger and sadness on social cognitive judgments are quite different (e.g., Bodenhausen, Sheppard, & Kramer, 1994; Tiedens, 2001). Thus adjustment group differences reported in studies using situational manipulation methodology may be related to the fact that the situations used induced different emotions in children who varied in adjustment (Dorsch & Keane, 1994). One methodological answer to this problem involves using mood induction techniques (e.g., Masters & Furman, 1976) to induce specific discrete emotions.

Using Mood Induction Techniques to Manipulate Specific Emotions in the Information Processor

In a study by den Bak and Rose-Krasnor (1991), happy, angry, or neutral moods were induced in 90 fourth and fifth graders. Children then were presented with four provocation vignettes involving either peer entry or object acquisition issues and asked to generate possible responses to the problems. Results showed that both positive and negative mood inductions resulted in fewer strategies generated compared with the neutral condition. In addition, the neutral group generated and preferred more prosocial strategies than did the other two groups, and the angry group generated more irrelevant responses and more often selected appeals to authority as a preference. This study illustrated that the induction of a positive mood does not always have positive effects on problem solving; in cases like these, it hindered effective SIP, just as the negative mood did. However, in this study there were too few participants to evaluate whether individual differences in social competence were associated with differential effects of the mood induction.

More recently, Harper, Lemerise, and Caverly (in press) randomly assigned first, second, and third graders to receive either a happy, angry, or neutral mood induction. Then three ambiguous provocation stories, illustrated with line drawings, were presented, and children's response evaluations of competent, hostile, and passive responses (order counterbalanced across stimuli) to the provocations were assessed. Social relational consequences, instrumental consequences, and self-efficacy were evaluated for each response type, and children indicated their preference for a social relational versus an instrumental goal for each story.

Results showed that mood induction primarily affected children's goal selection. Children who received an angry mood induction selected significantly more instrumental goals (i.e., they were more interested in getting their way than in being friends with the peer) than did children who received a neutral mood induction. Harper et al. also compared the goal selection of children who were low accepted–aggressive ($n = 39$) with those who were high accepted–nonaggressive ($n = 68$). High accepted–nonaggressive children chose very few instrumental goals and did not differ in the number of instrumental goals chosen across mood induction conditions. In contrast, low accepted–aggressive children chose significantly more instrumental goals in the angry mood induction condition than in the happy mood induction condition and significantly more instrumental goals in the angry condition than did high accepted–nonaggressive children in the neutral condition.

Mood induction condition did not influence children's response evaluations, but their overall goal orientations did. Children were classified according to their predominant goal orientation (instrumental goal orientation = 2 or 3 instrumental goals chosen, $n = 204$; social relational goal orientation = 2 or 3 social relational goals chosen, $n = 276$). Goal orientation was unrelated to gender, grade, peer acceptance level, or aggression level, but it was significantly related to mood induction condition. Children who received an angry mood induction were more likely to have an instrumental goal orientation. The response evaluations of the two goal orientation groups were compared. Compared with children with a social relational goal orientation, children with an instrumental goal orientation rated nonhostile responses (i.e., competent and passive responses) to provocation less favorably and had greater self-efficacy for hostile responses. Thus, in this study, angry mood was associated with a preference for instrumental goals, and a predominant preference for instrumental goals was associated with a response evaluation style that would tend to enable aggressive responding to provocation.

To summarize, emotions in the social information processor and their influence on SIP have been studied with both situational manipulations to elicit negative arousal and, to a lesser extent, with mood induction techniques to elicit specific discrete emotions. Across the studies using situational manipulations, children who were rejected–aggressive showed disruptions of SIP, making more hostile attributions of intent and more aggressive problem-solving decisions when negatively aroused (Dodge & Somberg, 1987; Dorsch & Keane, 1994; de Castro et al., 2003; Vitaro et al., 1989). One difficulty with using situational manipulations is that it is not clear whether these situations induced different discrete emotions in rejected–aggressive children than in nonaggressive children. Mood induction techniques that induce specific discrete emotions can be used to address this problem.

In the two studies in which mood induction was used, later stages of SIP were studied, but attribution of intent was not examined. In one study, response generation was examined in fourth and fifth graders who received a happy, angry, or neutral mood induction; children who received the neutral mood induction generated more strategies and more prosocial strategies than did children receiving happy and angry mood inductions (den Bak & Rose-Krasnor, 1991). In the other study (Harper et al., in press), first through third graders' consequential reasoning (response evaluation step) and goal selection were studied. Children who received an angry mood induction selected more instrumental goals than did children who received a neutral mood induction. Moreover, when children who varied in social adjustment (low accepted–aggressive vs. well accepted–nonaggressive) were compared, results showed that more competent children selected few instrumental goals and did not vary in the goals selected across mood induction conditions, but low accepted–aggressive children selected more instrumental goals when they received an angry mood induction than when they received a happy mood induction. For the sample as a whole, selecting predominantly instrumental goals was associated with less favorable evaluations for nonhostile responses to provocation and higher self-efficacy for hostile responses. The results of Harper et al. (in press) suggested that children's goals exert a selective effect on the subsequent stages of SIP. It could be that the finding that neutral moods were associated with better response generation than were happy and angry moods (den Bak & Rose-Krasnor, 1991) reflects the selective effects of happy and angry moods on goal selection, compared with the neutral mood induction. Overall, the results of these two studies indicated that children's emotions do affect SIP, but there is a need for more research using mood induction across all the SIP steps. In particular, mood may be especially important in early stage SIP (encoding and interpretation of cues), but these SIP steps have yet to be studied with mood induction techniques.

Manipulation of the Information Processor's Affective Ties

Lemerise and Arsenio (2000) hypothesized that children may be more motivated to engage in reflective processing when provocateurs are liked peers than when they are disliked peers. Accordingly, another method utilized to study the effects of emotion on SIP has been the manipulation of the affective ties participants have with provocateurs. For example, Hymel (1986) investigated intent attributions in second, fifth, and tenth graders. Sociometric measures were utilized to determine the names of liked and disliked peers. Each participant was randomly assigned to either a like or dislike condition and either positive or negative behavior valence. Four vignettes were presented; the content of the stories varied on the basis of the experimental condition involved. For example, in the like–positive condition, a liked peer encouraged the child after he did poorly on a test, whereas in the like–negative condition, a liked peer teased the participant for doing poorly on a test. Results showed that explanations of peers' behaviors were related to the valence of the behavior and to the affective tie with the peer. When positive behaviors were performed by liked peers, participants were more likely to attribute the behaviors to stable causes than when the same behaviors were performed by disliked peers. On the other hand, when negative behaviors were performed by disliked peers, these behaviors were more likely to be attributed to stable causes, and greater responsibility was assigned to disliked peers than when the same negative behaviors were performed by liked peers.

Using a similar design, DeLawyer and Foster (1986) assessed liking ratings and problem-solving in 37 fifth graders. The names of peers who were liked, disliked, and neutral for each participant were determined with sociometric measures. Children were asked how they would feel in general and about the provocateur and what they would do in response to each of the scenarios. Results showed that participants gave higher liking ratings to liked peers than to disliked peers, neutral peers, and hypothetical peers. Children also predicted that they would like disliked peers less even after they behaved the same way as liked peers, and girls said they would feel worse when interacting with disliked peers. These results indicated that even when disliked peers exhibited positive behaviors, they continued to elicit negative responses.

More recently, Peets, Hodges, Kikas, and Salmivalli (2007) investigated attributions of intent and problem-solving responses in 137 randomly selected fourth graders from a pool of 442 who had completed social and behavioral reputation measures in third grade. When students were in fourth grade, a social cognitive interview was administered. Each child supplied the name of a friend, enemy, and neutral peer that fit given descriptions. The names of these peers were then inserted into ambiguous situations (one provocation and one rebuff) as provocateurs. Consistent with the studies reviewed above, children attributed less hostility to friends and more to enemies, predicted less hostile behavior in response to provocations toward friends than toward enemies or neutral peers, and predicted passive strategies more often toward friends than toward enemies. Interestingly, even after controlling for the reputation of the peer, results still showed that participants differentiated between friends and enemies. Beyond highlighting the general consensus of the literature that friendships and antipathies are relevant to SIP, the method utilized (i.e., asking children to identify peers who fit relationship descriptions before asking them to reason about scenarios involving said peers) also illustrates that this is an effective method of investigating the effects of affective ties on SIP.

Burgess et al. (2006) investigated intent attributions and response decisions in fifth and sixth graders. Children nominated two best friends and three good friends; children were only allowed to nominate same-gender friends in the same grade. Children also nominated others as fitting certain descriptions (i.e., this child stays by him- or herself). On the basis of these nominations, children were identified as either shy/withdrawn, aggressive, or control. All children with a mutual friendship were invited to the lab and given an Attributions and Coping Questionnaire. This measure assessed the participants' and their friends' attributions and emotional reactions in hypothetical situations. Part 1 of this measure assessed SIP with peers in general, and Part 2 assessed SIP when the best or good friend was the provocateur. Children were asked to make intent attributions and predict how they would behave if the situation happened to them and how they would respond. Results showed that aggressive children were more likely to make attributions of external blame when a hypothetical peer was involved than did control and shy/withdrawn children. Consistent with the studies reviewed above, children were more likely to attribute prosocial intent to mutual friends than to hypothetical peers. In addition, aggressive and shy/withdrawn boys were more likely than control boys to report angry emotional reactions when a hypothetical peer was involved. Responses differed as well; aggressive and control children were less likely to endorse revenge when a good friend was involved. Also, children were generally more likely to choose an appeasement strategy when provocateurs were friends than when they were unfamiliar peers. These results are consistent with other research on the impact of friendships and antipathies on SIP; children take into account their relationships with provocateurs when making social decisions. Moreover, there is some indication that the SIP of aggressive children is more competent when the provocateur is a mutual friend.

In another study, Peets, Hodges, and Salmivalli (2008) studied intent attributions and response decisions in 209 Finnish fifth graders. Sociometric procedures were used to discern reciprocal nominations for liked, disliked, and neutral peers. For each child, a peer fitting each of these three relationship descriptions became the provocateur in ambiguous provocation scenarios. Children reasoned about four vignettes for each peer type. For each vignette, participants answered questions about the provocateurs' intentions; they also reasoned about outcome expectancies and self-efficacy concerning possible aggressive responses. In addition to the social cognitive interview, children completed a self-report measure gauging their own reactive aggression, proactive aggression, and victimization. Participants also nominated up to three peers who fit descriptions of aggressive and victimization behaviors. Results indicated that when the provocateur was a disliked peer, children attributed more hostility, expected fewer positive relational and instrumental outcomes for aggressive responses to the problem, and felt that they would do a better job of aggressing toward the target. In contrast, when the provocateur was a liked peer, children showed the exact opposite pattern of SIP, attributing less hostility, expecting better relational and instrumental outcomes, and feeling less skillful at enacting aggressive responses. In addition, children who were nominated by their peers as being victimized generally expected worse outcomes if they responded aggressively, regardless of their affective status with the provocateur. The results of this study illustrate that children show clear biases toward enemies that impact multiple stages of SIP. In addition, children who are repeatedly victimized by their peers adopt biases of their own, expecting worse outcomes if they aggress no matter what kind of relationship they share with the provocateur.

To summarize, research focusing on the influence of children's affective ties on the encoding and interpretation of cues stages of SIP has generally found that children tend to give friends "the benefit of the doubt" during ambiguous conflicts; they attribute nicer intentions to friends than to enemies or neutral peers (Burgess et al., 2006; Hymel, 1986; Peets et al., 2008, 2007). In addition, children attribute both liked peers' positive behaviors and disliked peers' negative behaviors to stable causes; also, disliked peers are blamed more often for negative behaviors than are liked peers (Hymel, 1986). Research on the response decision step has shown that children are less likely to endorse revenge as a response when the peer is an actual friend than when the peer is hypothetical and are more likely to choose an appeasement strategy (Burgess et al., 2006). Moreover, even when disliked and liked peers behave in similar, positive ways, children report more negative emotional responses toward the disliked peers (DeLawyer & Foster, 1986). Interestingly, when children reason about hypothetical characters who are either best friends, enemies, or neutral peers, similar results are found (Ray & Cohen, 1997).

CONCLUSIONS

When Lemerise and Arsenio (2000) originally proposed integrating emotion processes into Crick and Dodge's (1994) SIP model, they argued that the integration of emotion into the SIP model would expand its explanatory power and enhance our understanding of both socially competent and incompetent behavior. In general, the studies reviewed in this chapter tend to support this argument. In particular, children who are rejected–aggressive, compared with more socially competent, nonaggressive children, display a number of difficulties related to emotion processes and SIP. For example, aggression and peer difficulties have been linked to difficulties in accurately recognizing emotions and to biases to perceive anger. Moreover, these deficits and biases predict aggression longitudinally. When self-reports of emotions are obtained in conjunction with SIP measures, compared with their nonaggressive peers, aggressive individuals (ranging from young children to adolescents) also report both experiencing more anger and having more difficulty regulating angry feelings. These correlational data tend to support the Lemerise and Arsenio (2000) model, but it is also possible that the emotions are the product of SIP rather than a causal influence on SIP. For this reason, it is important to review the results from studies in which some aspect of emotion has been manipulated so that its causal influence can be examined.

Results from studies using experimental designs yield findings that agree with those from studies using correlational designs. Rejected–aggressive children display SIP deficits and biases, including hostile attributional biases, hostile and self-focused social goals, aggressogenic response evaluations, and unfriendly and aggressive social problem-solving, under conditions that raise negative arousal in general and under conditions that induce discrete negative emotions (anger, sadness). This pattern of converging findings has been obtained across studies using a variety of research methods and designs.

Interestingly, under relaxed and positive emotion conditions, when asked specifically about provocateurs' emotions and when reasoning about a mutual friend, aggressive children display patterns of SIP that are not appreciably different from those of more competent children. This set of findings not only highlights that SIP models describe an interaction between person and situation, but also suggests that interventions can build on the fact that rejected–aggressive children do not always display SIP problems.

Despite this generally consistent picture, there still is a great deal of research that remains to be done. We are just beginning to examine emotion regulation in conjunction with SIP. In addition, mood induction techniques, despite their advantages, have rarely been used to study SIP and have never been used to study early stage SIP (encoding and attributions). Finally, the SIP models that have guided much of this research have not been explicitly developmental (however, see Chapter 3, this volume for an interesting developmental model for SIP). It is clear that many of the processes described by SIP models undergo developmental change. For example, with regard to the more "cognitive" aspects of SIP, attention, processing speed, short-term memory, and working memory all improve over the course of childhood. Similarly, emotion discrimination, emotion knowledge/understanding, emotion regulation, and emotion display rules all have their own developmental trajectory, which will interact with SIP. There is a great deal of work that remains to be done to identify developmental "norms" for emotions and SIP. Such work will allow us to identify SIP patterns associated with risk at earlier ages when interventions are more likely to be effective. Finally, we would argue that research on relational aggression, bullying, and victimization would profit from a fuller consideration of how emotions and SIP interact.

REFERENCES

Arsenio, W. F., Adams, E., & Gold, J. (2009). Social information processing, moral reasoning, and emotion attributions: Relations with adolescents' reactive and proactive aggression. *Child Development, 80*, 1739–1755.

Arsenio, W. F., Gold, J., & Adams, E. (2004). Adolescents' emotion expectancies regarding aggressive and nonaggressive events: Connections with behavior problems. *Journal of Experimental Child Psychology, 89*, 338–355. Medline doi:10.1016/j.jecp.2004.08.001

Arsenio, W. F., & Lemerise, E. A. (2001). Varieties of childhood bullying: Values, emotion processes, and social competence. *Social Development, 10*, 59–73. doi:10.1111/1467-9507.00148

Bailey, C. A., & Ostrov, J. M. (2008). Differentiating forms and functions of aggression in emerging adults: Associations with hostile attribution biases and normative beliefs. *Journal of Youth and Adolescence, 37*, 713–722. doi:10.1007/s10964-007-9211-5

Bauminger, N., & Kimhi-Kind, I. (2008). Social information processing, security of attachment, and emotion regulation in children with learning disabilities. *Journal of Learning Disabilities, 41*, 315–332. Medline doi:10.1177/0022219408316095

Bengtsson, H. (2003). Children's cognitive appraisal of others' distressful and positive experiences. *International Journal of Behavioral Development, 27*, 457–466. doi:10.1080/01650250344000073

Bodenhausen, G. V., Sheppard, L. A., & Kramer, G. P. (1994). Negative affect and social judgment: The differential impact of anger and sadness. *European Journal of Social Psychology, 24*, 45–62. doi:10.1002/ejsp.2420240104

Burgess, K. B., Wojslawowicz, J. C., Rubin, K. H., Rose-Krasnor, L., & Booth-LaForce, C. (2006). Social information processing and coping strategies of shy/withdrawn and aggressive children: Does friendship matter? *Child Development, 77*, 371–383. Medline doi:10.1111/j.1467-8624.2006.00876.x

Camodeca, M., & Goosens, F. A. (2005). Aggression, social cognitions, anger and sadness in bullies and victims. *Journal of Child Psychology and Psychiatry, and Allied Disciplines, 46*, 186–197. Medline doi:10.1111/j.1469-7610.2004.00347.x

Camodeca, M., Goosens, F. A., Schuengel, C., & Terwogt, M. M. (2003). Links between social information processing in middle childhood and involvement in bullying. *Aggressive Behavior, 29*, 116–127. doi:10.1002/ab.10043

Crick, N. R., & Dodge, K. A. (1994). A review and reformulation of social information-processing mechanisms in children's social adjustment. *Psychological Bulletin, 115*, 74–101. doi:10.1037/0033-2909.115.1.74

de Castro, B. O., Merk, W., Koops, W., Veerman, J. W., & Bosch, J. D. (2005). Emotions in social information processing and their relations with reactive and proactive aggression in referred aggressive boys. *Journal of Clinical Child and Adolescent Psychology, 34*, 105–116. Medline doi:10.1207/s15374424jccp3401_10 de Castro, B. O., Slot, N. W., Bosch, J. D., Koops, W., & Veerman, J. W. (2003). Negative feelings exacerbate hostile attributions of intent in highly aggressive boys. *Journal of Clinical Child and Adolescent Psychology*, *32*, 56–65. Medline doi:10.1207/15374420360533068

DeLawyer, D., & Foster, S. (1986). The effects of peer relationship on the functions of interpersonal behaviors of children. *Journal of Clinical Child Psychology*, *15*, 127–133. doi:10.1207/s15374424jccp1502_4

den Bak, I., & Rose-Krasnor (1991, April). *Effects of emotion and goal value on social problem-solving*. Paper presented at biennial meeting of the Society for Research in Child Development, Seattle, WA.

DiLiberto, L., Katz, R. C., Beauchamp, K. L., & Howells, G. N. (2002). Using articulated thoughts in simulated situations to assess cognitive activity in aggressive and nonaggressive adolescents. *Journal of Child and Family Studies*, *11*, 179–189. doi:10.1023/A:1015125625312

Dodge, K. A. (1986). A social information processing model of social competence in children. In M. Permutter (Ed.), *Minnesota Symposium in Child Psychology* (Vol. 18, pp. 77–125). Hillsdale, NJ: Erlbaum.

Dodge, K. A., Lochman, J. E., Harnish, J. D., Bates, J. E., & Pettit, G. S. (1997). Reactive and proactive aggression in school children and psychiatrically impaired chronically assaultive youth. *Journal of Abnormal Psychology*, *106*, 37–51. Medline doi:10.1037/0021-843X.106.1.37

Dodge, K. A., & Somberg, D. R. (1987). Hostile attributional biases among aggressive boys are exacerbated under conditions of threats to the self. *Child Development*, *58*, 213–224. Medline doi:10.2307/1130303

Dorsch, A., & Keane, S. P. (1994). Contextual factors in children's social information processing. *Developmental Psychology*, *30*, 611–616. doi:10.1037/0012-1649.30.5.611

Eisenberg, N., Fabes, R. A., & Guthrie, I. K. (2000). Dispositional emotionality and regulation: Their role in predicting quality of social functioning. *Journal of Personality and Social Psychology*, *78*, 136–157. Medline doi:10.1037/0022-3514.78.1.136

Fine, S. E., Trentacosta, C. J., Izard, C. E., Mostow, A. J., & Campbell, J. L. (2004). Anger perception, caregivers' use of physical discipline, and aggression in children at risk. *Social Development*, *13*, 213–228. doi:10.1111/j.1467-9507.2004.000264.x

Fontaine, R. G. (2008). On-line social decision making and antisocial behavior: Some essential but neglected issues. *Clinical Psychology Review*, *28*, 17–35. Medline doi:10.1016/j.cpr.2007.09.004

Garner, P. W., & Lemerise, E. A. (2007). The roles of behavioral adjustment and conceptions of peers and emotions in preschool children's peer victimization. *Development and Psychopathology*, *19*, 57–71. Medline doi:10.1017/S0954579407070046

Gottman, J. M. (1986). Merging social cognition and social behavior: Commentary. *Monographs of the Society for Research in Child Development, 51*(2, Serial No. 213).

Graham, S., Hudley, C., & Williams, E. (1992). Attributional and emotional determinants of aggression among African-American and Latino young adolescents. *Developmental Psychology, 28*, 731–740. doi:10.1037/0012-1649.28.4.731

Harper, B. D., Lemerise, E. A., & Caverly, S. (in press). The effect of induced mood on children's social information processing: Goal clarification and response decision. *Journal of Abnormal Child Psychology.*

Hubbard, J. A., Smithmyer, C. M., Ramsden, S. R., Parker, E. H., Flanagan, K. D., Dearing, K. F., . . . Simons, R. F. (2002). Observational, physiological, and self-report measures of children's anger: Relations to reactive versus proactive aggression. *Child Development, 73*, 1101–1118.

Hymel, S. (1986). Interpretations of peer behavior: Affective bias in childhood and adolescence. *Child Development, 57*, 431–445. doi:10.2307/1130599

Keane, S. P., & Parrish, A. E. (1992). The role of affective information in the determination of intent. *Developmental Psychology, 28*, 159–162. doi:10.1037/0012-1649.28.1.159

Lemerise, E. A., & Arsenio, W. F. (2000). An integrated model of emotion processes and cognition in social information processing. *Child Development, 71*, 107–118. Medline doi:10.1111/1467-8624.00124

Lemerise, E. A., Fredstrom, B. K., Kelley, B. M., Bowersox, A. L., & Waford, R. N. (2006). Do provocateurs' emotion displays influence children's social goals and problem solving? *Journal of Abnormal Child Psychology, 34*, 555–567. Medline doi:10.1007/s10802-006-9035-x

Lemerise, E. A., Gregory, D. S., & Fredstrom, B. K. (2005). The influence of provocateurs' emotion displays on the social information processing of children varying in social adjustment and age. *Journal of Experimental Child Psychology, 90*, 344–366. Medline doi:10.1016/j.jecp.2004.12.003

Lengua, L. J., & Long, A. C. (2002). The role of emotionality and self-regulation in the appraisal-coping process: Tests of direct and moderation effects. *Applied Developmental Psychology, 23*, 471–493. doi:10.1016/S0193-3973(02)00129-6

Lengua, L. J., Sandler, I. N., West, S. G., Wolchik, S. A., & Curran, P. J. (1999). Emotionality and self-regulation, threat appraisal, and coping in children of divorce. *Development and Psychopathology, 11*, 15–37. Medline doi:10.1017/S0954579499001935

Masters, J. C., & Furman, W. (1976). Effects of affective states on noncontingent outcome expectancies and beliefs in internal or external control. *Developmental Psychology, 12*, 481–482. doi:10.1037/0012-1649.12.5.481

Miller, A. L., Gouley, K. K., Seifer, R., Zakriski, A., Eguia, M., & Vergnani, M. (2005). Emotion knowledge skills in low-income elementary school children: Associations with social status and peer experiences. *Social Development, 14*, 637–651. doi:10.1111/j.1467-9507.2005.00321.x

Murphy, B. C., & Eisenberg, N. (2002). An integrative examination of peer conflict: Children's reported goals, emotions, and behaviors. *Social Development, 11*, 534–557. doi:10.1111/1467-9507.00214

Musher-Eizenman, D. R., Boxer, P., Danner, S., Dubow, E. F., Goldstein, S. E., & Heretick, D. M. (2004). Social-cognitive mediators of the relation of environmental and emotion regulation factors to children's aggression. *Aggressive Behavior, 30*, 389–408. doi:10.1002/ab.20078

Nas, C. N., Orobio de Castro, B., & Koops, W. (2005). Social information processing in delinquent adolescents. *Psychology, Crime & Law, 11*, 363–375. doi:10.1080/10683160500255307

Nelson, D. A., & Crick, N. R. (1999). Rose-colored glasses: Examining the social information processing of prosocial young adolescents. *The Journal of Early Adolescence, 19*, 17–38. doi:10.1177/0272431699019001002

Peets, K., Hodges, E. V. E., Kikas, E., & Salmivalli, C. (2007). Hostile attributions and behavioral strategies in children: Does relationship type matter? *Developmental Psychology, 43*, 889–900. Medline doi:10.1037/0012-1649.43.4.889

Peets, K., Hodges, E. V. E., & Salmivalli, C. (2008). Affect-congruent social-cognitive behavioral strategies in children: Does relationship type matter? *Child Development, 79*, 170–185. Medline doi:10.1111/j.1467-8624.2007.01118.x

Pettit, G. S., Polaha, J. A., & Mize, J. (2001). Perceptual and attributional processes in aggression and conduct problems. In J. Hill & B. Maughan (Eds.), *Conduct disorders in childhood and adolescence* (pp. 292–319). Cambridge, England: Cambridge University Press.

Quiggle, N. L., Garber, J., Panak, W. F., & Dodge, K. A. (1992). Social information processing in aggressive and depressed children. *Child Development, 63*, 1305–1320. Medline doi:10.2307/1131557

Ray, G., & Cohen, R. (1997). Children's evaluations of provocations between peers. *Aggressive Behavior, 23*, 417–431. doi:10.1002/(SICI)1098-2337(1997)23:6<417::AID-AB2>3.0.CO;2-D

Schultz, D., Izard, C. E., & Bear, G. (2004). Children's emotion processing: Relations to emotionality and aggression. *Development and Psychopathology, 16*, 371–387. Medline doi:10.1017/S0954579404044566

Tiedens, L. Z. (2001). The effect of anger on the hostile inferences of aggressive and nonaggressive people: Specific emotions, cognitive processing, and chronic accessibility. *Motivation and Emotion, 25*, 233–251. doi:10.1023/A:1012224-507488

Vitaro, F., Pelletier, D., & Coutu, S. (1989). Effects of a negative social experience on the emotional and social-cognitive responses of aggressive-rejected children. *Perceptual and Motor Skills, 69*, 371–382.

Waschbusch, D. A., Pelham, W. E., Jennings, J. R., Greiner, A. R., Tarter, R. E., & Moss, H. B. (2002). Reactive aggression in boys with disruptive behavior disorders: Behavior, physiology, and affect. *Journal of Abnormal Child Psychology, 30* , 641–656. Medline doi:10.1023/A:1020867831811

Wilson, B. J. (2003). The role of attentional processes in children's prosocial behavior with peers: Attention shifting and emotion. *Development and Psychopathology, 15*, 313–329. Medline doi:10.1017/S0954579403000178

9

THE DEVELOPMENT OF MORAL EMOTIONS IN A CULTURAL CONTEXT

TINA MALTI AND MONIKA KELLER

For centuries moral philosophers and psychologists have discussed the centrality of moral emotions and moral cognition in human morality. Although the issue is far from resolved, some consensus has evolved that ordinary moral concepts and moral emotions are linked. For example, moral emotions such as compassion or guilt feelings are recognized as influencing a person's understanding of the prescriptive nature of norms of fairness and care (Nussbaum, 2001). Developmental studies have supported the conclusion that moral emotions are a salient feature of children's experience of rule violations and that they help children to differentiate moral judgments from other social judgments (Arsenio, Gold, & Adams, 2006).

In this research, we focus on the emotions children attribute to protagonists in moral conflict situations. These emotion attributions have a strong cognitive component, because they require a basic understanding of the conflict, that is, the protagonist's situation, actions, and related consequences for self and others (Harris, 1989). Moral emotions constitute motives to consider another person's welfare, and they function as a motivational force that impels moral action (Hoffman, 2000; Krettenauer, Malti, & Sokol, 2008). For example, feelings of guilt motivate reparative behavior, such as apologies (Miller, Chakravarthy, & Rekha, 2008). However, it is also clear that the relationship between moral emotions and moral action is complex. Thus, feelings of guilt do not necessarily prevent the violation of moral rules. Rather, their presence following a moral violation indicates moral awareness, or the beginnings of the moral self (Keller, 2004; Keller, Brandt, & Sigurdardottir, in press; Keller & Edelstein, 1993). A developmental analysis of moral emotions is therefore necessary, and it has both conceptual and applied value.

Even though the development of moral emotions is inevitably embedded in a child's sociocultural history, most developmental research on moral emotions has been conducted in Western cultures. The complex interaction between developmental processes and cultural experiences in the genesis of children's moral emotions has still to be disentangled. For example, which aspects of moral emotions are due to normative developmental processes, and what are the specific contributions of culture to experiencing the norms of fairness and care as emotionally salient? How do normative development and cultural constructions interact in children's emerging conceptions of moral emotions?

The research presented here is an initial attempt to answer these previously unresolved questions. In this chapter, we provide a conceptual framework for integrating findings from different research traditions on moral emotions in different cultural settings. Furthermore, we present data on emotions in the context of moral and interpersonal rule violations and in a morally relevant dilemma among children and adolescents from both the West and Asia. Previous studies have generated important insights into the development of moral emotions following rule violations in Western industrialized societies (see Arsenio et al., 2006, and Krettenauer et al., 2008, for reviews). Our integrative conceptual and methodological approach extends this line of research and allows us to assess developmental and cultural aspects of moral emotions. Utilizing cross-sectional and longitudinal data from different cultures, we investigate patterns of moral emotion attributions following hypothetical rule violations and in a situation that involves conflicting interpersonal and moral obligations. This also allows us to examine if young peoples' emotion attributions differ depending on the experimental procedure used (i.e., moral rule violation vs. moral dilemma).

THE DEVELOPMENT OF MORAL EMOTIONS: A THEORETICAL MODEL

Feelings of guilt, compassion, and shame have been considered key indicators of moral development. An understanding of complex moral emotions, such as guilt feelings, is assumed to emerge around the age of 7 years (Harris, 1989). Similarly, Keller, Gummerum, Wang, and Lindsay (2004) have shown that the attribution of guilt feelings to perpetrators over contract violations increases between ages 7 and 9 years. Around 7 years of age, children also seem to show a change in emotion attributions to transgressors by switching from a "happy victimizer" or positive attribution to the attribution of negative or guilt feelings (but see Arsenio et al., 2006, for a discussion of the complexities of this phenomenon).

The understanding of guilt feelings requires complex cognitive abilities, namely, the integration of the understanding of a moral rule's validity with the understanding that other's evaluation of the self depends on the self's own actions (Harris, 1989; Krettenauer et al., 2008). From a motivational perspective, moral emotions indicate that the self feels committed to a norm (Malti, Gummerum, Keller, & Buchmann, 2009; also see Gibbard, 2002). Thus, moral emotions provide an early foundation for the development of the moral self (Keller et al., in press).

We have interpreted the development of the moral self and related moral emotions in the framework of a naïve theory of action (Keller & Reuss, 1984). The development of the moral self entails sociomoral knowledge about persons, interactions, and norms. Cognitively, the self increasingly comes to understand the world of others by participating in social interactions. Affectively, the moral self is characterized by an empathic sharing of the consequences of its actions on others. Building on this cognitive-developmental approach (Kohlberg, 1984; Selman, 1980), we have described a sequential model of development: As a first step in differentiating the perspectives of the self and others, the self becomes aware that actions violating moral rules have negative consequences for others. However, the self does not take these consequences into account, thus leading to the happy victimizer phenomenon, whereby children attribute positive feelings to a protagonist violating a moral rule in order to achieve a personal goal (Nunner-Winkler & Sodian, 1988). In the second step, which involves coordinating the perspectives of the self and others, the child realizes that violating a moral norm not only has negative effects on others, but also gives rise in the self to the moral emotion of guilt. Cognitively, the self becomes aware that the evaluation of the self by others depends on his or her own actions. Guilt feelings indicate the self's awareness that he or she has acted in a morally wrong way. In the third step, which occurs in adolescence, a generalized third-person perspective is developed, giving rise to a self-evaluative system that determines how one ought to treat others to establish and maintain relationships built on trust. Feelings of guilt emerge when the person violates trust in a relationship. This moral self also includes positive moral feelings, such as pride, if the self has resisted moral temptation and acted in accordance with obligations and responsibilities (Keller & Edelstein, 1993). Guilt feelings of the mature moral self, such as "existential guilt" (Hoffman, 2000), emerge if moral ideals and moral principles are violated.

In this chapter, we argue that different experimental procedures assess moral emotions at different levels of our sequential model. Moral emotion attributions after rule violations indicate that a child realizes the negative emotional consequences of rule-transgressing behavior for the victimizer. By contrast, moral emotions in a moral dilemma allow the assessment of the ability to take a generalized third-person perspective, because the child must reflect on the emotional consequences of his or her actions, for both others and themselves in light of generalized norms.

MORAL EMOTIONS IN THE HAPPY VICTIMIZER PARADIGM

To date, emotions in the context of moral rule violations have been investigated most prominently in the happy victimizer research tradition. In this tradition, children are presented with scenarios in which a protagonist violates a moral rule (e.g., pushing somebody off a swing, stealing sweets) in order to achieve a personal goal. One of the earliest findings in this tradition is that children below the age of 6 years attributed positive feelings to the victimizer even though they acknowledged the validity of the moral norm (physical integrity or property rights) by giving genuine moral reasons (Nunner-Winkler & Sodian, 1988; Turiel, 1983). By ages 6 to 7 years, children start to attribute negative or mixed (i.e., positive and negative) emotions, thereby establishing a developmental benchmark in moral development (Lagattuta, 2005). However, some studies have complicated this picture. Keller, Lourenço, Malti, and Saalbach (2003) have shown that emotion attributions also depend on perspective: Children from Germany and Portugal attributed negative emotions more frequently and earlier to the self-as-victimizer than to a hypothetical other victimizer. Studies with adolescents have indicated that individual differences in self-attributed emotions continue to exist (Arsenio et al., 2006; Krettenauer & Eichler, 2006).

Research in the happy victimizer tradition can be seen to differentiate between Levels 1 and 2 of our sequential developmental model. Thus, children either do not take into account the consequences of rule violations for the emotions of victimizers (Level 1: happy victimizer attribution) or do realize the negative emotional consequences of these actions for victimizers (Level 2: "unhappy victimizer" attribution). However, this experimental procedure is limited in various ways. Because this method presents children and adolescents with a simple transgression, it does not elicit more complex forms of moral emotions. Thus, this experimental method does not address the third level of moral emotions, the generalized third-person perspective, because children do not have to choose between acting in accordance with or against a moral norm in a more complex situation involving conflicting moral concerns. Addressing this level of understanding moral emotions requires a research paradigm that connects back to the cognitive-developmental method of moral dilemmas.

MORAL EMOTIONS IN DILEMMA SITUATIONS

In contrast to the happy victimizer paradigm, we also examine research on the feelings of children and adolescents who find themselves in a morally relevant dilemma. The dilemma method requires them to reflect on an action choice that is either consistent with or violates their moral obligations, and the emotional consequences of their action choices, for both others and themselves (Keller, 1996, 2004; Keller & Edelstein, 1991, 1993; Keller & Reuss, 1984; Kohlberg, 1984). In the happy victimizer tradition, a moral violation is presented to the child—independent of whether the child might ever have committed such a violation—and the child can focus either on his or her selfish interests or on the harmful consequences for the other, or on both and thus coordinate these perspectives. The dilemma situation, in contrast, requires the reflection about different action choices and consequences in view of different norms and relationships between the persons, and this adds complexity, requiring the differentiation and coordination of different perspectives. Thus, children can feel unhappy about a choice that is consistent with a moral norm (e.g., keeping a promise to a friend and not following an interesting invitation of a third child) because they acknowledge the negative consequences for the third party involved in the moral dilemma, or they can feel happy about the choice because they decided to act in accordance with a moral norm of promise-keeping or friendship. Oser, Schmid, and Hattersley (2006) have described these two scenarios as the "unhappy moralist" effect and the "happy moralist" effect, respectively. These authors see the unhappy moralist as related to a lack of moral reversibility, in which the inability to achieve a personal goal (i.e., because a moral norm is violated and another person has to suffer) makes the self feel unhappy. Although a moral norm has guided a moral action choice, the accompanying emotions are inconsistent with this choice. On the other hand, the happy moralist has acted on the basis of a moral norm and established consistency between moral knowledge and emotions, for example, by feeling good about having made a morally right choice. This pattern indicates consistency in the moral self, for which personal values guide both actions and emotions (Blasi, 2004; Keller & Edelstein, 1993). Both patterns are consistent with what we have described as Level 3 moral emotions.

Research in the happy victimizer literature has indicated that children acquire from early on an understanding of the moral rule validity and the victim's suffering in contexts of rule violations; even so, they frequently attribute happy emotions to victimizers. In contrast, our research shows that in a cognitively more demanding moral dilemma in which selfish motives (e.g., fun) were put in conflict with normative demands (promise keeping, close friendship), some of the youngest 7-year-old children were not aware of the negative consequences of their action choices for others (Keller, 1996; Malti, 2007; Malti & Keller, 2009). There seemed to be a pattern of "everybody is happy whatever happens," with no evidence of moral awareness. Thus, the traditional happy victimizers seem to be already ahead developmentally, because they at least have an empathic awareness of the victim's feelings. The unhappy victimizers represent the next developmental step in both experimental procedures. However, it seems clear that the unhappy and happy moralists are later achievements developmentally.

MORAL EMOTIONS IN A CROSS-CULTURAL CONTEXT

Growing up in a Western or Asian culture is linked with different experiences in regard to social expectations and social interactions in relationships. For example, cross-cultural research has indicated that people in collectivist cultures tend to experience meeting interpersonal responsibilities to family and friends as personally satisfying. In contrast, people in individualistic cultures treat such responsibilities as obligations (Miller et al., 2008). Although distinguishing Asian and Western societies by the dimension of individualism and collectivism has been critically debated (Turiel, 2002), it seems that the value of relationships in the socialization process is emphasized more strongly in China than in Western society. Benevolence and concern for the well-being of other members of the community are central moral values in both the Confucian and the Marxist traditions (Bond, 1996). These values influence social interactions, thereby serving as mediators of cultural influence on children's social development (Chen & French, 2008). For example, research indicates that Chinese mothers primarily encourage connectedness, whereas Canadian mothers primarily encourage autonomy (Hoffman, 2000; Liu et al., 2005). Thus, Chinese and Western parents presumably have different fundamental belief systems regarding social harmony and autonomy (Wang & Leichtman, 2000). From a constructivist perspective, culturally guided social interaction processes interact with the child's emerging construction of norms involving fairness and care, as well as with the associated emotional experiences (Piaget, 1970).

The last decade has witnessed a growing interest in adults' moral emotions across cultures (e.g., Li & Fischer, 2007). Surprisingly, however, the question of whether the development of children's and adolescents' moral emotion attributions is affected by culture-specific constructions of social relationships, norms, and emotions has rarely been investigated. This illustrates the need to overcome the ethnocentric research tradition in this field and to investigate moral emotions from an integrative developmental and cross-cultural perspective.

Research has indicated both cross-cultural differences and normative developmental trends in the multifaceted and complex moral judgments of children and adolescents (e.g., Helwig, Arnold, Tan, & Boyd, 2007; Neff & Helwig, 2002). As research also shows that children's early moral cognition and moral affect are linked (Eisenberg, 1986; Kochanska, Padavich, & Koenig, 1996), we discuss selected studies of children's development of moral judgment across cultures as a basis for drawing conclusions about cultural differences and similarities in the development of moral emotions. In a study of sociomoral reasoning, Keller, Edelstein, Schmid, Fang, and Fang (1998) found that, compared with Icelandic children, Chinese children gave more empathic reasons to explain the needs of a new child in the context of a dilemma concerning promise keeping toward a close friend versus helping a new child who does not have any friends yet. However, this study also revealed that cultural differences decreased from childhood to adolescence, and at age 15 adolescents from both cultures gave priority to close friendship.

Other studies have found similar cross-cultural differences in children's reasoning about moral issues: For example, Gummerum and Keller (2008) showed that in considering the concept of close friendship, Chinese and Russian children referred more often to the normative categories of supporting and helping one's friend than did Icelandic children. Similarly, Yau and Smetana (2003) showed that young Chinese children's justifications for moral transgressions focused overwhelmingly on the intrinsic consequences of the acts for others' welfare and fairness. Another study by Wang and Leichtman (2000) revealed that 6-year-old Chinese children's moral narratives reflected social harmony and attention to others, whereas American children's narratives reflected the preeminent value placed on developing autonomy. Taken together, these studies indicate that children from Chinese culture refer more frequently to relationship concerns in their moral narratives and reasoning than do children from Western cultures. It is likely that these cultural differences are linked to similar differences in the affective consequences associated with the violation of moral and interpersonal norms.

THE DEVELOPMENT OF MORAL EMOTIONS IN A CULTURAL CONTEXT: EMPIRICAL FINDINGS

In the research that we present in this chapter, we used the sequential model of the development of moral emotions outlined in the beginning of the chapter to investigate the hypothesis that children in an Asian and a Western culture have different affective experiences in the moral domain. We first present a study replicating the Level 1–Level 2 distinction of moral emotions as assessed in traditional happy victimizer research using Chinese and Western samples. Second, we present a cross-cultural comparison of a Western and a Chinese sample with regard to moral emotions after decision making in an interpersonal moral dilemma. This experimental method allows the detection of different emotional patterns that transcend the traditional distinctions made in this research field.

Study 1: The Development of Happy Victimizers Across Cultures

In a cross-sectional study, forty-eight 3- to 4-year-old, forty 5- to 6-year-old, and forty 8- to 9-year-old Chinese children were interviewed. Additionally, thirty-eight 5- to 6-year-old and forty 8- to 9-year-old Icelandic children were assessed. Iceland is often referred to as a prototypical Western society (e.g., Edelstein, Keller, & Schröder, 1990; Keller et al., 1998).

Four different types of moral rule transgressions were presented to the children (violating physical integrity, stealing from a peer, stealing from an adult, not keeping a promise) in male and female versions. The scenarios were illustrated with cartoons in which characters showed affectively neutral expressions. Depending on the child's gender, either male or female versions of the following were assigned: (a) pushing another child off a swing, (b) stealing chocolate from another child in kindergarten, (c) stealing a doll from a store, and (d) not giving borrowed skates back to another child as promised.

In keeping with the traditional method in happy victimizer research, the Icelandic children were asked to attribute emotions to a hypothetical protagonist. For the cross-cultural comparison between the Icelandic and Chinese children, we thus could only draw on the emotions attributed to the hypothetical victimizer in two age groups (5–6 and 8–9 years). Overall, the Icelandic children in both these groups attributed predominantly negative emotions to the victimizer (79%). Only 20% of the younger Icelandic children were happy victimizers, a surprisingly low number. Thus, compared with the findings from previous Western research (Nunner-Winkler & Sodian, 1988), the Icelandic children did not demonstrate the expected change from positive to negative emotions, but even at the younger ages they scored high on moral emotions. In contrast, only 44% of the Chinese 5- to 6-year-olds and 8- to 9-year-olds attributed negative emotions to the hypothetical victimizer. Thus, like the Icelandic participants, the Chinese participants did not demonstrate more happy emotion attributions in the younger compared with the older age groups; even the oldest Chinese children revealed a very high frequency of happy victimizer responses. However, the direction of this finding is opposite because even the youngest Icelanders were unhappy victimizers, whereas even the oldest Chinese were happy victimizers.

This finding is highly surprising, given the many previous findings indicating that Chinese children and adolescents display more altruistic concern than do their Western counterparts (Keller et al., 1998). It was therefore necessary to change the experimental procedure and differentiate between the hypothetical protagonist and the self in the Chinese sample. This changed the empirical findings completely. When developmental differences in moral emotion attribution patterns to the other and to the self were tested in the Chinese sample, the findings revealed a significant interaction between age and context, $F(2, 1014) = 13.11, p < .001, \eta^2 = .03$. Post hoc comparison tests indicated a developmental effect only when the emotions were attributed to the self and not—as in the Icelandic sample—when they were attributed to the hypothetical violator (see Figure 9.1): 3- to 4-year-olds attributed fewer moral emotions to the self than did 5- to 6-year-olds, who in turn attributed fewer moral emotions to the self than did 8- to 9-year-olds.

One possible explanation for this finding is that the children in the Western sample identified with the hypothetical victimizer and therefore attributed predominantly moral feelings. The Chinese children seem not to have identified with the hypothetical violator, but rather they may have evaluated him or her as a bad or immoral person and therefore attributed positive emotions—an effect that seems to be even stronger in the older than in the younger children. However, the puzzle of the Icelandic data with the very infrequent happy victimizers remains. Although we did not assess self-attributed emotions in the Icelandic sample, it is extremely unlikely that these children would have attributed positive emotions to the self had they attributed negative

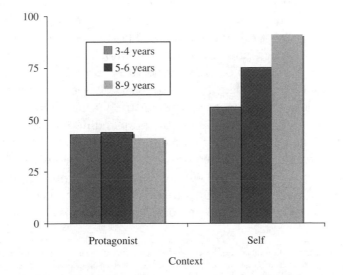

Figure 9.1. Frequencies (%) of moral (negative) emotion attributions to the protagonist and the self by age group in China.

emotions to hypothetical wrongdoers. This assumption was confirmed by some follow-up interviews with Icelandic children who were given the other–self dichotomy. None of the children attributed positive feelings to the self if they attributed negative feelings to the hypothetical violator, thus indicating that Icelandic children do not seem to distinguish between self and other in their emotion attributions. At the same time, the Chinese children made a stark distinction between other- and self-attributed emotions in this context. We therefore considered it justified to compare, for two of the age groups (5–6 years, 8–9 years), other-attributed negative emotions in Icelandic children with self-attributed negative emotions in Chinese children. The analysis revealed a significant interaction between age and culture, $F(1, 570) = 3.95$, $p < .05$: Older Chinese children attributed more moral emotions to the self than did younger Chinese children, whereas no age difference was obtained in the Icelandic sample.

In contrast to the classic study by Nunner-Winkler and Sodian (1988), a much higher proportion of the 5- to 6-year-old Icelandic children in this study attributed moral feelings to the hypothetical transgressor in the story. In contradistinction, the Chinese frequently attributed across all three age groups positive emotions to the hypothetical transgressor and did not reveal higher frequencies of immoral emotions in the younger than in the older age groups. Only when attributing feelings to the self, the findings revealed the more frequently found pattern of an increase in moral emotions across the three age groups. The spontaneous comments of the Chinese children about the transgressions indicated that they disapproved of both the violation and the transgressor. We therefore assume that identification with the transgressor may vary by culture. Our own further research with 5- to 6-year-old and 8- to 9-year-old German and Portuguese children supported the difference in other- and self-attributed emotions but also indicated a developmental decrease in both (Keller et al., 2003). Thus, Western children seem more prone to identify with the story character and project their own feelings onto this character, whereas the Chinese children seem to disapprove of the character and therefore project different emotions to this other than to the self.[1] Therefore, we can conclude that negative (moral) feelings are attributed by children only if they spontaneously identify with the transgressor and project the self's feelings onto the protagonist. If children identify with the story character and attribute moral emotions, these emotion attributions might have important implications for (mal)adaptive

---

[1]Although we did not assess self-attributed emotions following rule violations in the Icelandic sample, the finding that Icelandic children attributed predominantly negative emotions to hypothetical victimizers makes it extremely unlikely that they would have attributed positive emotions to the self. Our research clearly indicates that children tend to attribute negative (moral) emotions more frequently to the self than to the victimizer (Keller et al., 2003).

behavior, because they serve as a motive for moral action (Malti et al., 2009; Malti, Gasser, & Gutzwiller-Helfenfinger, in press). This assumption has been supported by research on the relation between moral emotion attributions and aggressive–prosocial behavior (see Arsenio et al., 2006, and Krettenauer et al., 2008, for reviews).

In our conceptual framework, the attribution of negative emotions in the happy victimizer approach exemplifies just the beginning of the second level of moral emotions. This second level indicates that children not only acknowledge that violating a moral norm has negative effects on others, but also that this violation is felt by the self and therefore gives rise to moral emotions (guilt feelings) in the self.

Study 2: Patterns of Moral Emotions in an Interpersonal-Moral Dilemma Across Cultures

In these studies, we investigated developmental and cultural differences in Chinese and Icelandic children and adolescents in more complex patterns of moral emotions. These patterns were assessed in a moral dilemma situation represented by a conflict between self-interest and different interpersonal-moral obligations (Keller et al., 1998). This methodological approach allows examining an emerging self-evaluation system of how a moral person should act and feel in order to establish and maintain interpersonal trust in relationships, and it indicates a third-person perspective governed by generalized norms of reciprocity and fairness. These self-evaluations imply a comparison between how one acts and how one ought to act and to anticipate moral feelings of guilt if one violates this moral self-ideal. Alternatively, positive moral emotions (pride) arise when one acts in accordance with the moral self-ideal. These emotions are characteristic of the emerging moral and relationship self in early adolescence (Keller, 2004).

On the basis of our own research and that of others (Arsenio et al., 2006), we expected the happy victimizer pattern to developmentally decrease and the unhappy victimizer pattern to increase in both cultures in this experimental setting. Because of our previous findings that young Chinese children focused more on relationship concerns than did young Icelandic children in this dilemma (Keller et al., 1998), we also assumed that the Chinese participants would give happy victimizer responses less frequently than the Icelandic participants. Yet, it also has to be kept in mind that the Icelandic children did not attribute happy emotions in the less complex experimental procedure, the happy victimizer task.

Concerning the pattern of happy and unhappy moralists (i.e., opting to fulfill an obligation but feeling happy or unhappy about it), our expectations were twofold. On the one hand, the readiness to sacrifice selfish or "first-order"

(Frankfurt, 1993) desires in favor of what is morally right seems to increase developmentally because of an increasing moral awareness of consequences of actions for self and others (Keller & Edelstein, 1993). On the other hand, we expected that regret of a moral choice because of selfish desires might be more characteristic of younger children and might indicate that the moral self has not yet been developed. This pattern might be more characteristic of younger children. We decided to call such a pattern of regret the "unhappy conformist," that is, one who follows a (moral) norm but feels unhappy about this choice because of exclusively hedonistic interests (rather than empathic concerns for the third party). We distinguished this pattern from both the pattern of a happy moralist, who acts in accordance with the moral norm and feels morally good about this, and the pattern of an unhappy moralist, who is unhappy following a moral action choice because he or she is aware that a conflicting obligation has been violated. This is the case when the moral dilemma is interpreted not in terms of selfish concerns versus moral obligation but in terms of two conflicting obligations as the dilemmas in the Kohlberg tradition (Kohlberg, 1984). We found previously (Keller et al., 1998) that Chinese children interpreted an interpersonal-moral dilemma in terms of conflicting obligations of close friendship and altruism, whereas Icelandic children interpreted it in terms of a conflict between selfish desires and friendship obligations. On the basis of these findings, we assumed that happy moralists would be more frequent among Icelandic and unhappy moralists would be found more frequent among Chinese children, because of the Chinese children's intensive moral socialization (cf. Fung, 1999).

In this study, Icelandic children and adolescents were assessed longitudinally, beginning at the age of 7 years. The sample included 121 participants from the city of Reykjavik who were about equally distributed according to social class and gender (see Edelstein et al., 1990, and Keller, 1996, for a detailed description). The children were reinterviewed at ages 9, 12, and 15 years. The Chinese participants (from Beijing) were studied cross-sectionally at the equivalent ages of 7, 9, 12, and 15 years ($N = 100$ per age group).

The children were interviewed about an interpersonal-moral dilemma (Selman, 1980), which contained selfish desires and altruistic obligations on the one side, and interpersonal responsibilities (close friendship) and moral obligations (promise keeping) on the other. In the dilemma, the protagonist (with whom the self has to identify) had promised to visit his or her (same-sex) best friend at a particular time. At precisely this time, the protagonist receives an invitation to an interesting event from a child who is new in the class (selected according to age and culture). The close friend had expressed a special need to see the protagonist and did not like the new child particularly. The cultural validity of the dilemma was established in pretests for each culture.

The children were asked to define the problem, to make an action choice and give reasons for it as well as for the alternative choice, and also to think about the consequences of the choice for others and the self, in particular concerning feelings and the strategies to compensate for consequences as well as to justify the choice from a moral point of view (Keller, 1996). Concerning the emotions of the other ("victim"), only the feelings attributed to the close friend could be scored, because the focus of the interview had (unfortunately) been only on the friends' feelings when a friendship obligation had been violated. For the present analysis, the following questions were used to assess the different patterns of moral emotions:

- *Action decision:* How does the protagonist decide in this situation? What are the reasons for the choice and which reasons would speak for the alternative option?
- *Emotion attribution to the protagonist:* How does the protagonist feel after this choice? Why would he or she feel this way?
- *Emotion attribution to friend/victim:* How will the friend feel with this decision? Why would he or she feel this way?

Emotion attributions were scored for both action decisions (e.g., visiting friend as promised, meeting with the new child). The emotions attributed to the protagonist and to the close friend were scored as positive or negative. Mixed feelings (which occurred only rarely) were scored as negative feelings, if they were based on a moral awareness. Content categories were defined for the reasons or justifications given for the action choices (new child/friend) and emotions (positive, negative, mixed). Reasons were assigned to qualitative categories according to the coding manual of Keller et al. (1998). These categories included (a) selfish-hedonistic reasons (interest in objects or relationships; for example, the protagonist/self feels good "because the movie is great" or "because it is fun to be with the new child" or the protagonist/self feels bad, "because the movie is not so good" or "the friends' toys are boring"); (b) moral and friendship reasons (reference to obligation of a promise or close friendship; for example, he feels bad "because she broke a promise" or "because he left his best friend behind"), and (c) interpersonal-altruistic reasons (altruistic obligations and empathy with the new child; for example, she feels bad "because the new child will be sad," or "because she should have helped the newcomer"). Concerning the emotions of the victim/friend it was only differentiated whether the reasons referred to selfish concerns (e.g., "he was bored and had no fun") or moral-interpersonal obligations (e.g., reference to the friend's feelings, the friendship, or the promise). Several pairs of coders achieved above 90% agreement for all categories across age groups and cultures.

In a next step, direction of choice, emotion attributions, and justifications were combined to create the different patterns of emotion attribution. These

TABLE 9.1
Frequencies (%) of Moral Emotion Patterns for Different Age Groups
in China and Iceland

Pattern	Age				
	7 years	9 years	12 years	15 years	Overall
China					
Premoral–happy victimizer	12	0	0	0	3
Unhappy victimizer	13	14	5	8	9
Unhappy conformist	5	7	0	0	3
Happy moralist	35	7	17	31	22
Unhappy moralist	35	80	78	61	63
Iceland					
Premoral–happy victimizer	24	14	4	2	11
Unhappy victimizer	38	50	25	22	33
Unhappy conformist	5	4	14	6	8
Happy moralist	19	14	45	50	32
Unhappy moralist	13	18	12	20	16

patterns were based on the theoretical considerations discussed previously. The frequencies (percentage) of the emotion patterns for the different age groups in China and Iceland are displayed in Table 9.1. To test for the effects of development and culture on the various patterns of moral emotions, a series of 4×2, between-subjects analyses of variance were computed; the factors were age (7, 9, 12, 15 years) and culture (China, Iceland).

Premoral–Happy Victimizer

The premoral category includes participants who opted for the friend or the new child for exclusively hedonistic reasons and who attributed exclusively positive emotions to the protagonist/self or to the friend (victim) when deciding to go to the new child (e.g., victimizer and victim feel good). In contrast, the happy victimizer pattern applies to participants who opted for the new child and attributed positive feelings to the self for hedonistic reasons (she or he has fun at the movie); however, in line with the happy victimizer research, they attributed negative emotions to the friend (victim) for empathic reasons (the friend feels bad because she or he is alone). Because of the infrequent occurrence of both patterns, they were combined. As there were empty cells for some age groups, the 7- and 9-year-old and the 12- and 15-year-old participants were pooled, thereby creating a new age factor with the values "younger" and "older." Younger participants in both cultures used the premoral–happy victimizer pattern more frequently than did older participants, $F(1, 761) = 18.77, p < .001, \eta^2 = .02$.

Unhappy Victimizers

This category includes participants who opted to go with the new child for hedonistic reasons (because it was a very good opportunity), but who attributed negative emotions to the self for reasons of friendship and promise (the friend felt unhappy, jealous, or betrayed). The analysis of variance revealed an interaction between age and culture, $F(3, 380) = 2.73$, $p < .05$, $\eta^2 = .02$. Post hoc tests indicated that Icelandic 9-year-olds used this pattern more frequently than did Icelandic 15-year-olds, whereas no age differences in the Chinese sample were obtained.

Unhappy Conformists

This response pattern applies to participants who opted to meet the friend for friendship or moral reasons (they are friends and/or she or he promised), but who attributed negative emotions to the self for hedonistic reasons (she or he regrets missing out on such a good opportunity). Because of the low cell frequencies for some categories, the 7- and 9-year-olds and the 12- and 15-year-olds were again pooled. There was an age by culture interaction, $F(1, 380) = 6.76$, $p < .05$, $\eta^2 = .02$: In China, younger participants used this pattern less frequently than did older participants, whereas there was no age effect for Icelandic children.

Happy Moralists

This category includes participants who decided to meet the friend and attributed positive feelings to the self for friendship and moral reasons and attributed positive feelings for the victim/friend. The findings revealed a statistically significant age by culture interaction, $F(3, 761) = 3.55$, $p < .05$, $\eta^2 = .01$: In the Icelandic sample, 7-year-olds used this pattern less frequently than did 15-year-olds, and 9-year-olds used it less frequently than did 12- and 15-year-olds. In the Chinese sample, no clear developmental trend was observed.

Unhappy Moralists

This category includes participants who opted to go with the new child for altruistic reasons, but who attributed negative emotions to the protagonist/self because of friendship and/or moral reasons. In this case, the somewhat negative feelings of victim/friend were frequently interpreted such that the friend would understand and share the reasons of the protagonist/self. In addition, this pattern includes participants who opted to go with the friend for friendship and or moral reasons, but who attributed negative emotions to protagonist/self because of altruistic reasons (because the newcomer was alone). The unhappy moralist pattern revealed a developmental increase in the Chinese sample, $F(3, 761) = 3.00\, p < .05$, $\eta^2 = .01$: 7-year-old Chinese children used this pattern less frequently than did Chinese 9- and 12-year-olds.

Taken together, these findings clearly indicate that both development and culture are important factors in children's and adolescents' patterns of moral emotions. It is very surprising that the traditional happy victimizer pattern in which the victimizer feels good even though anticipating the negative emotions of the victim occurred very rarely in the dilemma approach. However, developmental declines of this pattern were still evident in both cultures, thereby confirming the normative developmental trend in this pattern of emotion attribution. The few children who attributed positive emotions to the protagonist/self also attributed positive feelings to the victim/friend and did not reveal any understanding of the moral dimension of the conflict (everybody is happy). Nearly all the children—even the youngest 7-year-olds— were aware of the moral aspects of the friendship dilemma and understood the negative interpersonal consequences of a choice violating friendship and/or promise obligations. Therefore, only a few children attributed positive feelings to protagonist/self in light of friendship and/or promise violation and the attribution of negative feelings to the friend (victim). This finding reveals a salient difference from the happy victimizer research, which clearly supports the hypothesis that children attribute positive feelings to the violator in spite of the awareness of negative feelings of the victim—even if the victim is a friend (Arsenio & Lover, 1995).

This difference may have to do with the fact that in the traditional happy victimizer research, the moral violation is presented to the child, whereas in the moral dilemma the child has to make a choice that either violates or does not violate obligations. Thus, making a choice that violates friendship expectations might rather lead to guilt feelings than positive feelings. Therefore, the most frequent pattern among younger Icelandic children is the unhappy victimizer who breaks a promise and violates friendship obligations for selfish reasons, but anticipates pangs of conscience. This finding also shows that guilt feelings are not necessarily motives for action and that the awareness of guilt feelings does not prevent an action choice that violates obligations. Rather, guilt feelings are a sign of awareness that obligations have been violated, and they indicate that the child has acquired the basic competencies of the moral self (Keller, 2004). Thus, moral feelings have a double function: Internally, they indicate the presence of a moral self; externally, they also indicate to the other a moral failure and willingness to compensate for the failure. This latter aspect is evidenced by the more comprehensive data from the sociomoral interviews in which children were asked how the situation could be resolved afterward (Keller & Edelstein, 1993).

In contrast, the pattern of unhappy conformists occurred rather infrequently and showed a developmental decline only in the Chinese but not in the Icelandic children. This finding indicates that even the youngest Chinese children were aware of friendship obligations. It is in line with previous research documenting that close friendships in China as in Western societies contain strong obligations to support one's friend (Gummerum & Keller, 2008). Most of the older Icelandic children and adolescents turned out to be happy moralists. This pattern indicates that the focus of the Icelandic participants is on close friendship, and the dilemma is seen as a conflict of moral and/or friendship obligations versus hedonistic self-interest. Older children and adolescents become increasingly aware of their obligations and the consequences of their actions in relation to a close friend, and they link these consequences to the moral self, which at this point in development is a "relationship self" (Noam, 1999; Sullivan, 1953). Acting in accord with one's responsibilities to be a trustworthy and faithful friend is seen as obligatory in adolescence (Keller & Edelstein, 1993). Keller et al. (1998) found that nearly all adolescents, both Icelandic and Chinese, gave priority to close friendship in their decision making.

The most striking finding was that the Chinese children and adolescents predominantly were unhappy moralists: they felt unhappy whichever choice they made, because they had violated either moral and friendship or altruistic obligations. However, in contrast to the Icelandic children, nearly all of whom viewed the friend as having negative feelings about the violation of the friendship obligations, the Chinese children frequently interpreted the friend/victim as someone who can understand the action choice of helping a child who is new in the class. In spite of the interpretation of a shared understanding, however, guilt feelings remained. Thus, the Icelandic children interpreted the "morally right choice" as resisting a selfish temptation and acting in accordance with one's own moral ideals; pride or contentment logically follows from this interpretation. In contrast, the Chinese children seemed to focus on the inability to make both children happy or decide in accordance with both obligations, and this evaluation led to guilt feelings. This cultural difference in guilt feelings may be due to cultural differences relating to collectivism and the intensive moral education that Chinese children receive. However, Chinese children are also specifically socialized into altruism toward newcomers in school, more so than their Icelandic counterparts (Keller et al., 1998).

SUMMARY AND DIRECTIONS FOR FUTURE RESEARCH

In summary, our findings document that a developmental theory of moral emotions must integrate the universal logic inherent in normative development and the culture-specific patterns of emotions that are embedded in the culture-bound construction of the self (Keller, 2004). We proposed a sequential model that conceptualizes moral emotions at different developmental levels: Although moral emotions after rule violations indicate that a child anticipates the negative consequences of rule-transgressing behavior for the victimizer, moral emotions in a moral dilemma are more complex and express the ability to coordinate more than two perspectives and to take a generalized third-person perspective. In accord with this model, our findings indicate that the majority of older children attribute moral emotions to the self after rule-transgressing behavior. In contrast, the unhappy victimizer pattern occurs only rarely in older children within the moral dilemma task. Rather, the findings show that the decision to act morally developmentally increases, but this is associated with either happy feelings (the happy moralist) in Icelanders or unhappy feelings (the unhappy moralist) in Chinese. Taken together, these developmental trends suggest that although the complexity of moral emotions increases, interindividual differences in moral emotions remain well into adolescence. This supports the findings by Krettenauer and Eichler (2006) in the traditional happy victimizer paradigm. It is a challenging task for future research to analyze how these interindividual differences in moral emotions within different experimental procedures relate to moral judgment and affect moral action.

Although there were normative developmental effects, there were also stable cultural differences in moral emotions between children and adolescents from the two cultures. For example, the anticipation of positive (i.e., pride) and negative (i.e., guilt, shame) emotions in a moral dilemma might be influenced by culturally bounded constructions of the meaning of the situation and the corresponding emotions. Thus, it remains a question for future research whether the happy moralist pattern (i.e., feeling good about having made a morally right choice) is the only pattern that indicates consistency in the moral self, for which personal values guide both actions and emotions (Blasi, 2004; Keller & Edelstein, 1993), or if the unhappy moralist pattern and the expression of existential guilt feelings can likewise express the formation of the moral self. It should be noted that the meaning of close friendship may be culturally different as well. Thus, although Icelandic adolescents see close friendship as an intimate personal relationship, Chinese adolescents emphasize the interconnection of friendship and society (Keller, 2004). This difference might impact the emotions associated with the action decision in the moral dilemma.

Finally, the development of moral emotions may be influenced by other factors besides development and general cultural orientations, such as phenomena of social disintegration and modernization (Heitmeyer & Hüpping, 2008). For example, a first analysis of time-lagged assessments in China revealed striking differences in changes from altruistic concerns to more hedonistic self-interest in reasoning and related attribution of emotions in the moral dilemma. These changes in sociomoral reasoning and moral emotions might be related to rapid modernization and the capitalist–individualistic transformation of Chinese society. Thus, the normative development of moral emotions is both a universal and a socially dynamic process, which is mirrored in what children see as important in morally relevant situations. As moral emotions are of significance for the genesis of interindividual differences in moral behavior (Arsenio et al., 2006; Krettenauer et al., 2008), knowledge about developmental and cultural effects in moral emotions gives impetus to educational efforts aimed at promoting young people's moral development across cultures (Nucci & Narvaez, 2008). It is a task for future research to further disentangle the complex interactions between development and culture and their role in moral emotions.

REFERENCES

Arsenio, W., Gold, J., & Adams, E. (2006). Children's conceptions and displays of moral emotions. In M. Killen & J. Smetana (Eds.), *Handbook of moral development* (pp. 581–610). Mahwah, NJ: Erlbaum.

Arsenio, W. F., & Lover, A. (1995). Children's conceptions of sociomoral affect: Happy victimizers, mixed emotions, and other expectancies. In M. Killen & D. Hart (Eds.), *Morality in everyday life* (pp. 87–128). New York, NY: Cambridge University Press.

Blasi, A. (2004). Moral functioning: Moral understanding and personality. In D. K. Lapsley & D. Narvaez (Eds.), *Moral development, self, and identity* (pp. 335–348). Mahwah, NJ: Erlbaum.

Bond, M. H. (Ed.). (1996). *The handbook of Chinese psychology*. New York, NY: Oxford University Press.

Chen, X., & French, D. C. (2008). Children's social competence in cultural context. *Annual Review of Psychology, 59*, 591–616. Medline doi:10.1146/annurev.psych.59.103006.093606

Edelstein, W., Keller, M., & Schröder, E. (1990). Child development and social structure: A longitudinal study of individual differences. In P. B. Baltes, D. L. Featherman, & R. M. Lerner (Eds.), *Life-span development and behavior* (Vol. 10, pp. 151–185). Hillsdale, NJ: Erlbaum.

Eisenberg, N. (1986). *Altruistic emotion, cognition, and behavior*. Hillsdale, NJ: Erlbaum.

Frankfurt, H. G. (1993). On the necessity of ideals. In G. Noam & T. E. Wren (Eds.), *The moral self* (pp. 16–27). Cambridge, MA: MIT Press.

Fung, H. (1999). Becoming a moral child: The socialization of shame among young Chinese children. *Ethos, 27*, 180–209. doi:10.1525/eth.1999.27.2.180

Gibbard, A. (2002). *Wise choices and apt feelings*. Oxford, England: Clarendon Press.

Gummerum, M., & Keller, M. (2008). Affection, virtue, pleasure, and profit: Developing an understanding of friendship closeness in Western and Asian Societies.

International Journal of Behavioral Development, 32, 218–231. doi:10.1177/0165025408089271

Harris, P. L. (1989). *Children and emotion.* Oxford, England: Basil Blackwell.

Heitmeyer, W., & Hüpping, S. (Eds.). (2008). Youth, violence, and social disintegration. *New Directions for Youth Development, 119*, 25–37.

Helwig, C. C., Arnold, M. L., Tan, D., & Boyd, D. (2007). Mainland Chinese and Canadian adolescents' judgments and reasoning about the fairness of democratic and other forms of government. *Cognitive Development, 22*, 96–109. doi:10.1016/j.cogdev.2006.07.002

Hoffman, M. L. (2000). *Empathy and moral development: Implications for caring and justice.* Cambridge, MA: Cambridge University Press.

Keller, M. (1996). *Moralische sensibilität: Entwicklung in freundschaft und familie* [Moral sensitivity in friendship and family]. Weinheim, Germany: Psychologie-Verlags Union.

Keller, M. (2004). Self in relationship. In D. K. Lapsley & D. Narvaez (Eds.), *Moral development, self, and identity* (pp. 267–298). Mahwah, NJ: Erlbaum.

Keller, M., Brandt, A., & Sigurdardottir, G. (in press). "Happy" and "unhappy" victimizers: The development of moral emotions from childhood to adolescence. In W. Koops & A. Sanders (Eds.), *The development and structure of conscience.* Hove, England: Psychology Press.

Keller, M., & Edelstein, W. (1991). The development of socio-moral meaning making: Domains, categories, and perspective-taking. In W. M. Kurtines & J. L. Gewirtz (Eds.), *Handbook of moral behavior and development: Vol. 2. Research* (pp. 89–114). Hillsdale, NJ: Erlbaum.

Keller, M., & Edelstein, W. (1993). The development of the moral self from childhood to adolescence. In G. G. Noam & T. E. Wren (Eds.), in cooperation with G. Nunner-Winkler & W. Edelstein (Eds.), *The moral self* (pp. 310–336). Cambridge, MA: MIT Press.

Keller, M., Edelstein, W., Schmid, C., Fang, F., & Fang, G. (1998). Reasoning about responsibilities and obligations in close relationships: A comparison across two cultures. *Developmental Psychology, 34*, 731–741. Medline doi:10.1037/0012-1649.34.4.731

Keller, M., Gummerum, M., Wang, X. T., & Lindsay, S. (2004). Understanding perspectives and emotions in contract violation: Development of deontic and moral reasoning. *Child Development, 75*, 614–635. Medline doi:10.1111/j.1467-8624.2004.00696.x

Keller, M., Lourenço, O., Malti, T., & Saalbach, H. (2003). The multifaceted phenomenon of "happy victimizers": A cross-cultural comparison of moral emotions. *The British Journal of Developmental Psychology, 21*, 1–18. doi:10.1348/026151003321164582

Keller, M., & Reuss, S. (1984). An action–theoretical reconstruction of the development of social-cognitive competence. *Human Development, 24*, 211–220.

Kochanska, G., Padavich, D. L., & Koenig, A. L. (1996). Children's narratives about hypothetical moral dilemmas and objective measures of their conscience: Mutual relations and socialization antecedents. *Child Development, 67*, 1420–1436. Medline doi:10.2307/1131709

Kohlberg, L. (1984). *Essays on moral development: Vol. 2. The psychology of moral development*. San Francisco, CA: Harper & Row.

Krettenauer, T., & Eichler, D. (2006). Adolescents' self-attributed moral emotions following a moral transgression: Relations with delinquency, confidence in moral judgment, and age. *The British Journal of Developmental Psychology, 24*, 489–506. doi:10.1348/026151005X50825

Krettenauer, T., Malti, T., & Sokol, B. (2008). The development of moral emotion expectancies and the happy victimizer phenomenon: A critical review of theory and application. *European Journal of Developmental Science, 2*, 221–235.

Lagattuta, K. H. (2005). When you shouldn't do what you want to do: Young children's understanding of desires, rules, and emotions. *Child Development, 76*, 713–733. Medline doi:10.1111/j.1467-8624.2005.00873.x

Li, J., & Fischer, K. W. (2007). Respect as a positive self-conscious emotion in European Americans and Chinese. In J. L. Tracy, R. W. Robins, & J. P. Tangney (Eds.), *The self-conscious emotions: Theory and research* (pp. 224–242). New York, NY: Guilford Press.

Liu, M., Chen, X., Rubin, K. H., Zheng, S., Cui, L., Li, D., . . . Wang, L. (2005). Autonomy- vs. connectedness-oriented parenting behaviours in Chinese and Canadian mothers. *International Journal of Behavioral Development, 29*, 489–495.

Malti, T. (2007). Moral emotions and aggressive behavior in childhood. In G. Steffgen & M. Gollwitzer (Eds.), *Emotions and aggressive behavior* (pp. 185–200). Göttingen, Germany: Hogrefe.

Malti, T., Gasser, L., & Gutzwiller-Helfenfinger, E. (in press). Children's interpretive understanding, moral judgments, and emotion attributions: Relations to social behavior. *The British Journal of Developmental Psychology*.

Malti, T., & Keller, M. (2009). The relation of elementary school children's externalizing behaviour to emotion attributions, evaluation of consequences, and moral reasoning. *European Journal of Developmental Psychology, 6*, 592–614.

Malti, T., Gummerum, M., Keller, M., & Buchmann, M. (2009). Children's moral motivation, sympathy, and prosocial behavior. *Child Development, 80*, 442–460. Medline doi:10.1111/j.1467-8624.2009.01271.x

Miller, J., Chakravarthy, S., & Rekha, D. (2008). The moral emotions of guilt and satisfaction: A cross-cultural perspective. *European Journal of Developmental Science, 2*, 236–250.

Neff, K. D., & Helwig, C. C. (2002). A constructivist approach to understanding the development of reasoning about rights and authority within cultural contexts. *Cognitive Development, 17*, 1429–1450. doi:10.1016/S0885-2014(02)00126-0

Noam, G. G. (1999). The psychology of belonging: Reformulating adolescent development. In A H. Esman, L. T. Flaherty, & H. A. Horowitz (Eds.), *Adolescent psychiatry: Development and clinical studies* (Vol. 24, pp. 49–68). Hillside, NJ: Analytic Press.

Nucci, L., & Narvaez, D. (2008). (Eds.). *Handbook of moral and character education.* New York, NY: Routledge.

Nunner-Winkler, G., & Sodian, B. (1988). Children's understanding of moral emotions. *Child Development, 59,* 1323–1338. Medline doi:10.2307/1130495

Nussbaum, M. (2001). *Upheavals of thought: The intelligence of emotions.* Cambridge, England: Cambridge University Press.

Oser, F., Schmid, E., & Hattersley, K. (2006). The "unhappy moralist" effect: Emotional conflicts between being good and being successful. In L. Verschaffel, F. Dochy, M. Boekarts, & S. Vosniadou (Eds.), *Instructional psychology. Past, present and future trends* (pp. 149–168). Amsterdam: Elsevier.

Piaget, J. (1970). Piaget's theory. In P. Mussen (Ed.), *Carmichael's manual of child psychology* (pp. 703–732). New York, NY: Wiley.

Selman, R. L. (1980). *The growth of interpersonal understanding.* New York, NY: Academic Press.

Sullivan, H. S. (1953). *The interpersonal theory of psychiatry.* New York, NY: Norton.

Turiel, E. (1983). *The development of social knowledge: Morality and convention.* Cambridge, England: Cambridge University Press.

Turiel, E. (2002). *The culture of morality: Social development, context, and conflict.* Cambridge, England: Cambridge University Press.

Wang, Q., & Leichtman, M. D. (2000). Same beginnings, different stories: A comparison of American and Chinese children's narratives. *Child Development, 71,* 1329–1346. Medline doi:10.1111/1467-8624.00231

Yau, J., & Smetana, J. G. (2003). Conceptions of moral, social-conventional, and personal events among Chinese preschoolers in Hong Kong. *Child Development, 74,* 647–658. Medline doi:10.1111/1467-8624.00560

III

ASSESSMENT, INTERVENTIONS, AND CLINICAL PERSPECTIVES

10

THE ROLE OF ANGER IN CHILDREN'S REACTIVE VERSUS PROACTIVE AGGRESSION: REVIEW OF FINDINGS, ISSUES OF MEASUREMENT, AND IMPLICATIONS FOR INTERVENTION

JULIE A. HUBBARD, MICHAEL T. MORROW, LYDIA J. ROMANO, AND MEGHAN D. MCAULIFFE

A theoretical distinction has been made between two types of childhood aggression that serve different functions. Reactive aggression is defensive, retaliatory, and in response to real or perceived provocation. Proactive aggression, on the other hand, is displayed to reach a goal, whether that goal involves material or territorial gain or social dominance. Throughout the years, researchers and theorists have used different labels to describe this distinction, including hostile/instrumental, retaliatory/predatory, and effectual/ineffectual. Each of these pairs of labels refers to the same idea, namely, that when children display aggression, their behavior sometimes is driven by defense and retaliation, whereas at other times, it is driven by a cool and deliberate purpose.

Researchers originally hypothesized that distinct groups of aggressive children existed, with one group displaying primarily reactive aggression and the other group displaying primarily proactive aggression (Dodge, 1991). However, most studies to date have suggested the two subtypes of aggression tend to co-occur, with most aggressive children displaying some degree of both reactive and proactive aggression. Thus, the reactive/proactive distinction may be more useful in describing the function of particular episodes of children's aggressive behavior than in describing aggressive children themselves.

Even though aggressive children do not divide cleanly into reactive and proactive groups, the distinction may still be quite useful, especially for understanding the relation between anger and aggression. Years ago, Averill (1982) stressed that all anger does not result in aggression, and that all aggression is not the result of anger. The second half of this idea, that aggression can have other catalysts besides anger, is reflected in the distinction between reactive and proactive aggression. The conceptualization suggests that some episodes of children's aggressive behavior are strongly driven by anger, whereas other episodes are calm, driven instead by the desire to achieve a goal. Thus, learning more about the distinction between reactive and proactive aggression is essential to developing a greater understanding of the complex relation between anger and aggression. This work will require a precise assessment of reactive and proactive aggression, one that is careful to separate the assessment of anger from aggression, particularly reactive aggression. Unfortunately, many previous measures of the subtypes of aggression have confounded the assessment of these two constructs.

For this reason, we begin our review with a brief history of the measurement of reactive and proactive aggression. Next, we review and critique existing empirical work in children and adolescents demonstrating that anger is positively related to reactive aggression, but not proactive aggression. Finally, we end with a discussion of the need for intervention programs that target children's reactive and proactive aggression separately and that stress learning anger regulation skills as a critical component of decreasing reactive aggression.

A HISTORY OF THE ASSESSMENT OF REACTIVE AND PROACTIVE AGGRESSION IN CHILDREN

The majority of studies of childhood reactive and proactive aggression have assessed the subtypes of aggression with a six-item questionnaire developed by Dodge and Coie (1987). The rating scale was originally developed for use by teachers, although it has since been used by parents and correctional facility staff as well. The scale includes three items indexing reactive aggression: (a) "When this child has been teased or threatened, he or she gets angry easily and strikes back"; (b) "This child claims that other children are to blame in a fight and feels like they started the trouble"; and (c) "When a peer accidentally hurts this child, such as by bumping into him or her, this child assumes that the peer meant to do it, and then overreacts with anger or fighting." Three other items index proactive aggression: (d) "This child gets other children to gang up on a peer that he or she does not like"; (e) "This child uses physical force, or threatens to use force, in order to dominate other children"; and (f) "This child threatens or bullies other children in order to get his or her own way."

In many ways, the psychometric properties of the scale are strong. In the original paper in which the scale was developed, intrascale correlations and coefficient alphas were high, suggesting strong internal consistency. More impressive were data regarding convergent validity. Observational data on children's reactive and proactive aggression in playgroups over 5 consecutive days were collected, in addition to teacher ratings of the subtypes of aggression on these six items. Teacher ratings of reactive aggression correlated positively with directly observed reactive aggression, even after teacher ratings of proactive aggression were parceled out; the complementary finding held for proactive aggression. In contrast, the correlations between teacher ratings of each subtype of aggression and observations of the other subtype of aggression were nonsignificant.

However, discriminant validity was weaker. In particular, in the development of the scale, items were retained that had factor loadings of greater than .40 on both the reactive and proactive subscales. In addition, in the original study, the eigenvalue of the proactive factor was only .74. Finally, in subsequent studies, confirmatory factor analyses have been equivocal regarding the replication of a two-factor structure, with the reactive and proactive items loading onto separate factors. In several studies, a two-factor model represented the best fit for the data (Fite, Colder, & Pelham, 2006 [parent report]; Poulin & Boivin, 2000 [teacher and parent report]; and Smithmyer, Hubbard, & Simons, 2000 [correctional facility staff report]). However, one study failed to replicate this two-factor structure (Roach & Gross, 2003 [teacher report]).

In our view, though, the most concerning issue is that two of the three reactive aggression items explicitly describe anger. In items (a) and (c), both anger and aggression are described side by side ("gets angry easily and strikes back," "overreacts with anger or fighting"). It is difficult to interpret a finding showing that reactive aggression assessed via the Dodge and Coie (1987) scale is related to anger assessed via another method, when in fact the items in the scale describe anger as much as they describe aggressive behavior.

The next questionnaire measure to emerge was a teacher rating form by Brown and colleagues (Brown, Atkins, Osborne, & Milnamow, 1996). The psychometric properties of this scale were somewhat improved over the Dodge and Coie (1987) scale. However, the questionnaire suffered from many of the same difficulties with item wording, with several of the reactive-aggression items describing anger clearly but never actually mentioning aggressive behavior (e.g., "This child gets mad when she doesn't get her way," "This child gets mad when corrected," "This child gets mad for no good reason"). In spite of the improved psychometrics, this scale never "caught on" with researchers, who continued to rely on the Dodge and Coie (1987) scale.

In the last 5 years, two new self-report measures of reactive and proactive aggression have appeared. The first measure was developed by Raine and colleagues (Raine et al., 2006). It includes 11 items indexing reactive aggression and 12 items indexing proactive aggression. Internal consistency estimates for each subscale were strong, the authors provided compelling evidence that a two-factor model fit the data better than a one-factor model, and they replicated these results across two samples of 16-year-olds. However, our concerns with item wording continue. Many of the items on this questionnaire do not actually describe aggressive behavior at all, but rather simply anger (e.g., "Reacted angrily when provoked by others," "Gotten angry when frustrated," "Become angry or mad when you don't get your way"). Thus, this confusion of anger and aggression continues, even with more recently developed measures. In our view, it is critical to remember that all angry feelings do not lead to aggressive actions, that anger is an emotion and aggression is a behavior, and that these two constructs require separate and careful assessment.

Fortunately, another self-report measure has recently emerged (Little, Brauner, Jones, Nock, & Hawley, 2003; Little, Jones, Henrich, & Hawley, 2003), and its authors have been much more careful in their separation of anger and aggression. This measure assesses two forms (overt and relational) and two functions (reactive and proactive) of aggression. Six items assess overt aggression, with no reference to function (e.g., "I'm the kind of person who hits, kicks, or punches others"). Six more items repeat these items, but with the phrase "to get what I want" added to assess proactive overt aggression. Similarly, six other items repeat the first six items, but this time with phrases such as "When I'm hurt by someone" added to assess reactive overt aggression. The same pattern is followed to create six items each to assess basic relational aggression, proactive relational aggression, and reactive relational aggression. These items were very carefully worded to avoid any mention of anger. To create scores for reactive aggression, reactive overt aggression scores are regressed on to overt aggression scores, and reactive relational aggression scores are regressed on to relational aggression scores; the resulting residuals representing "pure" reactive aggression are then averaged together. The same approach is used to create proactive aggression scores. Little and colleagues collected data on this scale from two large samples of 5th- through 10th-grade German adolescents. In both samples, a model with two forms and two functions of aggression fit the data better than other models, and internal consistency estimates were good. Furthermore, results were replicated across different ages and genders.

Clearly, this scale represents an advance over previous questionnaires, and we are eager to see it used more extensively in future studies. However, the fact that the scale has only been developed in a self-report format is a limitation, because it can only be used to assess the subtypes of aggression in older children or adolescents. Little and colleagues (Little, Brauner, et al., 2003;

Little, Jones, et al., 2003) claimed that only self-report measures are appropriate for determining a behavior's function, because no one but the individual can know why he or she behaved in a particular way. However, we disagree. Observational studies of the subtypes of aggression have suggested that independent observers can reliably agree on the function of aggression (Boivin, Dodge, & Coie, 1995; Dodge & Coie, 1987; Hubbard, Dodge, Cillessen, Coie, & Schwartz, 2001; Price & Dodge, 1989), suggesting that parents, teachers, and peers may be able to do so as well. We consider the development of new teacher-, parent-, and even peer-report measures of reactive and proactive aggression that follow the format developed by Little and colleagues to be an important next step for the field.

QUESTIONNAIRE-BASED STUDIES OF ANGER AND REACTIVE VERSUS PROACTIVE AGGRESSION

The questionnaire measures of reactive and proactive aggression described previously have been used in a number of studies that support the hypothesis that childhood reactive aggression is related to difficulties with anger and its regulation, whereas proactive aggression is not. This conclusion has been supported in studies using the Dodge and Coie measure (de Castro, Merk, Koops, Verrman, & Bosch, 2005; Dodge & Coie, 1987; McAuliffe, Hubbard, Rubin, Morrow, & Dearing, 2006; Price & Dodge, 1989), the Brown and colleagues measure (McAuliffe et al., 2006), the Raine and colleagues measure (Raine et al., 2006), and the Little and colleagues measure (Little, Brauner, et al., 2003; Little, Jones, et al., 2003). The validity of findings from the first three measures is questionable, given the confound between anger and reactive aggression that we described above in each of these questionnaires. However, our faith in these findings is greatly enhanced when they converge with results using the measure by Little and colleagues.

The findings are also quite robust in other ways. Throughout these studies, anger relates to reactive but not proactive aggression across diverse samples, including elementary-school children, lower class African-American boys, German adolescents, Dutch behavior-disordered boys, and antisocial adolescents. In addition, the finding holds up across different methodologies for assessing anger, including hypothetical vignettes, peer nominations, and self-report scales.

However, in all of these studies, anger was assessed in a trait-like way. None of the studies included observational measures of children's anger or measures of the physiological arousal that likely accompanies anger. The next section of our review is devoted to studies using these laboratory-based approaches.

LABORATORY-BASED STUDIES OF ANGER
AND REACTIVE VERSUS PROACTIVE AGGRESSION

Theorists use terms such as "hot-headed" to refer to children engaged in reactive aggression and "cold-blooded" to refer to children engaged in proactive aggression. Thus, episodes of reactive aggression are thought to be characterized by high levels of physiological arousal. In contrast, episodes of proactive aggression are consistent with a profile of low physiological arousal (Dodge, 1991; Dodge & Pettit, 2003; Vitaro & Brendgen, 2005).

To date, only one study of the associations between the subtypes of aggression and physiological arousal has been published. This is also the only published investigation of the relations between reactive and proactive aggression and an observational measure of anger. In this project (Hubbard et al., 2002), teacher ratings of reactive and proactive aggression were gathered on 272 second-grade children. These children then participated in a laboratory procedure in which they lost a board game to a peer confederate who cheated. Physiological data on children's skin conductance reactivity (SCR) and observational data on children's anger expression were collected during each turn of the game. Findings revealed that reactive aggression, but not proactive aggression, was positively related to SCR and observed anger expression. Moreover, these relations held not only when SCR and anger expression were aggregated across the game, but also in terms of rate of increase over the time span of the game. That is to say, children higher in teacher-rated reactive aggression had steeper increases in their SCR and anger expression over the course of the game, whereas these increases were not related to proactive aggression.

Furthermore, the relations between observed anger and SCR were examined on a turn-by-turn basis over the course of the game. Higher levels of teacher-rated reactive aggression were associated with stronger turn-by-turn relations between children's SCR and their observed anger, although these relations did not vary by children's level of proactive aggression (Hubbard et al., 2004). Thus, reactive aggression in the classroom was related to a strong moment-by-moment connection between children's physiological arousal and their anger expression in a laboratory-based peer interaction. These findings point to the importance of understanding more about the connection between children's online physiological arousal and their anger expression. Some children may have a harder time keeping their physiological arousal from manifesting itself in observable anger (i.e., they have not mastered the display rules for dissembling their angry feelings), and these difficulties may be related to reactive aggression.

This project was an important starting point in our understanding of the relations among children's reactive and proactive aggression, their anger, and their physiological arousal. However, more work is clearly needed in several areas. First, this study did not address the question of whether proactive aggression is characterized by lack of physiological arousal and anger. Second, the study relied on the same Dodge and Coie teacher-rating measure of reactive and proactive aggression critiqued above. Third, teacher ratings of classroom-based reactive aggression were related to physiological arousal and observed anger in a laboratory-based peer-provocation situation; however, aggression itself was not elicited or measured in the laboratory context. In future work, we need to assess children's physiological arousal and observed anger during actual episodes of reactive and proactive aggression elicited through laboratory procedures. We would benefit from knowing more about whether children's physiological and emotional profiles differ in the moment when they are engaging in episodes of reactive versus proactive aggression.

In our laboratory, we have recently pilot-tested procedures designed to meet these goals (Hubbard et al., 2008). Specifically, we have developed new laboratory-based measures of reactive and proactive aggression, with accompanying measures of physiological arousal and anger expression. Our sample for this pilot work consisted of 36 fourth- and fifth-grade boys and girls from diverse racial/ethnic groups.

The three laboratory tasks all involved computer-based picture exchanges with virtual peers designed to provide an opportunity for participants to display either reactive or proactive aggression. In each task, participants prepared computer art pictures while they believed that a virtual peer was preparing his or her own picture in another room. Each participant took part in all three tasks, with a different virtual peer each time. During the reactive aggression tasks, the participant sent his or her picture to the virtual peer, who criticized it and spoiled it (two reactive tasks were used, one involving low provocation from the virtual peer and one involving high provocation). The participant then had an opportunity to comment on the virtual peer's picture and spoil it if he or she chose to do so. The proactive aggression task involved a similar picture exchange. However, in this case, the virtual peer was not provocative (he or she praised the participant's picture and did not spoil it), but the participant increased his or her chance of winning a chosen prize if he or she spoiled the virtual peer's picture. Thus, the reactive tasks involved peer provocation but no instrumental gain from aggression, whereas the proactive task involved no peer provocation but clear instrumental gain from aggression.

During each task, we collected the following measures: (a) behavioral aggression (amount participant spoiled the virtual peer's picture), (b) observationally coded verbal aggression, (c) the physiological arousal measures of SCR and heart rate (HR), and (d) observationally coded angry facial expressions and angry verbal intonations.

We used these pilot data to provide preliminary information on two hypotheses. First, we hypothesized that children's aggression would relate positively to their anger expression during the reactive tasks, but not the proactive task. Support for this hypothesis was found across all three laboratory tasks. In the low-provocation reactive task, verbal anger was positively correlated with behavioral reactive aggression, .34, $p = .05$, and with verbal reactive aggression, .52, $p = .001$. In the high-provocation reactive task, verbal anger was correlated with behavioral reactive aggression, .31, $p = .07$, and with verbal reactive aggression, .79, $p = .0001$. In contrast, no significant relations between anger and aggression emerged for the proactive task. These findings provide further support for the idea that reactive aggression is driven by and accompanied by angry feelings, and they provide initial empirical evidence that proactive aggression is marked by a lack of anger.

Our second hypothesis was that children's aggression would relate positively to their physiological arousal (SCR, HR) during the reactive tasks, but that these relations would be negative during the proactive task. Strong support emerged for this hypothesis, as can be seen in Table 10.1. The higher children's SCR and HR were in the reactive tasks, the more likely they were to engage in behavioral and verbal aggression during those tasks (five of eight correlations significant or marginal). Conversely, the lower children's SCR and HR were in the proactive task, the more likely they were to engage in behavioral and verbal aggression during that task (three of four correlations significant). These results suggest not only that elevated physiological arousal is a primary mechanism driving reactive aggression, but that proactive aggression is actually marked by a notable absence of physiological arousal. Children with the lowest levels of physiological arousal during the proactive task were the most likely to aggress against the virtual peer in an attempt to improve their chances of winning a desired prize. These data provide the first empirical support of theory suggesting that proactive aggression is literally cold-blooded, in that it is displayed when children are particularly calm and unaroused.

In our view, more laboratory-based assessments of the subtypes of aggression and accompanying physiological and emotional processes are needed. Only through such time- and labor-intensive approaches will we deepen our understanding of the way in which anger and physiology differentially drive episodes of children's reactive and proactive aggression. No other approach provides such rich, detailed, and in-the-moment information. That said, the research accumulated thus far provides compelling initial evidence to support the theory that differing emotional and physiological processes underlie reactive versus proactive aggression. Anger and physiological arousal appear to be hallmarks of reactive aggression, whereas proactive aggression is marked by a distinct absence of both these characteristics.

TABLE 10.1
Relations Among Measures of Reactive and Proactive Aggression and Measures of Physiological Arousal During Laboratory Tasks

Type of aggression	Low-provocation reactive task				High-provocation reactive task				Proactive task			
	SCR		HR		SCR		HR		SCR		HR	
	r	p	r	p	r	p	r	p	r	p	r	p
Behavioral reactive aggression		ns		ns		ns	.33	.05				
Verbal reactive aggression	.37	.03	.46	.01	.28	.10	.35	.04				
Behavioral proactive aggression									-.31	.07		ns
Verbal proactive aggression									-.58	.0001	-.35	.04

Note. SCR = skin conductance reactivity; HR = heart rate; ns = nonsignificant; r = reactive; p = proactive. Blank cells indicate data are not applicable.

INTERVENTIONS FOR REACTIVE
AND PROACTIVE AGGRESSION

In the preceding sections, we have reviewed and critiqued literature demonstrating that anger and physiological arousal drive episodes of children's reactive aggression, and that episodes of proactive aggression are marked by lack of emotion and arousal. Clearly, more work on the connection between anger and reactive aggression is needed, work that emphasizes observational and laboratory-based approaches as well as the development of new measures of the subtypes of aggression. However, as this work continues to progress, it will make sense to begin to consider the implications that it holds for intervention efforts aimed at aggressive children. This is the topic to which we turn in this final section of our chapter—how might research on the reactive-proactive aggression distinction influence intervention programs for aggressive children, and in particular, how does a focus on anger and its regulation fit into these programs?

In the 1970s and 1980s, efforts to intervene with aggressive children produced disappointing results (see Kazdin, 1987, for a review), at least partially because the interventions were usually short-term and involved only a single component (e.g., social skills training, parent management training). However, in the past decade, long-term, multicomponent interventions have been developed, and these treatments have shown more promise (for reviews, see Catalano, Arthur, Hawkins, Berglund, & Olson, 1998; Elliott, Hamburg, & Williams, 1998; Greenberg, Domitrovich, & Bumbarger, 2001).

These successes have brought some measure of hope to researchers invested in developing effective preventive treatments for aggressive children. However, there is general agreement that room for improvement exists in several respects. First, although these interventions have demonstrated effects on some constructs, these effects are by no means pervasive across all constructs assessed or even across different sources of data for the same construct. Furthermore, even those effects that are obtained are sometimes not maintained at future assessments. Finally, the amount of time, money, and labor required to obtain these effects is quite significant.

A long-term goal for our field is to develop intervention and prevention programs for aggressive children that demonstrate greater efficacy and, at the same time, that are cheaper, shorter, and easier to administer. Admittedly, this is a huge task. However, one possible pathway toward enhancing current intervention and prevention efforts for aggressive children may be to develop separate interventions targeting reactive aggression and proactive aggression. Separate interventions for the subtypes of aggression have been suggested by numerous researchers (e.g., Dodge, 1991; Dodge & Schwartz, 1997; Larson, 1994; Phillips & Lochman, 2003; Vitaro & Brendgen, 2005). These treatment packages could target the specific correlates of each subtype of aggression. Empirical support for these differential correlates is growing quickly. In particular, beyond anger and physiological arousal, reactive aggression has shown unique associations with difficulty encoding social cues, hostile attributional biases, aggressive problem solving, peer rejection, peer victimization, and internalizing symptoms. In contrast, this literature suggested that proactive but not reactive aggression is positively related to self-efficacy about enacting aggressive behavior, expecting positive outcomes from aggression, valuing instrumental goals over social goals, and future delinquency (for a review, see Hubbard, McAuliffe, Morrow, & Romano, in press). The idea behind distinct interventions for the subtypes of aggression is that aggressive behavior may be decreased more effectively if the specific behavioral, social, social cognitive, emotional, and physiological underpinnings of each subtype of aggression are targeted separately.

Clearly, children are sometimes aggressive for reactive reasons, and at other times, their aggression is more proactively driven. However, a differentiated approach to the treatment of reactive versus proactive aggression may make sense even for those aggressive children who display high levels of both subtypes of aggression. The idea is that careful targeting of the mechanisms driving each subtype of aggression may enhance the efficacy of our intervention efforts with all aggressive children.

Interventions for Reactive Aggression

Within an intervention for reactive aggression, we would be wise to include a strong element of exposure to anger. Thus, after children have been taught basic skills for regulating their angry feelings, situations should be structured within the context of the intervention group that will purposefully elicit angry feelings in the children. Adult leaders can then encourage children to practice their developing anger regulation skills, while coaching and supporting as much as is necessary. The "taunting circles" that Lochman uses in his Coping Power program (Larson & Lochman, 2002) probably come closest to this concept of exposure to anger. Other examples would be to ask children to negotiate the allocation of scarce resources or to play competitive games. If a group of aggressive children must divide up too few snacks, decide who gets to play with a Gameboy first, or handle losing a game, the opportunity to practice anger regulation skills will arise almost without fail.

Exposing children to actual anger-inducing experiences provides them with an opportunity to practice their anger regulation skills online. Role plays and other forms of simulated practice are important in the initial stages of teaching children skills and techniques for regulating anger. However, in later stages, we should challenge children to use their emerging anger regulation skills online in situations in which they experience high levels of angry arousal.

Creating interventions that incorporate these types of anger-inducing situations will require substantial innovation, planning, foresight, and courage. And, clearly, opportunities for children to practice anger regulation skills online would need to be accompanied by considerable support, coaching, and scaffolding. We believe, though, that this sort of real-world practice is at the heart of what is missing from current approaches to teaching children how to regulate their anger. And, it may be the key to obtaining faster and longer lasting generalization of anger regulation skills from the treatment setting to home and school environments.

Why, then, have we shied away from exposing children to their strong, angry feelings in the context of our intervention programs? One possibility is that the taboo against anger that exists in our society is being perpetuated by the very researchers who study and treat children's aggression. In spite of encouraging children to believe that "all feelings are okay," many of us do not feel comfortable with children's anger, especially if we feel responsible for it. We may even believe that the goal of our intervention programs is to prevent children from ever becoming angry, rather than teaching children adaptive ways of coping with the anger that they all experience. However, anger is remarkably normative in interactions between children and their peers (Snyder, Schrepferman, Brooker, & Stoolmiller, 2007). If children indeed experience anger many times a day, then our goal should be to help children learn effective and constructive ways to manage angry feelings, rather than pursuing the unrealistic goal of banishing angry feelings altogether.

It is also likely that we have avoided giving children full-fledged opportunities to practice their anger regulation skills in our interventions because we worry about the ethics and pragmatics involved in doing so. When children become angry, they are sometimes going to resort to aggression, no matter how much coaching and scaffolding we provide. How do we keep all of the children in our intervention groups safe under these circumstances? Many of us are already doing so. Anyone who has worked with groups of aggressive children has experience in planning for the disagreements and scuffles that inevitably result. Most of us use as much scaffolding, praise, and support as possible, but we also use as many time-outs and as much "safe holding" as necessary. We also make sure that our groups are adequately staffed to allow for individual attention when children require it. Planning for exposure to anger is not really any different from planning for these naturally occurring altercations; in fact, it is in some ways easier, because we can more readily predict when aggressive episodes may occur.

The risks involved in exposing children to anger are obvious. However, in our opinion, the benefits may well justify these risks. Only when children are placed in actual anger-provoking situations are they allowed the opportunity to practice their anger regulation skills, to learn that they can actually control their angry feelings, and to experience the power of feeling angry but not resorting to aggression. In the cognitive–behavioral tradition, these experiences may fundamentally change the meaning of anger for aggressive children. Through success experiences such as these, aggressive children may learn that anger is something that they can control, not something that controls them. For all of these reasons, we suggest that interventions for aggressive children, and particularly interventions that target reactive aggression specifically, would do well to include greater exposure to angry feelings.

Interventions for Proactive Aggression

In contrast, interventions for proactive aggression would likely target the social-cognitive constructs that have been shown to relate uniquely to this subtype of aggression. Proactive aggression has been uniquely linked to positive outcome expectations for aggression, self-efficacy about enacting aggressive behavior, and valuing instrumental goals over social goals (Arsenio, Gold, & Adams, 2004; Crick & Dodge, 1996; Dodge & Coie, 1987; Dodge, Lochman, Harnish, Bates, & Pettit, 1997; Hubbard et al., 2001; Smithmyer et al., 2000). Thus, children who often aggress proactively believe that they are "good at" aggression, they consider aggression to be an effective way of getting what they want, and they care more about meeting their own needs than getting along with others. Each of these cognitions should be included in an intervention to reduce proactive aggression. For example, interventions for aggressive children usually teach children appropriate strategies for achieving instrumental goals, such as negotiation and compromise, in the hopes that children will replace aggression with these socially competent behaviors. Beyond mastering these new skills, though, children may need help in reframing their social cognitions to support the newly learned strategies. They may need to be encouraged to think of themselves as competent negotiators and compromisers, and they may need to be pushed to realize that these approaches can be just as effective as aggression in achieving instrumental goals.

Beyond this focus on social cognition, interventions for proactive aggression should also include an emotional component. Previously, we have described findings indicating that children are particularly calm when they aggress proactively. These results suggest that interventions to reduce proactive aggression should target what Frick and colleagues refer to as callous-unemotional traits (e.g., Frick & Marsee, 2006; Frick & White, 2008). Specifically, programs should work on building empathy and compassion for others and more generally enhancing children's moral development. For example, exercises in emotional perspective taking could be included. In addition, children could be provided with opportunities to perform altruistic acts for others, with the goal of enhancing their understanding of the personal satisfaction that comes from caring about and helping others. Readers interested in similar interventions for reactive and proactive aggression for adults should consult the edited volumes by Cavell and Malcolm (2007) and Carr and McNulty (2006).

CONCLUSION

Throughout this review, we have suggested several future directions for researchers of the subtypes of aggression and anger in children to consider. Most important are two recommendations. First, we need more time- and labor-intensive observational and laboratory-based investigations of the subtypes of aggression and anger. Second, we need psychometrically strong and theoretically derived measures of reactive and proactive aggression in children, measures that do not confound assessment of reactive aggression with assessment of anger. Little and colleagues have paved the way in this regard, but development of teacher-, parent-, and peer-report measures that follow their lead are quite needed.

Yet, even with all that we still have to do, we are encouraged by all that we have learned thus far. Credible evidence is growing to suggest that reactive aggression is driven by anger and physiological arousal, but that proactive aggression is marked by a lack of anger and arousal. These findings may seem commonsensical and logically in keeping with theory. However, as our review suggests, conducting rigorous research to back up this theory is actually quite complex. However, we are making progress, and we will continue to do so, particularly if researchers undertake projects aimed at the goals described above. As evidence grows that reactive and proactive aggression are driven by very different emotional and physiological processes, our understanding of the nature of childhood aggression will grow as well.

As this work advances, it may make sense to consider developing interventions that separately target children's reactive versus proactive aggression. With an intervention for reactive aggression, we suggest that it will be especially important to include a focus on anger and its regulation. We look forward to work that increasingly applies what we are learning about relations between anger and the subtypes of aggression to treatments aimed at helping children manage their angry feelings and aggressive behaviors more effectively.

REFERENCES

Arsenio, W. F., Gold, J., & Adams, E. (2004). Adolescents' emotion expectancies regarding aggressive and nonaggressive events: Connections with behavior problems. *Journal of Experimental Child Psychology, 89,* 338–355.

Averill, J. R. (1982). *Anger and aggression: An essay on emotion.* New York, NY: Springer-Verlag.

Boivin, M., Dodge, K. A., & Coie, J. D. (1995). Individual–group behavioral similarity and peer status in experimental play groups of boys: The social misfit revisited. *Journal of Personality and Social Psychology, 69,* 269–279. doi:10.1037/0022-3514.69.2.269

Brown, K., Atkins, M. S., Osborne, M. L., & Milnamow, M. (1996). A revised teacher rating scale for reactive and proactive aggression. *Journal of Abnormal Child Psychology, 24,* 473–480. doi:10.1007/BF01441569

Carr, A., & McNulty, M. (Eds.). (2006). *The handbook of adult clinical psychology: An evidence-based practice approach.* New York, NY: Routledge/Taylor and Francis.

Cavell, T. A., & Malcolm, K. T. (Eds.). (2007). *Anger, aggression, and interventions for interpersonal violence.* Mahwah, NJ: Erlbaum.

Catalano, R. F., Arthur, M. W., Hawkins, D. J., Berglund, L., & Olson, J. J. (1998). Comprehensive community- and school-based interventions to prevent anti-social behavior. In R. Loeber & D. P. Farrington (Eds.), *Serious and violent juvenile offenders: Risk factors and successful interventions* (pp. 248–283). Thousand Oaks, CA: Sage.

Crick, N. R., & Dodge, K. A. (1996). Social information processing mechanisms on reactive and proactive aggression. *Child Development, 67,* 993–1002. doi:10.2307/1131875

de Castro, B. O., Merk, W., Koops, W., Verrman, J.W., & Bosch, J. D. (2005). Emotions in social information processing and their relations with reactive and proactive aggression in referred aggressive boys. *Journal of Clinical Child & Adolescent Psychology, 34,* 105–116. doi:10.1207/s15374424jccp3401_10

Dodge, K. A. (1991). The structure and function of reactive and proactive aggression. In D. J. Pepler & K. H. Rubin (Eds.), *The development and treatment of childhood aggression* (pp. 201–218). Hillsdale, NJ: Erlbaum.

Dodge, K. A., & Coie, J. D. (1987). Social information processing factors in reactive and proactive aggression in children's peer groups. *Journal of Personality and Social Psychology, 53,* 1146–1158. doi:10.1037/0022-3514.53.6.1146

Dodge, K. A., Lochman, J. E., Harnish, J. D., Bates, J. E., & Pettit, G. S. (1997). Reactive and proactive aggression in school children and psychiatrically impaired chronically assaultive youth. *Journal of Abnormal Psychology, 106,* 37–51. doi:10.1037/0021-843X.106.1.37

Dodge, K. A., & Pettit, G. S. (2003). A biopsychosocial model of the development of chronic conduct problems in adolescence. *Developmental Psychology, 39,* 349–371. doi:10.1037/0012-1649.39.2.349

Dodge, K. A., & Schwartz, D. (1997). Social information processing mechanisms in aggressive behavior. In D. M. Stoff & J. Breiling (Eds.), *Handbook of antisocial behavior* (pp. 171–180). New York, NY: Wiley.

Elliott, D. S., Hamburg, B. A., & Williams, K. R. (Eds.). (1998). *Violence in American schools: A new perspective*. New York, NY: Cambridge University Press. doi:10.1207/s15374424jccp3504_9

Fite, P. J., Colder, C. R., & Pelham, W. E. (2006). A factor analytic approach to distinguish pure and co-occurring dimensions of proactive and reactive aggression. *Journal of Clinical Child and Adolescent Psychology, 35*, 578–582.

Frick, P. J., & Marsee, M. A. (2006). Psychopathy and developmental pathways to antisocial behavior in your. In C. J. Patrick (Ed.), *Handbook of the psychopathy* (pp. 353–374). New York, NY: Guilford Press.

Frick, P. J., & White, S. F. (2008). Research review: The importance of callous-unemotional traits for developmental models of aggressive and antisocial behavior. *Journal of Child Psychology and Psychiatry, 49*, 359–375.

Greenberg, M. T., Domitrovich, C., & Bumbarger, B. (2001). The prevention of mental disorders in school-aged children: Current state of the field. *Prevention and Treatment, 4*(1). doi:10.1037/1522-3736.4.1.41a

Hubbard, J. A., Dodge, K. A., Cillessen, A. H. N., Coie, J. D., & Schwartz, D. (2001). The dyadic nature of social information processing in boys' reactive and proactive aggression. *Journal of Personality and Social Psychology, 80*, 268–280. doi:10.1037/0022-3514.80.2.268

Hubbard, J. A., McAuliffe, M. D., Morrow, M. T., & Romano, L. J. (in press). Reactive and proactive aggression in childhood: Processes, outcomes, and measurement. *Journal of Personality*.

Hubbard, J. A., Parker, E. H., Ramsden, S. R., Flanagan, K. D., Relyea, N., Dearing, K. F., . . . Hyde, C. T. (2004). The relations between observational, physiological, and self-report measures of children's anger. *Social Development, 13*, 14–39. doi:10.1111/j.1467-9507.2004.00255.x

Hubbard, J. A., Romano, L., McAuliffe, M. D., Morrow, M. T., Rubin, R. M., & Hyde, C. T. (2008). *Laboratory-based assessment of children's reactive and proactive aggression and relations to emotions and psychophysiology*. Manuscript in preparation.

Hubbard, J. A., Smithmyer, C. M., Ramsden, S. R., Parker, E. H., Flanagan, K. D., Dearing, K. F., . . . Simons, R. F. (2002). Observational, physiological, and self-report measures of children's anger: Relations to reactive versus proactive aggression. *Child Development, 73*, 1101–1118. doi:10.1111/1467-8624.00460

Kazdin, A. E. (1987). Treatment of antisocial behavior in children: Current status and future directions. *Psychological Bulletin, 102*, 187–203. doi:10.1037/0033-2909.102.2.187

Larson, J. (1994). Cognitive–behavioral treatment of anger-induced aggression in the school setting. In M. J. Furlong & D. C. Smith (Eds.), *Anger, hostility, and aggression: Assessment, prevention, and intervention strategies for youth* (pp. 393–440). Brandon, VT: Clinical Psychology.

Larson, J., & Lochman, J. E. (2002). *Helping schoolchildren cope with anger: A cognitive-behavioral intervention. The Guilford school practitioner series*. New York, NY: Guilford Press.

Little, T. D., Brauner, J., Jones, S. M., Nock, M. K., & Hawley, P. H. (2003). Rethinking aggression: A typological examination of the functions of aggression. *Merrill-Palmer Quarterly, 49,* 343–369. doi:10.1353/mpq.2003.0014

Little, T. D., Jones, S. M., Henrich, C. C., & Hawley, P. H. (2003). Disentangling the "whys" from the "whats" of aggressive behavior. *International Journal of Behavioral Development, 27,* 122–133. doi:10.1080/01650250244000128

McAuliffe, M. D., Hubbard, J. A., Rubin, R. M., Morrow, M. T., & Dearing, K. F. (2002). Reactive and proactive aggression: Stability of constructs and relations to correlates. *The Journal of Genetic Psychology, 167,* 365–382. doi:10.3200/GNTP. 167.4.365-382

Phillips, N. C., & Lochman, J. E. (2003). Experimentally manipulated change in children's proactive and reactive aggressive behavior. *Aggressive Behavior, 29,* 215–227. doi:10.1002/ab.10028

Poulin, F., & Boivin, M. (2000). Reactive and proactive aggression: Evidence of a two-factor model. *Psychological Assessment, 12,* 115–122. doi:10.1037/1040-3590.12.2.115

Price, J. M., & Dodge, K. A. (1989). Reactive and proactive aggression in childhood: Relations to peer status and social context dimensions. *Journal of Abnormal Child Psychology, 17,* 455–471. doi:10.1007/BF00915038

Raine, A., Dodge, K., Loeber, R., Gatzke-Kopp, L., Lynam, D., Reynolds, C., . . . Liu, J. (2006). The reactive-proactive aggression questionnaire: Differential correlates of reactive and proactive aggression in adolescent boys. *Aggressive Behavior, 32,* 159–171. doi:10.1002/ab.20115

Roach, C. N., & Gross, A. M. (2003). Assessing child aggression: A tale of two measures. *Child & Family Behavior Therapy, 25,* 19–38. doi:10.1300/J019v25n04_02

Smithmyer, C. M., Hubbard, J. A., & Simons, R. F. (2000). Proactive and reactive aggression in delinquent adolescents: Relations to aggression outcome expectancies. *Journal of Clinical Child Psychology, 29,* 86–93. doi:10.1207/S15374424-jccp2901_9

Snyder, J., Schrepferman, L., Brooker, M., & Stoolmiller, M. (2007). The roles of anger, social reinforcement, and conflict with parents and peers in the early development of physical aggression. In T. Cavell and K. Malcolm (Eds.), *Anger, aggression, and interventions for interpersonal violence* (pp. 187214). Mahwah, NJ: Erlbaum.

Vitaro, F., & Brendgen, M. (2005). Proactive and reactive aggression: A developmental perspective. In R. E. Tremblay, W. Hartup, & J. Archer (Eds.), *Developmental origins of aggression* (pp. 178–201). New York: Guilford Press.

11

THE ETIOLOGY OF YOUTH VIOLENCE: A COGNITIVE–EMOTIONAL MODEL

JASON GOLD AND MICHAEL LEWIS

Research consistently shows that childhood abuse places children at risk for a wide range of problematic outcomes, ranging from chronic low self-esteem to dissociative states and from social difficulties to extremely violent behavior (Erickson & Egeland, 1996; Kolko, 1996; National Research Council, 1993). Furthermore, child abuse has been implicated in the development of youth violence, sexual violence, child abuse, and intimate relationship violence (English, Widom, & Branford, 2001; Rickert, Wiemann, Vaughan, & White, 2004). For example, abused children are nine times more likely to become involved in criminal activities than their nonabused peers (Crowley, Mikulich, Ehlers, Hall, & Whitmore, 2003).

However, many abused children do not develop psychological or behavioral problems. Although some individual differences in response to abuse may vary as a function of factors as different as the child's age and the severity, chronicity, timing, and form of abuse (Kendall-Tackett, Williams, & Finkelhor, 1993; Manly, Kim, Rogosch, & Cicchetti, 2001), these links have limited explanatory power in accounting for outcomes. In fact, the study of adjustment

This work is funded by a National Institute of Mental Health Grant (MH59391/DA11153) entitled "Maltreated Children's Emotions and Self-Cognitions."

following abuse continues to be hampered by basic questions, such as how to define abuse and how to account for the great diversity in outcomes (Cicchetti & Manly, 2001). Despite considerable study, the processes by which abusive parenting impacts the development of violent delinquent behavior remains largely unidentified.

We believe that the mechanism by which harsh and abusive parenting results in violent behavior involves a specific set of emotional and attributional processes. In Figure 11.1 we propose a model in which abusive parenting, that is, parenting that utilizes physically and/or verbally aggressive disciplinary techniques, is related to delinquent behavior both directly and indirectly through its relation to adolescents' proneness to shame and tendencies to blame others and avoid blame. Although abusive parenting may relate directly to delinquent behavior, the mediating effect of adolescents' emotions and attributions are proposed to have a stronger effect. Nonabusive parenting that utilizes techniques such as the use of reason, negotiation, and taking away privileges is not expected to have a direct effect on delinquency. However, shame and attributions of avoiding blame and blaming others are expected to be related to delinquent behavior. Furthermore, as shame and attributions develop within specific contexts, we would expect that cultural factors, such as ethnicity and social class, may impact the effect of physical discipline on violent behavior.

In this chapter, we first examine what is known about several contributors to aggression and violence, including harsh and abusive parenting, attributions and violent behavior, shame and violence, and the link between attributions and shame. We then describe the results of a study designed to examine how well these components fit into the model depicted in Figure 11.1.

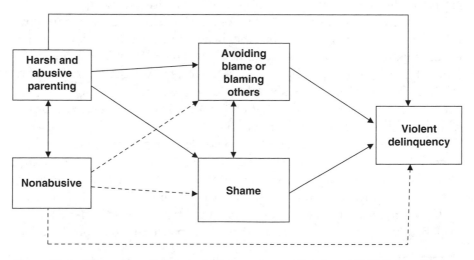

Figure 11.1. General mediation model between parenting type, attributions, shame, and violent delinquency.

Subsequently, we show that poverty rather than ethnicity appears to have the most potential to impact certain features of our model. Finally, we explore the implications our model has on designing interventions that alter adolescents' violent behavior.

HARSH AND ABUSIVE PARENTING

Physical punishment, such as spanking or hitting a child with an open hand, is often defined as a normative, culturally accepted behavior as it is intended to cause physical pain but not injury. Yet, physical punishment, even accepted forms, has been associated with negative outcomes in the general population, and many argue that it presents a significant risk for all children (Gershoff, 2002). Although physical punishment is most commonly applied to younger children, its use often continues well into adolescence (Wauchope & Straus, 1990).

It is not uncommon for physical punishment to be accompanied by other harsh, inappropriate methods of parenting, such as verbal abuse (Baumrind, Larzelere, & Cowan, 2002). Verbal punishment includes all types of negative, critical statements made to children—ranging from yelling at the child to threats of physical harm. Whether belittling, spurning, or ridiculing, these are all verbal expressions that directly shame or blame the child (McGee, Wolfe, Yuen, Wilson, & Carnochan, 1995). Verbal abuse is considered by many to be a form of maltreatment (Brassard & Hardy, 1997). Like physical abuse, verbal abuse is often associated with shame proneness and hostility (Alessandri & Lewis, 1996).

The literature consistently identifies childhood abuse with an increased risk for violent criminal behavior (Lansford et al., 2002). Compared with non-maltreated adolescents, juveniles exposed to abuse have been found to have high rates of self-reported delinquency, involvement in serious and violent behavior, and arrests for criminal acts and recidivism (Kelley, Thornberry, & Smith, 1997; National Council on Crime and Delinquency, 1999). Research has confirmed the relation between abuse and delinquency in community samples, samples of maltreated children, and in criminal offenders (e.g., Lansford et al., 2002; Maxfield & Widom, 1996).

ATTRIBUTIONS AND VIOLENT BEHAVIOR

Attributions, or individual's beliefs about why events occur, play a vital role in the developmental processes associated with child abuse. Parental rejection may increase abused children's likelihood of attributing blame to themselves for their maltreatment. Moreover, children's interpretations of why they have been the target of abuse appears to more predictive of clinical symptomatology than their abuse status alone (Hazzard, Celano, Gould, Lawry, & Webb, 1995). For example, the impact of sexual abuse and physical abuse is greater if victims believe that they are at fault or continue to blame themselves for the abuse (Feiring, Taska, & Lewis, 1998, 2002).

Specific attributional patterns have been implicated in the development and maintenance of violent behavior. One attribution that has been frequently studied is to avoid blame in conflict situations by disconnecting from others. Findings have indicated that criminal males and females reported more feelings of alienation or disconnection to others than did their nonoffending peers (Caspi et al., 1997). Violent individuals also scored higher in measures of alienation than did their peers with histories of nonviolent offenses. Additionally, emotional disconnection is also considered a key feature of psychopathy, a construct of deviant affective and behavioral features closely linked with delinquency (Neumann, Kosson, Forth, & Hare, 2006). Through the use of psychopathy measures, connections between emotional disconnection and violent behavior have been confirmed in several studies in correctional, forensic, and psychiatric populations (Douglas, Ogloff, Nicholls, & Grant, 1999; Skeem, Mulvey, & Grisso, 2003).

The tendency to blame others for one's own harmful behavior has also been identified as a trait associated with violent behavior (Cramer & Kelly, 2004). As opposed to self-blame, which may be associated with constructive, adaptive responses to conflict, blaming others often provides justification for aggressive responses (Averill, 1982). Lochman (1987) found that when compared with their nonaggressive peers, delinquent boys were more likely to blame others for being aggressive during conflict situations. Although failures in taking personal responsibility have been widely associated with chronic violent behavior (Wasserman, Miller, & Cothern, 2000), research into the emotions and contexts associated with the tendency to blame others has been relatively limited.

SHAME AND VIOLENCE

Shame is a state in which negative, global, and stable attributions about the self are made as a result of a perceived failure to meet standards (Lewis, 1992). Shame is highly aversive and has been associated with a wide range of socioemotional problems, from poor self-esteem and depression to aggressive, violent behavior (Lewis, 1992). Cerezo and Frias (1994) described the hostile, aggressive behavior that many abused children exhibit in relation to their experiences of shame.

Both the expression and suppression of shame appear to be related to aggressive, externalizing behaviors. Several studies have found that shame-prone individuals are more likely to exhibit hostility, anger, and abusiveness (Tangney & Dearing, 2002). Some researchers have even proposed that repeating patterns of shame and rage are the mechanism that drives violent behavior (Retzinger, 1991). Others have explained shame's association with hostile, aggressive behavior through a process of bypassed or suppressed shame (Lewis, 1992). Suppressed shame occurs when a person manages negative feelings of shame through displacement or dissociation—redirecting these feelings away from the self. For example, an individual prone to shame might frequently blame others for their own shame-inducing behavior, thus insulating themselves from their own intensely negative feelings. Another example of this process is available in the literature on intimate relationship violence. According to Dutton (1999, 2002), male batterers are often jealous and insecure, and they frequently exhibit hostility and overcontrolling behavior in an attempt to mask underlying fear and shame. This research has also indicated that male batterers were often subjected to shame and humiliation in their own childhoods, further supporting the view that shame plays a role in the perpetuating cycles of violence.

THE SHAME–ATTRIBUTION LINK

Negative attributions about the self (i.e., self-blame) and subsequent feelings of shame have been found to play a crucial role in the development of clinical symptomatology and have been related to poor adjustment following traumatic events (Tangney & Dearing, 2002). Research on sexual abuse, in particular, has yielded particularly strong findings in this regard. Feiring et al. (1999) found that sexually abused children's reports of shame and attributions of self-blame (i.e., "This happened to me because I am a bad person") mediated the relation between the degree of abuse and the development of depressive and posttraumatic stress disorder symptoms. Immediately after disclosure of sexual abuse, the severity of abuse had a direct effect on behavior problems, but the degree of abuse also had an indirect effect. Children's attributions of self-blame and shame about abuse were significantly related to behavior after discovery. However, 1 year later, shame and negative attributions continued to predict behavior problems, but abuse severity no longer had a direct effect nor was it related to self-attributions and shame. Finally, decreases in shame over time predicted long-term recovery (Feiring et al., 2002). This study demonstrated that shame and attributions are important mediators that explain the variability in psychopathology following abuse.

OUR MODEL: JUVENILE OFFENDER SAMPLE

We recently tested the conceptual model illustrated in Figure 11.1, which links harsh and abusive parenting to violent delinquency through distinct patterns of attributions and shame. The participants were 112 adolescents (12- to 19-year-olds, 90 males) who were incarcerated in a juvenile detention facility pending criminal charges. Abusive parenting was measured by using the Parent-Child Conflict Tactics Scale–Child Assessment (Straus, Hamby, Finkelhor, Moore, & Runyan, 1998), which measures the type, rate, and severity of exposure to parental maltreatment. Attributional patterns and shame were measured using the Test of Self-Conscious Affect–2 (Tangney & Dearing, 2002). This self-report measure assesses adolescents' proneness to shame and their tendency to respond to situations with detachment or unconcern and to externalize blame. Violent behavior (i.e., starting physical fights, weapons use, forcing others into sexual activity) was measured using an adapted version of the Violent and Nonviolent Delinquency Scales (see Broidy et al., 2003). Because this scale relied on adolescents' self-reports, institutional disciplinary reports were considered as another measure of violent delinquency. There was a significant relation between self-reported violent delinquency and violent institution disciplinary reports, suggesting that adolescents' self-reports were a valid measure of violent delinquent behavior.

As illustrated in Figure 11.2, adolescents who were abused had more violent delinquent behavior (see figure for beta weights). As shown, shame was

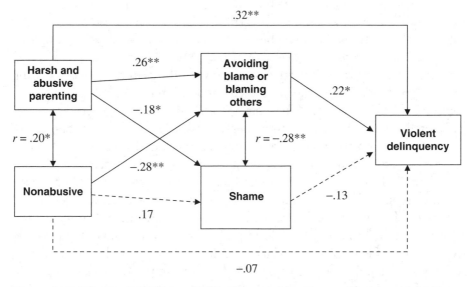

Figure 11.2. Standardized beta weights of regressions of parenting type, attributions, shame, and violent delinquency. *p = .05. **p < .01.

negatively related to avoiding blame and blaming others and to violent delinquent behavior. In addition, blaming others or avoiding blame was positively related to violent delinquency. In terms of parenting, abusive parenting was related to less shame and more avoiding blame and blaming others; although nonabusive parenting was related to more shame, there was no relation between nonabusive parenting, avoiding blame or blaming others, and violent delinquency. Overall, there was no direct relation between nonabusive parenting and violent behavior, but there was for abusive parenting. And, finally, abused adolescents who engaged in violent delinquent behavior were less prone to shame and more prone to avoiding blame or blaming others. Although these results support and extend previous findings linking physically abusive parenting to violent delinquency, these findings also highlight the role of emotions and attributions in mediating the relationship between abusive parenting and delinquency.

The findings regarding blaming others and low levels of shame appear to suggest that adolescents who engage in violent delinquency experience less shame. There are, however, reasons to expect that the opposite may, in fact, be the case. The psychotherapy literature identifies several mechanisms by which individuals protect themselves from the experience of shame (Lansky, 2005). For example, by blaming others, individuals redirect their shame from a focus on inner defects to external causes, converting their shame into anger or rage (Morrison, 1989). From this view, our violent offenders' tendencies to blame others or to avoid blame reduce their expressions of shame and increases anger and the likelihood of further aggressive or violent behavior.

Figure 11.2 also illustrates that the path to violent delinquency was not simply explained by abusive parenting; rather, parental abuse seems to influence violent behavior through the mediating effect of adolescents' attributions of avoiding blame and blaming others as well as shame. Several studies have linked violent behavior to individuals' failures in taking responsibility for their own behavior and in avoiding blame or blaming others in conflict situations (for a review, see Orobio de Castro, Veerman, Koops, Bosch, & Monshouwer, 2002). These attributions appear to play a key role in maintaining violent behavior, as individuals who avoid blame or see others as responsible for episodes of conflict may fail to realize that they themselves engage in problematic behaviors. With limited insight into their behavior, they also have little motivation to engage in treatment. The influence of these attributions may be reflected in the high rates of recidivism associated with chronic, violent juvenile offending (Loeber, Farrington, & Waschbusch, 1998). However, any attempt to model the etiology of violent delinquency would be incomplete without considering the influence of the contexts in which it develops.

ETHNICITY AS A POTENTIAL CONTEXT

One way of trying to understand the impact of context on violent behavior has been to focus on ethnic differences (Council for Children with Behavioral Disorders, 1996). Ethnic groups are often distinct in terms of belief systems, values, parental disciplinary practices, normative expectations for adaptive and maladaptive behavior, and explanations of mental illness (Pumariega, 2003). As these groups have distinct social processes, we would expect these differences to be reflected in normal and abnormal development.

Previous work has suggested that ethnicity has the potential to impact the factors in our model. Ethnic differences have been reported in relation to parents' use of physical discipline and the experience of shame and blame-related attributions, and in official rates of violent behavior (Aber, Brown, & Jones, 2003; Kelly, Power, & Wimbush, 1992; Mennen, 1995). However, the meaning of these differences and the impact that they have on actual violent behavior remains widely debated (Polaha, Larzelere, Shapiro, & Pettit, 2004; U.S. Public Health Service, 2001). Some studies have found ethnic group differences that challenge the traditionally strong positive relation between physical discipline and violent behavior (Deater-Deckard & Dodge, 1997; Lansford et al., 2002), but others have not (McLoyd & Smith, 2002; Stormshak, Bierman, McMahon, Lengua, & Conduct Problems Prevention Research Group, 2000). Our juvenile offender sample consisted of African American, Hispanic, and Caucasian adolescents. When we examined our model by ethnic groups, we found that the model held for all three groups. In other words, although abuse affected violence through attributions and shame, there were no ethnic differences in our causal model.

Some researchers have argued that poverty is linked to adolescent psychopathology through increases in economic stressors and decreases in positive parenting behaviors (Conger, Rueter, & Conger, 2000). Others, noting high rates of psychopathology among minority children living in urban poverty, have suggested that both ethnicity and poverty impact behavioral development (Schwab-Stone et al., 1995). According to the U.S. Census Bureau, 32% of African American and 28% of Hispanic children live in poverty (DeNavas-Walt, Proctor, & Smith, 2007). Furthermore, African American and Hispanic children are more likely to experience persistent poverty and to live in isolated urban neighborhoods (Huston, McLoyd, & Garcia-Coll, 1997). In these high-risk environments, the toxic effects of community and interpersonal violence are endemic (Grant et al., 2005). Unfortunately, consistent exposure to such risk factors appears strongly related to psychopathology. Several studies have found that minority youth in urban poverty are at heightened risk for a wide range of behavior problems, including violent delinquency (Duckworth, Hale, Clair, & Adams, 2000). It appears that for these youths, ethnicity may be embedded in the context of poverty.

POVERTY AS A SOCIAL CONTEXT

Research on the developmental impact of poverty has consistently found strong links between poverty and the development of behavior problems. Poverty affects children's mental health through multiple pathways, such as poor housing, homelessness, multiple moves from one dwelling to another, and inadequate health care (Brooks-Gunn & Duncan, 1997). Similar to ethnicity, poverty has the potential to impact elements of our model.

The parental stressors associated with poverty are substantial and have been associated with harsh and unpredictable discipline, poor supervision, and a lack of behaviors associated with warmth and love (Conger et al., 2000). Poverty consistently exposes children to experiences that foster negative attributions and shame. Inequality, social stigma, and perceived failures can fuel negative attributions and feelings of shame. Unfortunately for those in poverty, these experiences are often unremitting. Lewis (1992) suggested that those in poverty

> are shamed by how they are treated as students in our school systems; they are shamed by the inability to find jobs; they are shamed by the police; they are shamed by their mere identity as a minority in a majority society. (p. 158)

When considered from this perspective, we would expect the higher rates of violent behavior found in poverty-stricken neighborhoods (Sampson, Raudenbush, & Earls, 1997). As nearly all of the participants in our juvenile offender sample came from households with income levels below the poverty line, we were unable to explore differences in the impact of poverty on violent delinquency. However, other research has found low socioeconomic status to be a risk factor for the development of violent and aggressive behavior (see U.S. Public Health Service, 2001, for a review). It also highlights the importance of these processes in the development of violent behavior and the need to consider them when designing clinical interventions.

IMPLICATIONS FOR TREATMENT

Several research initiatives (for a review, see Loeber, Farrington, & Petechuk, 2003) led the U.S. Office of Juvenile Justice and Delinquency Prevention to conclude that successful interventions aimed at preventing and reducing violent behavior *"must* [italics added] address a range of risk and protective factors" (Wasserman et al., 2003, p. 1). Risk-driven approaches to treating violent behavior propose that we need to identify key risk factors before we can design interventions to counteract them (Farrington, 2007). However, the relationship between risk and outcome is notoriously complex (for a review, see Cicchetti & Rogosch, 1996). Single risk factors rarely predict the development of a disorder; rather, exposure to multiple risks appears to have cumulative effects (Coie et al., 1993). Similarly, there are considerable individual differences in response to risk, and their impact appears to vary according to developmental stage (Wasserman et al., 2003). Finally, many disorders share the same fundamental risk factors (Cicchetti & Rogosch, 1996).

In addition to understanding overall risk functions, we have to consider how different types of risk impact individuals. For example, individual risk factors for violence range considerably and include a wide array of biological, environmental, and psychological factors (for a review, see U.S. Public Health Service, 2001). Now consider that equally complex sets of risk factors are operating at the family, school, peer group, and community levels (Shader, 2003). Although adequately defining levels of risk has been a challenge to the field, understanding interactions between levels of risk is essential in developing effective interventions. Despite the considerable work on the association between risk and violence, there remains a lack of effective, conceptually driven treatments that can be easily accessed and modified for use in practice.

When considering specific, high-risk factors for the development of violent behavior, our conceptual model has clinical utility. As this model is theory-based, features of many existing treatments may be used to target the factors that mediate risk and violent behavior. As our model considers the direct effect of abusive parenting on violent delinquency, a key component involves interventions designed to reduce children's exposure to abuse. Existing interventions have focused on decreasing negative or "coercive" parenting, altering poor parental disciplinary practices, and increasing family cohesion and organization (Patterson, 1995). Given the strong relation between abusive parenting and violent behavior, it is not surprising that these family-focused interventions are among the most promising for reducing violent behavior (Dumas, 1989).

Attributions of blame and shame are key factors in our model and have direct implications for clinical practice. Cognitive–behavioral interventions attempt to restructure cognitions in order to impact problematic emotions and behaviors (Lambert, Bergin, & Garfield, 2004). From their inception, cognitive–behavioral treatments were used to reduce shame-inducing cognitions (Ellis, 1962). They have received empirical support for their treatment of a wide variety of emotional and behavioral problems (Cooper, 2008) and are among the most widely used approaches to treat violent offenders (Little, 2005). Meta-analyses of treatment programs have shown that the use of cognitive–behavioral interventions in treating incarcerated populations significantly reduced recidivism rates (Little, 2005).

Although previous work with juvenile offenders has focused on restructuring thoughts specific to delinquency (i.e., self-justificatory thinking, deficient social reasoning, schemas of dominance and entitlement, etc.), our model would suggest a concentration on blame-related cognitions and emotions of shame. The distorted thought processes associated with violent behavior, such as blaming others and avoiding blame, are amenable to cognitive restructuring (Tangney & Dearing, 2002). Despite variations in program delivery, this problem-focused approach is designed to identify and change the dysfunctional beliefs, thoughts, and actions that contribute to chronic violent behaviors (Office of Juvenile Justice and Delinquency Prevention, 2008).

In addition to the use of cognitive–behavioral interventions, feelings of shame can be further reduced by techniques designed to help individuals view perceived insults or failures more accurately and in context. In context, small slights rarely warrant global attributions of worthlessness and shame or violent responses. As these small situational precipitants often result in violence that is not explained by an individual's prior behavior or other frequently measured characteristics (Tolan, Gorman-Smith, & Loeber, 2000), it may in fact be the impact of perceived shame that triggers violent behavior. By consistently placing shame-inducing incidents into larger contexts, adolescents can begin to focus on specific situations or behaviors as opposed to shame-related judgments about their global selves (Tangney & Dearing, 2002).

POVERTY AND TREATMENT

Our model also stresses the importance of larger, cultural factors when considering interventions. Although several interventions have been designed to reduce the impact of poverty on children and families (Olds et al., 2004), our model suggests a focus on how cultural factors impact blame-related attributions and negative self-conscious emotions. The apparent impact of these factors can be found in the literature on subcultures of inner-city violence. In his ethnographic account, Anderson (1999) explains the following:

> In some of the most economically depressed and drug-and-crime-ridden pockets of the city, the rules of civil law have been severely weakened, and in their stead a "code of the street" often holds sway. At the heart of this code is a set of prescriptions and proscriptions or informal rules, of behavior organized around a desperate search for respect that governs public social relations, especially violence among so many residents,

particularly young men and women. Possession of respect—and the credible threat of violence—is highly valued. (pp. 9–10)

Our conceptual model would predict the connections between the low threshold for inferring disrespect and violence that have been observed in aggressive youth from this subculture (Dodge, Bates, & Pettit, 1990; Dodge & Somberg, 1987). As respect is defined as pride in receiving the deference that one deserves (Anderson, 1999), we would expect that its opposite, disrespect, would be associated with shame and/or humiliation (Lewis, 1992). Individuals then direct these powerful feelings away from the self—with rage—in the form of violent behavior. According to our model, targeting the distorted attributions underlying perceived incidents of disrespect would reduce the experience of painful emotions and, in turn, violent acting out. Expanding our view of context will allow us to better understand individual motivations and beliefs and to expand our ability to plan and execute specific interventions. At a larger level, an expanded view of context is necessary if we are to design treatment programs that meet the needs of historically marginalized or disenfranchised populations.

CONCLUSIONS

Although research has found childhood abuse to be implicated in the development of numerous types of violent behavior, the mechanism by which this process occurs has yet to be identified. We propose that process by which harsh and abusive parenting results in violent behavior is through the effect of attributional and emotional processes, particularly shame. In our model, specific cognitive and emotional responses to trauma are at the root of problem behavior. As harsh and abusive parenting is a strong elicitor of shame and blame-related attributions, we would expect these factors to be particularly strong indicators of outcome for abused children. For children who are exposed to repeated incidents of punitive, abusive parenting, patterns of shame and attributions of self-blame often become chronic, increasing their risk for psychopathology.

We tested this conceptual model with a juvenile offender population. As the model predicted, abused adolescents who engaged in violent delinquent behavior (i.e., crimes against people, such as assault and rape) reported less shame and tended to avoid blame or blame others. Furthermore, we found that the path to violent delinquency was not simply explained by abusive parenting, but that parental abuse seems to influence violent behavior through the mediating effect of adolescents' attributions of avoiding blame and blaming others, and shame. However, we believe that attempts to model the etiology of violent delinquency would be incomplete without considering the contexts in which they develop. Although we found no differences at the level of ethnicity, nearly all of the participants in our juvenile offender sample came from households with income levels below the poverty line. For these adolescents, we propose that ethnicity may be embedded in the larger context of poverty.

When considering specific, high-risk factors for the development of violent behavior, our conceptual model has clinical utility. As this model is theory based, features of many existing treatments may be used to target the factors that mediate risk and violent behavior. As our model considers the direct effect of abusive parenting on violent delinquency, a key component involves interventions designed to reduce children's exposure to abuse. At the level of attributions, the distorted thought processes associated with violent behavior—such as blaming others and avoiding blame—are amenable to treatment with cognitive–behavioral therapy techniques. This problem-focused approach is designed to identify and change the dysfunctional beliefs, thoughts, and actions that contribute to chronic violent behaviors and has been used successfully in the treatment of violent offenders. At the level of emotions, interventions that place shame-inducing incidents into larger contexts can help aggressive individuals focus on specific situations or behaviors as opposed to the shame-related judgments about their global selves that often precede violent behavior. Finally, our model also stresses the importance of contextual factors, such as of poverty, when designing and implementing clinical interventions.

REFERENCES

Aber, J. L., Brown, J. L., & Jones, S. M. (2003). Developmental trajectories toward violence in middle childhood: Course, demographic differences, and response to school-based intervention. *Developmental Psychology, 39*, 324–348. Medline doi:10.1037/0012-1649.39.2.324

Alessandri, S. M., & Lewis, M. (1996). Differences in pride and shame in maltreated and nonmaltreated preschoolers. *Child Development, 67*, 1857–1869. Medline doi:10.2307/1131736

Anderson, E. (1999). *Code of the street: Decency, violence, and the moral life of the inner city.* New York, NY: W.W. Norton.

Averill, J. R. (1982). *Anger and aggression.* New York, NY: Springer-Verlag.

Baumrind, D., Larzelere, R. E., & Cowan, P. A. (2002). Ordinary physical punishment: Is it harmful? Comment on Gershoff (2002). *Psychological Bulletin, 128*, 580–589. Medline doi:10.1037/0033-2909.128.4.580

Brassard, M., & Hardy, D. (1997). Psychological maltreatment. In M. Helfer, R. Kempe, & R. Krugman (Eds.), *The battered child* (pp. 392–412). Chicago, IL: University of Chicago Press.

Broidy, L. M., Nagin, D. S., Tremblay, R. E., Bates, J. E., Brame, B., Dodge, K. A., . . . Vitaro, F. (2003). Developmental trajectories of childhood disruptive behaviors and adolescent delinquency: A six-site, cross-national study. *Developmental Psychology, 39,* 222–245. Medline doi:10.1037/0012-1649.39.2.222

Brooks-Gunn, J., & Duncan, G. J. (1997). The effects of poverty on children. *The Future of Children, 7,* 55–71. Medline doi:10.2307/1602387

Caspi, A., Begg, D., Dickson, N., Harrington, H., Langley, J., Moffitt, T. E., & Silva, P. A. (1997). Personality differences predict health-risk behaviors in young adulthood: Evidence from a longitudinal study. *Journal of Personality and Social Psychology, 73,* 1052–1063. Medline doi:10.1037/0022-3514.73.5.1052

Cerezo, M. A., & Frias, D. (1994). Emotional and cognitive adjustment in abused children. *Child Abuse & Neglect, 18,* 923–932. Medline doi:10.1016/S0145-2134(05)80003-1

Cicchetti, D., & Manly, J. T. (2001). Operationalizing child maltreatment: Developmental processes and outcomes. *Development and Psychopathology, 13,* 755–757.

Cicchetti, D., & Rogosch, F. A. (1996). Equifinality and multifinality in developmental psychopathology. *Development and Psychopathology, 8,* 597–600. doi:10.1017/S0954579400007318

Coie, J. D., Watt, N. F., West, S. G., Hawkins, D., Asarnow, J. R., Markman, H. J., . . . Long, B. (1993). The science of prevention. *The American Psychologist, 48,* 1013–1022. Medline doi:10.1037/0003-066X.48.10.1013

Conger, K. J., Rueter, M. A., & Conger, R. D. (2000). The role of economic pressure in the lives of parents and their adolescents: The Family Stress Model. In L. J. Crockett & R. J. Silbereisen (Eds.), *Negotiating adolescence in times of social change* (pp. 201–233). Cambridge, England: Cambridge University Press.

Cooper, M. (2008). *Essential research findings in counseling and psychotherapy: The facts are friendly.* Newbury Park, CA: Sage.

Council for Children with Behavioral Disorders. (1996). Guidelines for providing appropriate services to culturally diverse youngsters with emotional and behavioral disorders: Report of the task force of the CCBD Ad Hoc Committee on Ethnic and Multicultural Concerns. *Behavioral Disorders, 21,* 137–144.

Cramer, P., & Kelly, F. D. (2004). Defense mechanisms in adolescent conduct disorder and adjustment reaction. *The Journal of Nervous and Mental Disease, 192,* 139–145. Medline doi:10.1097/01.nmd.0000110285.53930.44

Crowley, T. J., Mikulich, S. K., Ehlers, K. M., Hall, S. K., & Whitmore, E. A. (2003). Discriminative validity and clinical utility of an abuse–neglect interview for adolescents with conduct and substance abuse problems. *The American Journal of Psychiatry, 160,* 1461–1469. Medline doi:10.1176/appi.ajp.160.8.1461

Deater-Deckard, K., & Dodge, K. A. (1997). Externalizing problems and discipline revisited: Nonlinear effects and variation by culture, context and gender. *Psychological Inquiry, 8,* 161–175. doi:10.1207/s15327965pli0803_1

DeNavas-Walt, C. B., Proctor, D., & Smith, J. (2007). *Income, poverty and health insurance coverage in the United States: 2006.* (U.S. Census Bureau, Current Population Reports, P60-233). Washington, DC: U.S. Government Printing Office.

Dodge, K. A., Bates, J. E., & Pettit, G. S. (1990, December 21). Mechanisms in the cycle of violence. *Science, 250,* 1678–1683. Medline doi:10.1126/science.2270481

Dodge, K. A., & Somberg, D. R. (1987). Hostile attributional biases among aggressive boys are exacerbated under conditions of threat to the self. *Child Development, 58,* 213–224. Medline doi:10.2307/1130303

Douglas, K. S., Ogloff, J. R., Nicholls, T. L., & Grant, I. (1999). Assessing risk for violence among psychiatric patients: The HCR-20 violence risk assessment scheme and the Psychopathy Checklist: Screening Version. *Journal of Consulting and Clinical Psychology, 67,* 917–930. Medline doi:10.1037/0022-006X.67.6.917

Duckworth, M. P., Hale, D. D., Clair, S. D., & Adams, H. E. (2000). Influence of interpersonal violence and community chaos on stress reactions in children. *Journal of Interpersonal Violence, 15,* 806–826. doi:10.1177/088626000015008002

Dumas, J. E. (1989). Treating antisocial behavior in children: Child and family approaches. *Clinical Psychology Review, 9,* 197–222. doi:10.1016/0272-7358(89)90028-7

Dutton, D. G. (1999). Traumatic origins of intimate rage. *Aggression and Violent Behavior, 4,* 431–447. doi:10.1016/S1359-1789(98)00027-5

Dutton, D. G. (2002). Personality dynamics of intimate abusiveness. *Journal of Psychiatric Practice, 8,* 216–228. Medline doi:10.1097/00131746-200207000-00005

Ellis, A. (1962). *Reason and emotion in psychotherapy.* Secaucus, NJ: Citadel.

English, D., Widom, C., & Branford, C. (2001). *Childhood victimization and delinquency, adult criminality, and violent criminal behavior: A replication and extension.* Washington, DC: National Institute of Justice.

Erickson, M. F., & Egeland, B. (1996). The quiet assault: A portrait of child neglect. In L. Berliner, J. Briere, S. Bulkley, C. Jenny, & T. Reid (Eds.), *The handbook of child maltreatment* (pp. 4–20). Newbury Park, CA: Sage Publications.

Farrington, D. P. (2007). Childhood risk factors and risk-focused prevention. In M. Maguire, R. Morgan, & R. Reiner (Eds.), *The Oxford handbook of criminology* (4th ed., pp. 602–640). Oxford, England: Oxford University Press.

Feiring, C., Taska, L., & Lewis, M. (1998). The role of shame and attributional style in children's and adolescents' adaptation to sexual abuse. *Child Maltreatment, 3,* 129–142. doi:10.1177/1077559598003002007

Feiring, C., Taska, L., & Lewis, M. (1999). Age and gender differences in children's and adolescents' adaptation to sexual abuse. *Child Abuse & Neglect, 23,* 115–128. Medline doi:10.1016/S0145-2134(98)00116-1

Feiring, C., Taska, L., & Lewis, M. (2002). Adjustment following sexual abuse discovery: The role of shame and attributional style. *Developmental Psychology, 38,* 79–92. Medline doi:10.1037/0012-1649.38.1.79

Gershoff, E. T. (2002). Parental corporal punishment and associated child behaviors and experiences: A meta-analytic and theoretical review. *Psychological Bulletin, 128*, 539–579. Medline doi:10.1037/0033-2909.128.4.539

Grant, K. E., McCormick, A., Poindexter, L., Simpkins, T., Janda, C. M., Thomas, K. J., . . . Taylor, J. (2005). Exposure to violence and parenting as mediators between poverty and psychological symptoms in urban African American adolescents. *Journal of Adolescence, 28*, 507–521. Medline doi:10.1016/j.adolescence.2004.12.001

Hazzard, A., Celano, M., Gould, J., Lawry, S., & Webb, C. (1995). Predicting symptomatology and self-blame among child sex abuse victims. *Child Abuse & Neglect, 19*, 707–714. Medline doi:10.1016/0145-2134(95)00028-7

Huston, A. C., McLoyd, V. C., & Garcia-Coll, C. (1997). Poverty and behavior: The case for multiple methods and levels of analyses. *Developmental Review, 17*, 376–393. doi:10.1006/drev.1997.0447

Kelley, B. T., Thornberry, T. P., & Smith, C. A. (1997). *In the wake of childhood maltreatment*. Washington, DC: U.S. Department of Justice, Office of Justice Programs, Office of Juvenile Justice and Delinquency Prevention.

Kelly, M. L., Power, T. G., & Wimbush, D. D. (1992). Determinants of disciplinary practices in low-income Black mothers. *Child Development, 63*, 573–582. Medline doi:10.2307/1131347

Kendall-Tackett, K. A., Williams, L. M., & Finkelhor, D. (1993). Impact of sexual abuse on children: A review and synthesis of recent empirical studies. *Psychological Bulletin, 113*, 164–180. Medline doi:10.1037/0033-2909.113.1.164

Kolko, D. J. (1996). Clinical monitoring of treatment course in child physical abuse: Psychometric characteristics and treatment comparisons. *Child Abuse & Neglect, 20*, 23–43. Medline doi:10.1016/0145-2134(95)00113-1

Lambert, M. J., Bergin, A. E., & Garfield, S. L. (2004). Introduction and historical overview. In M. J. Lambert (Ed.), *Bergin and Garfield's handbook of psychotherapy and behavior change* (5th ed., pp. 3–15). New York, NY: Wiley.

Lansford, J. E., Dodge, K. A., Pettit, G. S., Bates, J. E., Crozier, J., & Kaplow, J. (2002). A 12-year prospective study of the long-term effects of early child physical maltreatment on psychological, behavioral, and academic problems in adolescence. *Archives of Pediatrics & Adolescent Medicine, 156*, 824–830.

Lansky, M. R. (2005). Hidden shame. *Journal of the American Psychoanalytic Association, 53*, 865–890. Medline doi:10.1177/00030651050530031101

Lewis, M. (1992). *Shame: The exposed self*. New York, NY: The Free Press.

Little, G. L. (2005). Meta-analysis of moral reconation therapy. Recidivism results from probation and parole implementations. *Cognitive–Behavioral Treatment Review, 14*, 14–16.

Lochman, J. E. (1987). Self- and peer perceptions and attributional biases of aggressive and nonaggressive boys in dyadic interactions. *Journal of Consulting and Clinical Psychology, 55*, 404–410. Medline doi:10.1037/0022-006X.55.3.404

Loeber, R., Farrington, D. P., & Petechuk, D. (2003). *Child delinquency: Early inter-vention and prevention* (Child Delinquency Bulletin Series). Washington, DC: U.S. Department of Justice, Office of Juvenile Justice and Delinquency Prevention.

Loeber, R., Farrington, D. P., & Waschbusch, D. A. (1998). Serious and violent juve-nile offenders. In R. Loeber & D. P. Farrington (Eds.), *Serious and violent juvenile offenders. Risk factors and successful intervention* (pp. 313–345). Thousand Oaks, CA: Sage.

Manly, J. T., Kim, J. E., Rogosch, F. A., & Cicchetti, D. (2001). Dimensions of child maltreatment and children's adjustment: Contributions of developmental timing and subtype. *Development and Psychopathology, 13*, 759–782.

Maxfield, M. G., & Widom, C. S. (1996). The cycle of violence. *Archives of Pediatrics & Adolescent Medicine, 150*, 390–395.

McGee, R. A., Wolfe, D. A., Yuen, S. A., Wilson, S. K., & Carnochan, J. (1995). The measurement of maltreatment: A comparison of approaches. *Child Abuse & Neglect, 19*, 233–249. Medline doi:10.1016/0145-2134(94)00119-F

McLoyd, V. C., & Smith, J. (2002). Physical discipline and behavior problems in African American, European American, and Latino children: Emotional support as a moderator. *Journal of Marriage and the Family, 64*, 40–53. doi:10.1111/j.1741-3737.2002.00040.x

Mennen, F. (1995). The relationship of race/ethnicity to symptoms in childhood sexual abuse. *Child Abuse & Neglect, 19*, 115–124. doi:10.1016/0145-2134(94)00100-9

Morrison, A. P. (1989). *Shame: The underside of narcissism*. Hillsdale, NJ: Analytic Press.

National Council on Crime and Delinquency. (1999). *Development of an empirically based risk assessment instrument for the Virginia Department of Juvenile Justice: Final Report*. Madison, WI: Author.

National Research Council. (1993). *Understanding child abuse and neglect*. Washing-ton, DC: National Academies Press.

Neumann, C. S., Kosson, D. S., Forth, A. E., & Hare, R. D. (2006). Factor structure of the Hare Psychopathy Checklist: Youth Version in incarcerated adolescents. *Psychological Assessment, 18*, 142–154. Medline doi:10.1037/1040-3590.18.2.142

Office of Juvenile Justice and Delinquency Prevention. (2008). *Model programs guide: Cognitive-behavioral treatment*. Retrieved March 12, 2009, from http://www.dsgonline.com/mpg2.5/cognitive_behavioral_treatment_prevention.htm

Olds, D. L., Kitzman, H., Cole, R., Robinson, J., Sidora, K., Luckey, D. W., . . . Holmberg, J. (2004). Effects of nurse home-visiting on maternal life-course and child development: Age-six follow-up of a randomized trial. *Pediatrics, 114*, 1550–1559. Medline doi:10.1542/peds.2004-0962

Orobio de Castro, B., Veerman, J. W., Koops, W., Bosch, J. D., & Monshouwer, H. J. (2002). Hostile attribution of intent and aggressive behavior: A meta-analysis. *Child Development, 73*, 916–934. Medline doi:10.1111/1467-8624.00447

Patterson, G. R. (Ed.). (1995). *Coercion—A basis for early age of onset for arrest*. New York, NY: Cambridge University Press.

Polaha, J., Larzelere, R. E., Shapiro, S. K., & Pettit, G. S. (2004). Physical discipline and child behavior problems: A study of ethnic group differences. *Parenting, Science and Practice, 4*, 339–360. doi:10.1207/s15327922par0404_6

Pumariega, A. J. (2003). Cultural competence in systems of care for children's mental health. In A. J. Pumariega & N. C. Winters (Eds.), *Handbook of child and adolescent systems of care: The new community psychiatry* (pp. 82–106) New York, NY: Jossey-Bass.

Retzinger, S. M. (1991). *Violent emotions: Shame and rage in marital quarrels.* London, England: Sage.

Rickert, V. I., Wiemann, C. M., Vaughan, R. D., & White, J. W. (2004). Rates and risk factors for sexual violence among an ethnically diverse sample of adolescents. *Archives of Pediatrics & Adolescent Medicine, 158*, 1132–1139. Medline doi:10.1001/archpedi.158.12.1132

Sampson, R. J., Raudenbush, S. W., & Earls, F. (1997, August 15). Neighborhoods and violent crime: A multilevel study of collective efficacy. *Science, 277*(5328), 918–924. doi:10.1126/science.277.5328.918

Schwab-Stone, M. E., Ayers, T. S., Kasprow, W., Voyce, C., Barone, C., Shriver, T., . . . Weissberg, R. P. (1995). No safe haven: A study of violence exposure in an urban community. *Journal of the American Academy of Child and Adolescent Psychiatry, 34*, 1343–1352.

Shader, M. (2003). *Risk factors for delinquency: An overview.* Washington, DC: U.S. Department of Justice, Office of Justice Programs, Office of Juvenile Justice and Delinquency Prevention.

Skeem, J. L., Mulvey, E. P., & Grisso, T. (2003). Applicability of traditional and revised models of psychopathy to the Psychopathy Checklist: Screening version. *Psychological Assessment, 15*, 41–55. Medline doi:10.1037/1040-3590.15.1.41

Stormshak, E. A., Bierman, K. L., McMahon, R. J., Lengua, L., & Conduct Problems Prevention Research Group. (2000). Parenting practices and child disruptive behavior problems in early elementary school. *Journal of Clinical Child Psychology, 29*, 17–29. Medline doi:10.1207/S15374424jccp2901_3

Straus, M. A., Hamby, S. L., Finkelhor, D., Moore, D., & Runyan, D. (1998). *Parent–Child Conflict Tactics Scale, revised.* Durham, NH: Family Research Laboratory, University of New Hampshire.

Tangney, J. P., & Dearing, R. L. (2002). *Shame and guilt.* New York, NY: Guilford Press.

Tolan, P. H., Gorman-Smith, D., & Loeber, R. (2000). Developmental timing of onsets of disruptive behaviors and later delinquency of inner-city youth. *Journal of Child and Family Studies, 9*, 203–220. doi:10.1023/A:1009471021975

U.S. Public Health Service. (2001). *Youth violence: A report of the Surgeon General.* Washington, DC: U.S. Department of Health and Human Services.

Wasserman, G. A., Keenan, K., Tremblay, R. E., Cole, J. D., Herrenkohl, T. I., Loeber, R., . . . Petechuk, D. (2003, April). Risk and protective factors of child delinquency. *Child Delinquency Bulletin Series*. Washington, DC: U.S. Department of Justice, Office of Juvenile Justice and Delinquency Prevention.

Wasserman. G. A., Miller, L. S., & Cothern, L. (2000, April). Prevention of serious and violent juvenile offending. *Juvenile Justice Bulletin*. Washington, DC: U.S. Department of Justice, Office of Juvenile Justice and Delinquency Prevention.

Wauchope, B. A., & Straus, M. A. (1990). Physical punishment and physical abuse of American children: Incidence rates by age, gender, and occupational class. In M. A. Straus, R. J. Gelles, & C. Smith (Eds.), *Physical violence in American families: Risk factors and adaptations to violence in 8,145 families* (pp. 133–148). New Brunswick, NJ: Transaction.

12

THE COPING POWER PROGRAM FOR ANGER AND AGGRESSION IN CHILDREN: TARGETING AROUSAL AND COGNITION

NICOLE P. POWELL, JOHN E. LOCHMAN, CAROLINE L. BOXMEYER, TAMMY D. BARRY, AND LAURA YOUNG

Children's angry and aggressive behaviors are influenced by a multitude of factors, including the interrelated processes of emotion regulation and social cognition. This chapter first reviews the roles of temperament and emotional arousability in angry and aggressive behaviors, and then summarizes the role of emotional factors on social-cognitive processes related to children's anger and aggression. Coping Power, an empirically supported intervention designed to target key deficits in aggressive children's emotion regulation and social-cognitive processes, is then described, along with examples of program activities that target emotion regulation processes.

THE ROLE OF TEMPERAMENT AND EMOTIONAL AROUSABILITY IN ANGRY AND AGGRESSIVE BEHAVIORS

Examination of individual child-level factors that contribute to the development of conduct problems has demonstrated a consistent link between such problems and children's temperamental features. The construct of temperament has been conceptualized to encompass three dimensions, including surgency–extraversion, negative affectivity, and effortful control (Rothbart,

Ahadi, Hershey, & Fisher, 2001). Surgency–extraversion is defined by high impulsivity, high-activity level, sensation seeking, and low shyness; negative affectivity includes discomfort, sadness, fear, anger or frustration, and low soothability; and effortful control is characterized by inhibitory control, attentional control, and perceptual sensitivity. Each of the three temperament dimensions has been linked to externalizing behaviors in youth. Direct correlations have been found between concurrent aggression in young children and high surgency–extraversion (e.g., Berdan, Keane, & Calkins, 2008; Rothbart et al., 2001), high negative affectivity (e.g., Rothbart et al., 2001), and low effortful control (e.g., Olson, Sameroff, Kerr, Lopez, & Wellman, 2005).

Additional research has focused on protective and risk factors in the relation between child temperament and aggressive behavior. For example, Berdan and colleagues (2008) demonstrated protective effects for actual and perceived peer acceptance in prekindergarten-age girls who were high in surgency–extraversion. Other research has demonstrated associations between temperamental features and behavior problems, but only under conditions of poor parenting practices such as harsh discipline and low monitoring (e.g., Colder, Lochman, & Wells, 1997; Scaramella & Conger, 2003)

Emotional arousability is a construct related to temperament that has also been linked to anger and aggression in children. Emotional arousability refers to the ease with which an emotional response can be elicited in an individual. Children with high levels of negative emotional arousabilty tend to become easily frustrated and angry, which can lead to the enactment of aggressive behaviors. Children displaying this pattern are characterized as reactively aggressive, while proactively aggressive children demonstrate a pattern of low emotional arousability with goal-directed, calculated aggressive acts (e.g., bullying).

Eisenberg and Fabes (1992) described how social behavior is likely influenced by an interaction between a youth's emotional arousability and emotion regulation skills. Specifically, they stated that reactively aggressive youth display high negative emotionality and low emotion regulation skills. These youth are easily aroused, struggle to regulate their emotions, and consequently lash out with aggressive responses. Furthermore, proactively aggressive youth are also poor emotion regulators, but they do not experience the high negative emotionality. Proactively aggressive youth show low levels of emotional reactivity but a strong desire to meet their own needs and a poor ability to regulate their behavior and emotions in striving for these goals. This profile of low emotionality and low emotion regulation is also thought to be associated with lower levels of sympathy toward others, which if present could serve to inhibit aggressive responding (Eisenberg & Fabes, 1992).

Reactive and proactive aggression have been found to differentially correlate with other problem behaviors and outcomes. Compared with proactive aggression, reactive aggression is more strongly associated with emotion dys-regulation (Dodge, Lochman, Harnish, Bates, & Pettit, 1997), impulsivity (Day, Bream, & Pal, 1992; Dodge et al., 1997), comorbid psychiatric diagnoses (Dodge et al., 1997), and feelings of anger (e.g., Lochman, Dunn, & Wagner, 1997). In contrast, proactive aggression is associated with a higher risk for delin-quency, oppositional defiant disorder, and conduct disorder (Vitaro, Gendreau, Tremblay, & Oligny, 1998).

Emotional arousability is also associated with physiological processes, including heart rate and skin conductance (a measure of sweat gland activity reflecting activation of the sympathetic nervous system). Typically, heart rate and skin conductance increase under conditions of emotional arousability; however, individuals with aggressive behavior problems may demonstrate atypical patterns of physiological reactivity. Children displaying aggressive and antisocial behavior have been consistently shown to have low resting heart rates (e.g., Ortiz & Raine, 2004), but under conditions of emotional arousal high heart rate reactivity has been shown to correlate with conduct problems (Lorber, 2004). In regard to skin conductance, aggressive children tend to show lower resting levels (Lorber, 2004); however, findings are inclu-sive about patterns of skin conductance reactivity for aggressive children (Lorber, 2004). Some studies have indicated that children with behavior problems demonstrate a lower skin conductance reactivity in response to stress or provocation (e.g., Snoek, van Goozen, Matthys, Buitelaar, & van Engeland, 2004), whereas others have demonstrated differential effects depend-ent on different classifications of aggressive children. Increased skin conduc-tance reactivity may be associated with highly reactive aggressive children, but not with children who are low on reactive aggression or those who display proactive aggression (Hubbard et al., 2004, 2002).

THE CONTEXTUAL SOCIAL-COGNITIVE MODEL OF PROCESSES LEADING TO ADOLESCENT ANTISOCIAL BEHAVIOR

Although aggressive and antisocial behaviors are easily identified because of their noticeably adverse effects, understanding their predictors is a much more complicated task. There are a number of personal and contextual fac-tors that are thought to contribute to the development of antisocial behavior over time. Researchers examining the development of these behaviors and their correlates have found that personal and familial factors (Patterson, Reid, & Dishion, 1992; Tolan, Gorman-Smith, Huesmann, & Zelli, 1997), innate characteristics (Berdan et al., 2008; Tarter, Alterman, & Edwards, 1985), and neighborhood context (Kroneman, Loeber, & Hipwell, 2004; Sampson & Laub, 1994) all contribute to their development.

With this growing body of empirical support for multiple predictors of antisocial behavior, researchers have sought an ecological framework in which to understand this behavior (Conduct Problems Prevention Research Group, 1992; Tolan et al., 1997) and to conceptualize ways to influence its developmental trajectory. One such framework, the contextual social-cognitive model, is composed of many of the most influential, imminent, and malleable factors thought to predict antisocial behavior. This model provides a conceptual framework of those factors in a youth's social and psychological development and family context that strongly predict antisocial behavior and its related problem behaviors (Lochman & Wells, 2002a).

The contextual social-cognitive model indicates that family and community background factors (e.g., neighborhood problems, low socioeconomic status, maternal depression, low social support, marital conflict) directly influence children's antisocial behaviors. These background characteristics also indirectly influence antisocial behavior through their impact on certain mediational processes (e.g., parenting practices, child social cognition, child self-regulation, child's perception of peer context; Lochman & Wells, 2002a). As these mediational processes are thought to be particularly malleable, this model has been the basis for intervention efforts targeting a reduction in antisocial behavior and its subsequent maladaptive outcomes (Lochman & Wells, 2002a, 2002b, 2003, 2004).

The Social Information Processing Model of Children's Social Adjustment

In the quest to understand the predictors and correlates of childhood antisocial behavior, the social information processing (SIP) model of children's social adjustment (Crick & Dodge, 1994; Dodge, 1986) narrows the focus from a child's general environment to his or her internal cognitive processes. This model delineates the mental steps children progress through as they process social information and come to a final response decision. More specifically, it serves as a way to categorize the various errors and biases that aggressive youth use during SIP, which result in maladaptive cognitions and poor decision making. Like the contextual social-cognitive model, the SIP model provides an ideal framework for determining treatment approach, the cognitive targets of intervention efforts, and the desired treatment outcomes.

The SIP model involves cyclical progression through six critical stages. When presented with social information, youth (a) attend to and encode the information, (b) interpret the social cues they have encoded, (c) choose a goal or desired outcome for the social situation, (d) access from memory their repertoire of possible responses or construct new responses if necessary, (e) evaluate these possible responses and select the one they view as most favorable, and

(f) enact the chosen response (Crick & Dodge, 1994). The child has then progressed from perception of the social stimuli through cognitive appraisal and decision-making processes, culminating in a social response.

An aggressive youth's progression through the SIP model is often speckled with numerous errors, biases, misperceptions, and distortions (e.g., Dodge, Pettit, McClaskey, & Brown, 1986; Lochman & Dodge, 1994). Because of the proposed link between these social-cognitive processes and subsequent social behaviors, the SIP model provides another scaffold for intervention.

The Role of Emotional Factors

The SIP errors discussed above bind the contextual social-cognitive model and the SIP model together. SIP errors are an integral part of the contextual social-cognitive model, as children's social cognitions act as a mediational process in the model, with cognitive errors contributing to behavior problems (Lochman & Wells, 2002a). With this model overlap in mind, it is easier to conceptualize the role of emotion on aggression and antisocial behavior as predicted by both of these models if we consider the general impact of emotion on social cognition.

In their reformulated SIP model, Crick and Dodge (1994) discussed the importance of integrating the role of emotion into their model. They introduced emotion into each stage, often reiterating that there is likely a bidirectional relationship between emotion and each stage's cognitions. Specifically, Crick and Dodge proposed that during encoding (Stage 1), one's internal emotional arousal in response to a social situation is one of the cues that must be encoded. During Stage 2, interpretation, Crick and Dodge posited that emotions have the potential to substantially impact a child's interpretation of a social event, and vice versa. Emotional arousal is believed to color these interpretations or decrease their general accuracy.

Moving into the later SIP stages, Crick and Dodge (1994) proposed that emotion plays a heavy role during the goal clarification stage (Stage 3). In fact, they classify this entire stage as an "arousal-regulating process" (p. 81). A particular emotion felt toward a peer will likely influence a child's goal in interacting with that peer (e.g., anger toward a peer may elicit a retaliatory goal). Similarly, at Stage 4 (response access) the emotion felt toward a peer is thought to influence the specific behaviors selected in response to that peer, and these response choices are likely to arouse or assuage the youth's emotion state, depending on the selected behavior. For example, feeling anger toward a peer, the youth may access the response of "punching him," which may in turn amp up the level of emotional arousal as the enactment of this response is anticipated. In selecting a response (Stage 5), these youth may predict the outcome to their selected response by considering the likely emotional reaction it will elicit in others.

Lemerise and Arsenio (2000) would agree that emotion plays a definite role in SIP. As such, they proposed several additional ways in which emotion likely factors into the SIP errors made by aggressive youth. In relation to the first two SIP stages, Lemerise and Arsenio stated that the peer's affective cues, in addition to one's own internal cues, must be encoded and interpreted. In fact, they proposed that keeping an eye on one's own emotional state and that of peers throughout the course of SIP acts as a gauge for how the interaction is progressing. They also proposed that the emotional tie to the peer is a salient detail, as negative interactions with a friend versus a stranger may be perceived in dramatically different ways.

At the goal clarification stage, Lemerise and Arsenio (2000) proposed that the perception of a peer's affect can also influence the nature of the chosen goal, with the perception of positive affect from a peer being more likely to encourage a prosocial goal choice. Additionally, children's ability to regulate their own emotional arousal may dictate whether they can keep their arousal in check in order to fully consider the situation and select a prosocial goal, or whether their choice is completely dictated by their strong emotional experience. Also, similar to Stage 2, the emotional tie to the person with whom they are interacting is a powerfully persuasive factor that can strongly influence the nature of their goal choice. In Stages 4 and 5, Lemerise and Arsenio again proposed that level of emotionality and difficulty with emotion regulation impair the response generation, evaluation, and decision-making processes. Children with higher emotionality and an inability to regulate those emotions will be less capable of considering their response choices carefully and viewing the situation from numerous perspectives.

Emotion-Related Deficits in Aggressive Youth

Crick and Dodge (1994) and Lemerise and Arsenio (2000) focused on the emotion-related social-cognitive deficits caused by children's inability to accurately perceive their own and their peers' emotions, the intensity of the youth's emotions (emotional arousal), the emotional ties felt toward the peer with whom they are interacting, and their ability to regulate their own emotions. Research conducted with aggressive youth strongly supports the idea that these youth demonstrate clear differences in these areas compared with their nonaggressive peers.

Aggressive youth are thought to have substantial difficulties with emotion identification. It is the incorrect perception of intentional anger in others that often spurs on aggressive youths' angry responding. Cohen and Strayer (1996) found that conduct disorder was often related to a decreased ability to recognize others' emotions. Similarly, Blair (1999) found a relation between adolescent psychopathy and increased problems recognizing sadness and fear.

If aggressive youth were able to accurately perceive emotion, particularly fear or regret in their peers during a social interaction, this might serve to inhibit their aggressive response.

A growing focus on emotional and physiological arousal in aggressive youth during social interactions has illuminated the issue of arousal, which seems to hinder SIP abilities. Williams, Lochman, Phillips, and Barry (2003) found that moderately aggressive boys showed a greater increase in heart rate following threat induction than did less aggressive boys. Increase in heart rate was also related to increased social-cognitive errors, illuminating the relation between arousal state and SIP errors.

Furthermore, aggressive youth have also been found to consistently demonstrate poor emotion regulation abilities and to struggle to manage their anger expression. These serve as meditational processes, alongside social cognitions, in the contextual social-cognitive model. In clarifying this influence, Eisenberg et al. (1996, 1997) found that prosocial behavior was related to lower emotional intensity and moderate emotion regulation skills.

THE COPING POWER PROGRAM

Using the contextual social-cognitive model described earlier as a framework for identifying intervention objectives, Coping Power (Lochman & Wells, 1996) has been developed as a multicomponent intervention for aggressive preadolescent to early adolescent children. The Coping Power child component (Lochman, Wells, & Lenhart, 2008) was derived from the earlier empirically supported Anger Coping program (Lochman, Burch, Curry, & Lampron, 1984; Lochman, 1992) and has 34 weekly sessions. The child component has been delivered primarily in a small-group format, although an individually delivered version is currently being tested. The accompanying parent component uses behavioral parent training (Wells, Lochman, & Lenhart, 2008) and is also delivered in a group format.

Behavioral, Emotional, and Social-Cognitive Outcomes

Coping Power intervention research has indicated that the program has had significant effects on children's emotional, social-cognitive, and behavioral functioning. Beneficial outcomes have been demonstrated through successive studies including efficacy, effectiveness, and dissemination research.

Efficacy Research

Research on Coping Power's predecessor, the 18-session Anger Coping program, indicated that preventive effects occurred only on some outcomes and suggested the need for a broader, multicomponent intervention to have more a lasting impact on serious antisocial outcomes, leading to the development of Coping Power. Lochman and Wells (1996) tested the effects of Coping Power with 183 aggressive boys who were randomly assigned to one of three conditions: a cognitive–behavioral child group component (CC), a combined child component and behavioral parenting training component (COM) and an untreated cell (C). The two intervention conditions took place during fourth to fifth grades or fifth to sixth grades, and the intervention lasted for 1.5 school years.

Analyses of outcomes at the time of the 1-year follow-up indicated that the intervention cells (CC, COM) produced reductions in children's self-reported covert delinquent behavior and in parent-reported alcohol and marijuana use by the child, and improvements in their teacher-rated functioning at school during the follow-up year, in comparison to the high-risk control condition (Lochman & Wells, 2002a, 2004). Normative comparison analyses, in which the intervention and control conditions were compared with a nonrisk group of boys ($N = 63$) from the same schools, indicated that the intervention moved at-risk boys into normative ranges for substance use, delinquency, and school behavior, in contrast to at-risk control boys, who significantly differed from the normative group.

The intervention effects on delinquency, parent-reported substance use, and teacher-rated improvement outcomes at the 1-year follow-up were found to be mediated by intervention-produced improvements in children's internal locus of control, their perceptions of their parents' consistency, their attributional biases, their person perception, and their expectations that aggression would not work for them (Lochman & Wells, 2002a).

Effectiveness Research

On the basis of these efficacy findings, we conducted an effectiveness study to examine the effects of Coping Power (combined child and parent components) as an indicated preventive intervention directed at high-risk aggressive children, along with the effects of a universal preventive intervention (Lochman & Wells, 2002b). A total of 245 male and female aggressive fourth graders were randomly assigned to one of four conditions: indicated intervention + universal intervention (IU), indicated intervention + universal control (I), indicated control + universal intervention (U), and indicated control + universal control (C). The universal intervention consisted of a series of teacher in-service meetings and classroom-wide meetings for parents about the upcoming middle school transition. At postintervention, the three intervention conditions (IU, I, U) produced lower rates of substance use than did the control cell (Lochman & Wells, 2002b). All three intervention cells also produced significant positive effects in measures of self-regulation, social competence, and parenting practices, although some of the effects were more apparent for Coping Power and some for the universal intervention (Lochman & Wells, 2002b). Children who received both interventions displayed improvements in their social competence, and teachers rated these children as improving most in problem solving and anger coping. The children receiving both interventions also tended to display less pronounced anger in response to vignettes about social problems, and they tended to have more marked decreases in teacher-rated aggression over time. At a 1-year follow-up, Coping Power children were significantly lower than controls on teacher-rated physical aggression and self-reported substance use and delinquency (Lochman & Wells, 2003), replicating the follow-up results on three similar key outcomes from the prior Coping Power efficacy study (Lochman & Wells, 2004). Longer term follow-up analyses have found that Coping Power continued to have significant positive effects on teacher-rated aggression 3 years after the end of intervention (Lochman et al., 2006).

Dissemination Research

A field trial of Coping Power has been implemented in 57 schools to examine whether Coping Power can be delivered in an effective manner by existing school staff. In this field study, school counselors were trained to use Coping Power with high-risk children at the time of transition to middle school. The 57 elementary schools were randomly assigned to one of three conditions: Coping Power intensive training (CP-IT), Coping Power basic training (CP-BT), or control. Basic training consisted of a 3-day initial workshop and monthly follow-up consultation. Intensive training included these training elements, as well as technical assistance and feedback given to counselors about their completion of objectives and the engagement of participants, on the basis of ratings of audiotapes of sessions. Nineteen schools were in each condition, with 183 children in CP-BT, 168 children in CP-IT, and 180 in control. Coping Power was delivered during the fourth and fifth grades.

Counselors who were trained intensively in Coping Power (CP-IT) produced significantly greater reductions in children's externalizing behavior problems according to teacher, parent, and child reports (Lochman, Boxmeyer, Powell, Qu, Wells, & Windle, 2009). The CP-IT counselors also produced greater improvements in children's positive social and academic skills in comparison to target children in both the control and the CP-BT conditions. The CP-IT condition produced significantly higher levels of counselor engagement with children according to audiotape coders, in comparison to CP-BT. The significant outcomes noted for CP-IT may be due in part to this condition producing more active, positive, and structured engagement with the children in their groups. Thus, intensity level of the training of counselors was found to be critically important for the successful dissemination of this program.

Affective decision-making data was collected for the second cohort in this field study at postintervention. Children completed the Iowa Gambling Task (IGT) on laptop computers, and a portable Biolog instrument assessed skin conductance and heart rate continuously during the task. In everyday situations, quick decisions often are based on affective or intuitive factors rather than on reasoning. Affective or intuitive decision making is considered to be a prefrontal function that is compromised in individuals who do not have affective responses to punishment, and who are thus unable to learn from their mistakes. In our sample, poor affective decision making on the IGT was concurrently associated with less parent-rated social skill and with more parent- and youth-rated problem behaviors. Of particular importance, Coping Power children were found to have better affective decision making on the IGT in comparison to control children (Lochman & Matthys, 2008). Thus, this form of affective decision making appears to be malleable when children receive an intervention like Coping Power that places strong emphasis on children's outcome expectations and on their anticipated consequences for their behavior.

Child Component Activities

The child component of the Coping Power program (Lochman et al., 2008) incorporates a number of intervention activities that address the role of emotion in aggression. The intervention manual includes seven sessions devoted to teaching children to recognize the physiological cues of anger and to utilize a range of coping skills to manage anger more effectively. Other units of the intervention address aspects of children's social information processing that are associated with anger and aggression (Crick & Dodge, 1994; Lochman, Whidby, & Fitzgerald, 2000), including perspective-taking activities to reduce hostile attributions and social problem-solving activities to improve social behavior. A description of the ways in which Coping Power addresses the role of emotion in aggression is provided below.

Awareness of Feelings and Physiological Arousal

The intervention unit on anger management begins with a series of activities designed to increase group members' abilities to accurately identify different emotions in themselves and others. The leader first facilitates a general discussion about emotions by asking the group members to define the word *emotion* and to list examples of different emotional states. The leader then shows pictures of faces depicting various emotions (e.g., joyful, sad, unsure, confident, lonely) and asks the group members to label the emotion in each picture. Next, the group members are asked to identify the picture that best reflects their current emotional state. To convey that emotions are physiological events that can change quite rapidly, the leader checks back in with each group member several times during the session to identify changes in emotional state.

To increase group members' abilities to recognize specific emotions in themselves and others, the leader guides the group in identifying the behavioral, physiological, and cognitive cues of several common emotions (e.g., happy, sad, scared, angry). The leader creates three column headings on a board or flip chart identifying "what people can see," "what you feel inside your body," and "the thoughts inside your head." Focusing on one emotion at a time, the group members provide responses for each column. For example, the group members may identify seeing someone's hands trembling as a behavioral indicator of anxiety, sweaty palms as a physiological indicator of their own anxiety, and a thought such as "I am going to fail this test" as a cognitive indicator of anxiety. A number of behavioral, physiological, and cognitive cues are elicited for each emotion. To deepen group members' awareness of nonverbal cues of emotions, the leader guides the group in a game of "feelings charades," in which the group members take turns selecting emotions from a hat and acting them out nonverbally while their peers try to guess what emotion was depicted.

The leader seeks to convey that although experiencing any emotion is acceptable, different ways of coping with emotions are more socially acceptable than others. For example, it is natural to feel angry if someone takes your backpack; however, it would not be acceptable to physically attack that person. The leader also conveys that some feelings may be difficult to express and that one can not always tell what other people are feeling because they may be concealing their true emotions. The leader has each child complete a "feelings bottle" worksheet, identifying emotions that are easier to express and those that are more difficult to express (and more likely to be "bottled up"). The leader also elicits examples of stimulus events that evoke specific emotions (e.g., getting a good grade on a test might make you happy; speaking in front of the class might make you scared; being teased might make you angry).

In the second session on awareness of feelings, the discussion begins to center more specifically on anger arousal. The group views a videotape depicting an anger-arousing situation (i.e., a child being told that he can't go out and play until he finishes his homework) and the child's resulting physiological cues of anger (e.g., red face, feeling hot, clenched fists). To personalize the lesson, the leader asks students to describe a situation from the past week that made them feel angry and the changes they noticed in their bodies as their anger increased. The leader uses the examples shared to introduce the critical lesson of the unit: that it is easier to manage anger effectively at low to moderate levels than at high levels, and that physiological changes can serve as important "cues" or signals that you are becoming angry and need to stop and think about how to best handle the situation.

Identifying Early Signs of Anger Arousal

Several in-session activities and homework assignments are implemented to improve students' abilities to identify varying intensity levels of anger, including the earliest signs of anger arousal. The students are taught to use "feelings thermometers" to measure their emotions. As an introductory activity, the students are given worksheets that list a range of words describing a particular emotion and are asked to write the words next to the appropriate level on the thermometer (e.g., "bothered" indicates a low level of anger, "mad" indicates a moderate level of anger, "enraged" indicates a very high level of anger). The students then record examples of triggers for each level of anger on the thermometer (e.g., missing a basketball shot might make you a little angry; being teased for wearing glasses might make you moderately angry; hearing someone make fun of your mother might make you extremely angry), as well as the physiological cues they experience at each level of anger. To point out the reciprocity in relationships, the students are also asked to describe the things they do that might trigger various levels of anger in others. As a homework assignment, the students are asked to record at least one anger-arousal event each day, marking the level of anger they experience on the thermometer and providing a brief description of the situation that triggered their anger. The leader is encouraged to complete the worksheet and to share a few appropriate examples first, to normalize the experience of anger and to model the assignment.

Skills for Managing Anger Arousal

Once the group members have learned to accurately identify anger arousal cues, they begin to learn specific skills for managing anger (e.g., distraction, deep breathing, coping self-statements). Each technique is first introduced through group activities and discussion. Role-play activities are then used to model and practice each technique. The main goal of the anger management activities is to expose the group members to anger-arousing situations in the safe therapeutic setting and to help them gain experience coping with their anger effectively. The anger management intervention unit includes a hierarchical series of exposure-based activities, beginning with activities designed to evoke low levels of anger and leading up to activities designed to evoke moderate to high levels of anger.

The group members first practice trying to "keep their cool" during activities designed to elicit low levels of anger, such as trying to recall the numbers on playing cards or building a tower of dominoes while being teased by their peers. The group leader uses these introductory activities to boost each child's sense of efficacy in controlling his or her anger and to elicit input about the types of anger coping strategies already in use. The group leader then asks the students to generate examples of anger-arousing situations that might be managed by simply distracting yourself, or shifting your thoughts to something else. Sample situations might include not being called on by the teacher or learning that you got a bad grade on a test. The group members then participate in role plays utilizing distraction (e.g., counting ceiling tiles, thinking about a fun activity that will take place later in the day) to stay in control in such situations.

The group members are then taught to use coping self-statements to stay in control during anger-arousal situations. The group members are provided with a list of sample coping statements (e.g., "He's just trying to make me mad," "I'm not going to give him want he wants," "I am going to stay calm, just relax, and ignore what he is saying," "I'll grow up not blow up"). They select their favorite coping statements from the list and also generate their own coping statements. In a first-tier exposure activity, the group members take turns playing the role of a puppet that is being teased. Rather than talking back to the other puppets, the puppet being teased recites coping statements out loud to stay calm. When all of the group members have demonstrated they are able to control their anger effectively during the puppet teasing activity, the leader initiates a similar exposure activity with direct peer taunting. The group member being teased can walk up and down a floor-size thermometer to show how angry he or she feels during the teasing and also to show how well the self-instruction is working to reduce that anger. During these teasing activities, the group leader can serve as a coach (e.g., by whispering coping self-statements in the ear of the target group member, or by suggesting other coping strategies to try). The group leader can also provide suggestions between "takes" and suggest that scenes be replayed until the group member demonstrates an ability to handle his or her anger effectively. It is important for the leaders to establish rules for the role play (e.g., no physical contact, no racial slurs) and to stop the action if necessary to make sure rules are enforced.

Throughout the unit on emotional awareness and anger management, the group members continue to complete weekly homework assignments in which they record daily anger-arousal events, describing the level of anger experienced and the coping strategies implemented. The group leader reinforces students for completing these monitoring logs and for gains made in learning to manage their anger effectively both in and outside of group sessions.

Parent Component Activities

A main principle underlying the Coping Power parent component (Wells et al., 2008) is that parents can be more effective with their children when they are calm and in control of their emotions. Toward this end, the content of several sessions is directed toward helping parents to develop effective stress management strategies. In addition, several other sessions focus on parenting techniques that support a calm and controlled emotional climate in the home. In the following section, we review the activities that are geared, either directly or indirectly, toward emotion regulation in the home setting.

Stress Management

Several sessions that occur early in the Coping Power parent component curriculum pertain to parents' abilities to manage stress in their own lives. Often, families of at-risk and aggressive students are dealing with multiple psychosocial stressors, in addition to the stress of parenting a child with behavior problems (e.g., Barry, Dunlap, Cotton, Lochman, & Wells, 2005). It is not uncommon for families participating in the Coping Power program to report experiencing simultaneous major stressors such as single parenthood, financial problems, and conflict with teachers and administrators at their children's schools. Psychosocial stress has been shown to negatively impact on effective parenting practices (Deater-Deckard & Scarr, 1996; Webster-Stratton, 1988), and reductions in parental stress have been associated with behavioral improvements in children (Blader, 2006; Harwood & Eyberg, 2006). As a result, a stress management module was included in the Coping Power parent component. In sequencing the sessions, the stress management component was placed at the beginning of the curriculum for two main reasons. First, if parents are better able to manage the stress in their lives, it is expected that stressors will cause less interference with their engagement with the program and their ability to implement new skills. Second, parents tend to receive these sessions well and may be more likely to be regular attenders if their early experiences with the program are positive.

The stress management sessions included in the Coping Power parent component include instruction on active relaxation, pleasant events scheduling, organizational strategies, and adaptive cognitions. An early activity in this module is designed to increase parents' awareness of the multiple roles they assume and how these demands compete with their ability to attend to their personal needs. The physiological, psychological, and behavioral effects of stress are discussed, and parents are assisted in identifying concrete steps that they can take to carve out time for stress-reducing activities. Leaders also provide instruction in active relaxation techniques and provide advice on time management. Parents are also presented with a cognitive model of stress management that links thoughts with feelings and subsequent behaviors. Leaders assist parents in reframing stressful events in more positive or neutral terms. For example, cognitions such as "my child's behavior is out of control and there is nothing I can do about it," which may increase a parent's stress level, are reframed in more adaptive terms ("I can help my child to improve his behavior") to decrease negative emotions and to increase the probability that effective parenting practices will be implemented.

Maintenance of a Positive Emotional Climate in the Home

The Coping Power program uses several strategies to promote a positive emotional climate in the home, including improving the parent–child relationship and reducing opportunities for parent–child conflict by setting up consistency and structure. The Coping Power parent component is based on the work of several leading child clinician-researchers and emphasizes the importance of a close, warm relationship between parent and child in behavior management and healthy child development. Sessions occurring early in the program focus on the benefits of parent–child "special time," and parents are encouraged to define in objective terms their plans for ensuring that these opportunities for positive contact occur regularly (e.g., parents agree to spend 15 minutes, four times each week engaging with their child in an activity of the child's choosing). Leaders instruct parents to refrain from using special time for teaching or lecturing, and instead to follow the child's lead and provide support and praise.

Parents are also encouraged to provide regular praise and positive attention to their children for appropriate behaviors. As a preliminary step, parents identify problem behaviors and define the prosocial opposite for each behavior. Parents then provide praise and positive attention for the prosocial behavior, with the anticipated effect of increasing these behaviors and decreasing the negative opposites. In addition, parents are encouraged to ignore minor disruptive behaviors (i.e., annoying, nonharmful behaviors such as back-talking and mimicking) with the goals of extinguishing these behaviors through nonattention, as well as to eliminate a potential source of family conflict by reducing parental corrective feedback.

Other sessions in the parent component focus on setting up structure for behavior management in the home, with the intention of reducing opportunities for argument and conflict. For example, parents are encouraged to set up "house rules" and to collaborate with their children in advance to define consequences for rule violations. As homework completion is often a major source of tension in the home, parents are encouraged to work with their children to set up specific rules and expectations relating to academics. This strategy of defining expectations and potential consequences in advance serves to ensure mutual understanding between parents and children and reduces the likelihood that parents will become overly emotional when enforcing rules, leading to less stressful and more adaptive interactions between parents and children.

Parental Support of Children's New Skills

Finally, a goal of the Coping Power parent component is to encourage practice and generalization of children's newly developing skills by enlisting parents' help. Parents are informed about the skills their children are learning in the Coping Power child component and are asked to look for opportunities to encourage their children to practice the techniques. For example, parents learn about coping statements and can be provided with a list of the specific coping statements their children selected to use. When parents notice their children becoming angry during interactions with family members at home, they can then remind their children to use the coping statements and provide reinforcement of the children's efforts.

CONCLUSION

In this chapter, we have reviewed the role of emotional processes in children's angry and aggressive behaviors. Emotion regulation influences several processes related to children's aggressive behaviors, including physiological reactivity and social-cognitive functioning. Understanding how emotional processes impact children's angry and aggressive behaviors has influenced and informed the development of intervention programs for children with externalizing problems. Coping Power, reviewed in this chapter, is one such program and contains a variety of therapeutic activities that target emotion regulation processes in the treatment of childhood aggression. It is important that outcome research on Coping Power supports the program's effectiveness in reducing aggressive behavior and improving self-regulation and anger coping skills (Lochman & Wells, 2002b). Although not all children demonstrating aggressive behavior problems have deficits in emotion regulation processes (i.e., children who display predominately proactive forms of aggression), the relation between emotion regulation and aggressive behavior underscores the importance of assessment in this area, and, if indicated, targeting interventions to address emotion regulation difficulties.

REFERENCES

Barry, T. D., Dunlap, S. T., Cotton, S. J., Lochman, J. E., & Wells, K. C. (2005). The influence of maternal stress and distress on disruptive behavior problems in boys. *Journal of the American Academy of Child and Adolescent Psychiatry, 44*, 265–273. Medline doi:10.1097/00004583-200503000-00011

Berdan, L. E., Keane, S. P., & Calkins, S. D. (2008). Temperament and externalizing behavior: Social preference and perceived acceptance as protective factors. *Developmental Psychology, 44*, 957–968. Medline doi:10.1037/0012-1649.44.4.957

Blader, J. C. (2006). Which family factors predict children's externalizing behaviors following discharge from psychiatric inpatient treatment? *Journal of Child Psychology and Psychiatry, and Allied Disciplines, 47*, 1133–1142. Medline doi:10.1111/j.1469-7610.2006.01651.x

Blair, R. J. (1999, April). *Responsiveness to distress cues in the child with psychopathic tendencies*. Poster session presented at the biennial meeting of the Society for Research in Child Development, Albuquerque, NM.

Cohen, D., & Strayer, J. (1996). Empathy in conduct disordered and comparison youth. *Developmental Psychology, 32,* 988–998. doi:10.1037/0012-1649.32.6.988

Colder, C. R., Lochman, J. E., & Wells, K. C. (1997). The moderating influence of children's fear and activity level on relations between parenting practices and childhood symptomatology. *Journal of Abnormal Child Psychology, 25,* 251–263. Medline doi:10.1023/A:1025704217619

Conduct Problems Prevention Research Group. (1992). A developmental and clinical model for the prevention of conduct disorder: The FAST Track Program. *Development and Psychopathology, 4,* 509–527. doi:10.1017/S0954579400004855

Crick, N. R., & Dodge, K. A. (1994). A review and reformulation of social information-processing mechanisms in children's social adjustment. *Psychological Bulletin, 115,* 74–101. doi:10.1037/0033-2909.115.1.74

Day, D. M., Bream, L. A., & Pal, A. (1992). Proactive and reactive aggression: An analysis of subtypes based on teacher perceptions. *Journal of Clinical Child Psychology, 21,* 210–217. doi:10.1207/s15374424jccp2103_2

Deater-Deckard, K., & Scarr, S. (1996). Parenting stress among dual earner mothers and fathers: Are there gender differences? *Journal of Family Psychology, 10,* 45–59. doi:10.1037/0893-3200.10.1.45

Dodge, K. A. (1986). A social information processing model of social competence in children. In M. Perlmutter (Ed.), *The Minnesota Symposium on Child Psychology* (Vol. 18, pp. 77–125). Hillsdale, NJ: Erlbaum.

Dodge, K. A., Lochman, J. E., Harnish, J. E., Bates, J. E., & Pettit, G. S. (1997). Reactive and proactive aggression in school children and psychiatrically impaired chronically assaultive youth. *Journal of Abnormal Psychology, 106,* 37–51. Medline doi:10.1037/0021-843X.106.1.37

Dodge, K. A., Pettit, G. S., McClaskey, C. L., & Brown, M. M. (1986). Social competence in children. *Monographs of the Society for Research in Child Development, 51*(Serial No. 213), 1–85. doi:10.2307/1165906

Eisenberg, N., & Fabes, R. A. (1992). Emotion, regulation, and the development of social competence. In M. S. Clark (Ed.), *Review of personality and social psychology: Vol. 14. Emotion and social behavior* (pp. 119–150). Newbury Park, CA: Sage.

Eisenberg, N., Fabes, R. A., Karbon, M., Murphy, B. C., Wosinski, M., Polazzi, L., . . . Juhnke. C. (1996). The relations of children's dispositional prosocial behavior to emotionality, regulation, and social functioning. *Child Development, 67,* 974–992. Medline doi:10.2307/1131874

Eisenberg, N., Fabes, R. A., Shepard, S. A., Murphy, B. C., Guthrie, I. K., Jones, S., . . . Maszk, P. (1997). Contemporaneous and longitudinal prediction of children's social functioning from regulation and emotionality. *Child Development, 68,* 642–664. Medline doi:10.2307/1132116

Harwood, M. D., & Eyberg, S. M. (2006). Child-directed interaction: Prediction of change in impaired mother-child functioning. *Journal of Abnormal Child Psychology, 34,* 335–347. Medline doi:10.1007/s10802-006-9025-z

Hubbard, J. A., Parker, E. H., Ramsden, S. R., Flanagan, K. D., Relyea, N., Dearing, K. F., . . . Hyde, C. T. (2004). The relations among observational, physiological, and self-report measures of children's anger. *Social Development, 13,* 14–39. doi:10.1111/j.1467-9507.2004.00255.x

Hubbard, J. A., Smithmyer, C. M., Ramsden, S. R., Parker, E. H., Flanagan, K. D., Dearing, K. F., . . . Simons, R. F. (2002). Observational, physiological, and self-report measures of children's anger: Relations to reactive versus proactive aggression. *Child Development, 73,* 1101–1118. Medline doi:10.1111/1467-8624.00460

Kroneman, L., Loeber, R., & Hipwell, A. E. (2004). Is neighborhood context differently related to externalizing problems and delinquency for girls compared to boys? *Clinical Child and Family Psychology Review, 7,* 109–122. Medline doi:10.1023/B:CCFP.0000030288.01347.a2

Lemerise, E. A., & Arsenio, W. F. (2000). An integrated model of emotion processes and cognition in social information processing. *Child Development, 71,* 107–118. Medline doi:10.1111/1467-8624.00124

Lochman, J. E. (1992). Cognitive–behavioral intervention with aggressive boys: Three-year follow-up and preventive effects. *Journal of Consulting and Clinical Psychology, 60,* 426–432. Medline doi:10.1037/0022-006X.60.3.426

Lochman, J. E., Boxmeyer, C., Powell, N., Qu, L., Wells, K., & Windle, M. (2009). Dissemination of the Coping Power program: Importance of intensity of counselor training. *Journal of Consulting and Clinical Psychology, 77,* 397–409.

Lochman, J. E., Burch, P. R., Curry, J. F., & Lampron, L. B. (1984). Treatment and generalization effects of cognitive behavioral and goal setting interventions with aggressive boys. *Journal of Consulting and Clinical Psychology, 52,* 915–916. Medline doi:10.1037/0022-006X.52.5.915

Lochman, J. E., Chen, L., Qu, L., Roth, D., Barth, J., & Wells, K. (2006, May). *Influence of neighborhood characteristics on the Coping Power program's effects on children's behavior and parenting processes.* Paper presented in a symposium (D. Gorman-Smith, Chair) at the annual meeting of the Society for Prevention Research, San Antonio, TX.

Lochman, J. E., & Dodge, K. A. (1994). Social cognitive processes of severely violent, moderately aggressive, and nonaggressive boys. *Journal of Consulting and Clinical Psychology, 62,* 366–374. Medline doi:10.1037/0022-006X.62.2.366

Lochman, J. E., Dunn, S. E., & Wagner, E. E. (1997). Anger. In G. Bear, K. Minke, & A. Thomas (Eds.), *Children's needs II* (pp. 149–160). Washington, DC: National Association of School Psychology.

Lochman, J. E., & Matthys, W. (2008, May). *Impaired decision-making: A vulnerability factor for the development of substance use disorders in children and adolescents with aggressive behavior and disruptive behavior disorders.* Poster session presented at the 16th annual meeting of the Society for Prevention Research, San Francisco, CA.

Lochman, J. E., & Wells, K. (1996). A social-cognitive intervention with aggressive children: Prevention effects and contextual implementation issues. In R. D. Peters

& R. J. McMahon (Eds.), *Prevention and early intervention: Childhood disorders, substance use, and delinquency* (111–143). Newbury Park, CA: Sage.

Lochman, J. E., & Wells, K. C. (2002a). Contextual social-cognitive mediators and child outcome: A test of the theoretical model in the Coping Power program. *Development and Psychopathology, 14,* 971–993. doi:10.1017/S0954579402004157

Lochman, J. E., & Wells, K. C. (2002b). The Coping Power program at the middle school transition: Universal and indicated prevention effects. *Psychology of Addictive Behaviors, 16,* S40–S54. Medline doi:10.1037/0893-164X.16.4S.S40

Lochman, J. E., & Wells, K. C. (2003). Effectiveness study of Coping Power and classroom intervention with aggressive children: Outcomes at a one-year follow-up. *Behavior Therapy, 34,* 493–515. doi:10.1016/S0005-7894(03)80032-1

Lochman, J. E., & Wells, K. C. (2004). The Coping Power program for preadolescent aggressive boys and their parents: Outcome effects at the one-year follow-up. *Journal of Consulting and Clinical Psychology, 72,* 571–578. Medline doi:10.1037/0022-006X.72.4.571

Lochman, J. E., Wells, K. C., & Lenhart, L. (2008). *Coping Power: Child group facilitators' guide.* New York, NY: Oxford University Press.

Lochman, J. E., Whidby, J. M., & Fitzgerald, D. P. (2000). Cognitive-behavioral assessment and treatment with aggressive children. In P.C. Kendall (Ed.), *Child and adolescent therapy: Cognitive-behavioral procedures* (2nd ed., pp. 31–87). New York, NY: Guilford Press.

Lorber, M. F. (2004). Psychophysiology of aggression, psychopathy, and conduct problems: A meta-analysis. *Psychological Bulletin, 130,* 531–552. Medline doi:10.1037/0033-2909.130.4.531

Olson, S. L., Sameroff, A. J., Kerr, D. C. R., Lopez, N. L., & Wellman, H. M. (2005). Developmental foundations of externalizing problems in young children: The role of effortful control. *Development and Psychopathology, 17,* 25–45. Medline doi:10.1017/S0954579405050029

Ortiz, J., & Raine, A. (2004). Heart rate level and antisocial behavior in children and adolescents: A meta-analysis. *Journal of the American Academy of Child and Adolescent Psychiatry, 43,* 154–162. Medline doi:10.1097/00004583-200402000-00010

Patterson, G. R., Reid, J. B., & Dishion, T. J. (1992). *Antisocial boys.* Eugene, OR: Castalia.

Rothbart, M. K., Ahadi, S. A., Hershey, K. L., & Fisher, P. (2001). Investigations of temperament at three to seven years: The Children's Behavior Questionnaire. *Child Development, 72,* 1394–1408. Medline doi:10.1111/1467-8624.00355

Sampson, R. J., & Laub, J. H. (1994). Urban poverty and the family context of delinquency: A new look at structure and process in a classic study. *Child Development, 65,* 523–540. Medline doi:10.2307/1131400

Scaramella, L. V., & Conger, R. D. (2003). Intergenerational continuity of hostile parenting and its consequences: The moderating influence of children's negative emotional reactivity. *Social Development, 12,* 420–439.

Snoek, H., van Goozen, S. H. M., Matthys, W., Buitelaar, J. K., & van Engeland, H. (2004). Stress responsivity in children with externalizing behavior disorders. *Development and Psychopathology, 16,* 389–406.

Tarter, R. E., Alterman, A. I., & Edwards, K. L. (1985). Vulnerability to alcoholism in men: A behavior–genetic perspective. *Journal of Studies on Alcohol, 46,* 329–356. Medline

Tolan, P. H., Gorman-Smith, D., Huesmann, L. R., & Zelli, A. (1997). Assessment of family relationship characteristics: A measure to explain risk for antisocial behavior and depression among urban youth. *Psychological Assessment, 9,* 212–223. doi:10.1037/1040-3590.9.3.212

Vitaro, F., Gendreau, P. L., Tremblay, R. E., & Oligny, P. (1998). Reactive and proactive aggression differentially predict later conduct problems. *Journal of Child Psychology and Psychiatry, and Allied Disciplines, 39,* 377–385. Medline doi:10.1017/S0021963097002102

Webster-Stratton, C. (1988). Mothers' and fathers' perceptions of child deviance: Roles of parent and child behaviors and parent adjustment. *Journal of Consulting and Clinical Psychology, 56,* 909–915. Medline doi:10.1037/0022-006X.56.6.909

Wells, K. C., Lochman, J. E., & Lenhart, L. (2008). *Coping Power: Parent group facilitators' guide.* New York, NY: Oxford University Press.

Williams, S. C., Lochman, J. E., Phillips, N. C., & Barry, T. D. (2003). Aggressive and non-aggressive boys' physiological and cognitive processes in response to peer provocations. *Journal of Clinical Child and Adolescent Psychology, 32,* 568–576. Medline doi:10.1207/S15374424JCCP3204_9

INDEX

ABOUT THE EDITORS

William F. Arsenio, PhD, was a preschool teacher and early education advocate before beginning his graduate studies in psychology and child development. He received his doctoral degree from Stanford University in 1986, followed by a postdoctoral fellowship at the University of California, Berkeley. He is currently a professor of psychology and director of clinical research training at the Ferkauf Graduate School of Psychology, Yeshiva University, Bronx, New York.

Dr. Arsenio is a fellow of the American Psychological Association. He has served on the editorial board of *Human Development* and was a consulting editor for the *Child Development* monographs. He is currently an associate editor for *Merrill-Palmer Quarterly*, a consulting editor for *Child Development*, and an editorial board member for *Early Education and Development* and *Merrill-Palmer Quarterly*. Dr. Arsenio is interested in how children and adolescents' affective tendencies and abilities influence their social competence, moral development, and aggression. An additional focus is on young children's affective competence and its connection with school adjustment and academic performance.

Elizabeth A. Lemerise, PhD, received her doctoral degree from The New School for Social Research in 1988, followed by a postdoctoral fellowship at Vanderbilt University. She is currently University Distinguished Professor of

Psychology and director of the Social Development Laboratory at Western Kentucky University. Dr. Lemerise is a coeditor of *Social Development* and was an editorial consultant for *Child Development*. She is interested in how different kinds of emotion processes influence children's social information processing, with a focus on comparing the social information processing of children who vary in social adjustment. Additionally, Dr. Lemerise is interested in how children's participation in friend and enemy relationships influences their adjustment and social cognition.